From Drinking to Alcoholism: a Sociological Commentary

From Drinking to Alcoholism: a Sociological Commentary

David Robinson

*Addiction Research Unit,
Institute of Psychiatry,
University of London*

JOHN WILEY & SONS

London · New York · Sydney · Toronto

Library of Congress Cataloging in Publication Data:

Robinson, David, 1941 –

From drinking to alcoholism.
Includes indexes.

1. Liquor problem — England — London. 2. Alcoholism.
I. Title. [DNLM: 1. Alcohol drinking. 2. Alcoholism.

WM274 R659f]

HV5450.L65R6 362.2'92'0942 75–26597

ISBN 0 471 01357 9 (Cloth)
ISBN 0 471 01358 7 (Pbk)

Typeset by Lightbown & Co., 72 Union Street,
Ryde, Isle of Wight and printed by
The Pitman Press Ltd., Bath, Avon.

Preface

This book is about drinking and about alcoholism. As such it is about an ordinary everyday activity and about one of the major health and social problems of our time. The ordinariness of the everyday activity can be judged by the fact that roughly four out of five adults in England will have had an alcoholic drink of some kind in the past month. The magnitude of the problem can be judged by the fact that the consumption of alcohol has been implicated as a significant contributory factor not only in a whole range of physical and mental illnesses, but also in divorce, desertion and family disintegration; in household, work and traffic accidents; in violence, murder and suicide; and in loss of jobs and destitution; in short, in almost every situation in which harm is done by one individual to himself or to someone else.

Given the many and various problems associated with alcohol consumption it is not surprising that we often hear the call for 'a multidisciplinary approach'. The World Health Organization Expert Committee on Mental Health[1] for example, after discussing:

> '. . . the effects of illness resulting from alcohol . . . dependence and the associated crime, accidents, family disruption, suicide, premature death, loss of productivity, as well as associated hospital, prison and welfare costs'.

felt that the problems involved in the aetiology, prevention and control of these conditions and in the treatment of dependent persons 'extend beyond the competence of any single profession or group'. Pittman puts the position quite simply when he says that:

> 'Alcoholism is a multidisciplinary problem which involves researchers and practitioners from the biological and natural sciences, the psychological sciences and the social sciences',[2]

while Catanzaro casts his net even wider:

> 'Professionals from a wide variety of disciplines must be involved, including physicians, social workers, psychologists, nurses, clergymen, vocational rehabilitation counselors, lay alcoholism counselors, judges, educators, sociologists and many others'.[3]

Significantly, perhaps, sociologists come immediately before the unspecified 'many others' at the end of Catanzaro's list of people to be involved. I say significantly because people who write about alcoholism and related problems often include sociologists in their list of people who should be involved in some way and yet they very rarely give any indication of what sociologists actually do or what kind of help they can be expected to give. In fact, given its widespread social significance, there have been surprisingly few sociologists involved in any way with 'the problem of alcoholism'.

Since the range of problems associated with alcohol consumption is so wide I have made no attempt to cover every topic about which the sociologist may have something to say. I have concentrated instead on some of the core issues which underpin any discussion of alcohol and alcoholism, such as: alcohol consumption and alcohol problems; the question of cause; the relationship between alcoholism and disease; and help, helpers and the goal of treatment. I have indicated the various kinds of work which sociologists have done in relation to alcohol, drinking and its associated problems and, in addition I have pointed out the major areas which sociologists appear to have neglected and which, I feel, are in need of systematic study. At heart the book is about becoming an alcoholic, and in particular about how people define alcohol-related problems in their own and other people's lives, and how they consider these problems were caused and how they should be handled. The emphasis of the book, therefore, is not directly on such questions as 'what is alcoholism?' or 'how many alcoholics are there?' or 'how does alcoholism affect people?' but rather on the core sociological question of 'what in particular settings are alcoholics and alcoholism taken to be?'

Some of the material comes from a questionnaire survey of the general population in a South London borough and from extended interviews with medical practitioners, and members of other agencies and organizations in the study locality who are called upon to handle drink-related problems. However, in addition to the interview-based studies, particular attention was focused on the question of referral to the out-patient department of a local psychiatric hospital. The aim was to place the discussion of becoming an alcoholic within a specific setting in order to see how 'the question of definition' was handled both by those in that setting and by those who made referrals to it. Clearly, referral behaviour is a research area of particular interest since any person who makes a referral does have to, in a sense, come clean about his notions of what counts as alcoholism, alcohol-related problems, help and treatment.

The book is informed by a perspective which says that 'alcoholism' and 'becoming an alcoholic' are very much what people take them to be when they employ such notions in the course of their everyday lives. This is not to say that alcoholism and the alcoholic are not also a product of bio-chemical apparatus and processes; they are of course. But biochemical and physiological states and processes are 'noticed', 'recognized', 'assessed', 'responded to' and 'treated' — and these activities occur in specific social contexts. It is this which gives the transformation 'from drinking to alcoholism' its distinctly social features.

In relation to a work of this kind there are many people whose help is gratefully acknowledged: Griffith Edwards for being persuaded to agree to the kind of 'soft' research which is drawn upon in this volume: the Maudsley Alcoholism Pilot Project team of Alan Cartwright, Yvonne Salter, Stan Shaw, Beryl Skinner and Terry Spratley for being such congenial collaborators when, in a marriage of local convenience, we joined forces to look at certain questions of mutual interest; Martin Robertson Ltd. and the publishers of the Journal of Alcoholism, the Quarterly Journal of Studies on Alcohol and the Japanese Journal of Studies on Alcohol for permission to use material from some of my previously published pieces; Howard Hershon, Jim Orford and Michael Russell for those recurrent discussions about what it might be that the sociologist is really up to in the addiction business; Martin Plant for his detailed comments on an earlier draft; Roger Johnson and Diana Leat for their interest and encouragement; Stella Egert for helping to trace and extract material from hospital case notes and finally, Terrie Heighington and Serena Dalrymple for providing so much more than just secretarial assistance.

DAVID ROBINSON

Institute of Psychiatry
London
May 20th, 1975

References

1. *Expert Committee on Mental Health, Alcoholism sub-committee, Second* Report, World Health Organization Tech. Rep. Ser. No. 48, Geneva, 1952.
2. Pittman, D. J. (Ed.), *Alcoholism,* Harper and Row, New York, 1967.
3. Catanzaro, R. J. (Ed.), *Alcoholism; the total treatment approach,* Charles, C. Thomas, Springfield, Illinois, 1968.

Acknowledgements

Permission was generously granted to reproduce short extracts from *Alcoholism,* Penguin Books Ltd. © Neil Kessel and Henry Walton; *The Treatment of Alcoholics: an evaluative study,* by Sidney Cahn, © Oxford University Press Inc; *Alcoholism,* Harper and Row, © David Pittman 1967; J. Orford, Personality Factors in Alcoholism, a psychological approach, *Update,* June 1972 © Update Publications; *Alcoholism: the total treatment approach,* Catanzaro, R. J. (Ed.) © Charles C. Thomas Publisher, 1968; *Alcoholism, progress in research and treatment,* Bourne, P. and Fox, R. (Eds.) © Academic Press Inc; and *Research Advances in Alcohol and Drug Problems,* Vol. 1, Gibbins, R., Israel, Y., Kalant, K., Popham, R. E., Schmidt, W., and Smart, R. G. (Eds.) © John Wiley and Sons Inc; 1974. The passage from Bacon S. D. Introduction to Cahalan, D., Cisin, I. H. and Crossley, H. M. *American Drinking Practices; a national study of drinking behaviour and attitudes,* Rutgers Center of Alcohol Studies; Monog. No. 6, New Brunswick, N.J.; 1969, was reprinted by permission from Monographs of the Rutger Center of Alcohol Studies, No. 6, Introduction, 1969. Copyright by Journal of Studies on Alcohol, Inc, New Brunswick, N.J. 08903. The passage from Fillmore, K. M. 'Drinking and problem drinking in early adulthood and middle age; an exploratory 20-year follow-up study', was reprinted by permission from *Quarterly Journal of Studies on Alcohol,* Vol. 35, pp. 819–840, 1974. Copyright by Journal of Studies on Alcohol, Inc; New Brunswick, N.J. 08903. Parts of Robinson, D. 'The alcohologist's addiction; some implications of having lost control over the disease concept of alcoholism', were reprinted by permission from *Quarterly Journal of Studies on Alcohol,* Vol. 33, pp. 1028–1042, 1972. Copyright by Journal of Studies on Alcohol, Inc; New Brunswick, N.J. 08903. The passage from Heath, D. B. 'Drinking patterns of the Bolivian Camaba', was reprinted by permission from *Quarterly Journal of Studies on Alcohol,* Vol. 19, pp. 491–508, 1958. Copyright by Journal of Studies on Alcohol, Inc; New Brunswick, N.J. 08903.

Contents

Chapter 1

Alcohol, Alcoholism and Sociology

> 'Alcohol is a drug with many appealing properties. It relieves anxiety and tension. It is an anaesthetic which can relieve physical and emotional pain. It helps relieve inhibitions. It can be made into a tasty and readily available beverage'. *Catanzaro*[1].

Of all the substances which men have learnt to ingest, alcohol is certainly amongst the most significant. Widespread in use and highly valued as a ritual and social artefact it has been tightly woven into the fabric of everyday life. While no one can be certain, of course, about which plant the primitive gatherers first cultivated Keller is confident that it was vitis, the grapevine, because:

> '. . . as legend tells us its fruit provided food that could be eaten both moist, as grapes, and dry, as raisons, and with little effort could be converted into a drink of magical properties and potency: one that relieved fatigue and assuaged pain, evoked gaiety, enhanced bravery, promoted friendship — and even facilitated communion with the invisible spirits that seemed to control men's fate'.[2]

But whatever its origins and its various uses, the base of any manufactured alcoholic beverage is ethyl alcohol; one of the many compounds of carbon, hydrogen and oxygen.[3] Depending on the particular combination of parts, these three chemical elements join to form ethyl alcohol, methyl alcohol — commonly used in paint strippers and anti-freeze mixtures — propyl alcohol, isopropyl alcohol, amyl alcohol and many more. Ethyl alcohol itself is a clear, colourless, rather volatile liquid, with a strong burning taste and very little smell. In fact, the distinctive smell on a drinker's breath is usually due to the other things in the beverage rather than to the actual alcohol.

The precise amount of ethyl alcohol in any particular drink varies from the four per cent in brewed beers and ales, through the fermented drinks and wines which usually have from 12 to 16 per cent alcohol to the distilled spirits with approximately 50 per cent alcohol, which is more usually expressed as 85–100 proof. The term proof originated in the early days of distillation when the buyer would mix a quantity of gunpowder with the drink and then put a match to it. If it burned it was 'proof' of the alcoholic content. Eventually the precise strength of the distilled drink was expressed as a number; with pure alcohol being 200 proof. Pure alcohol, however, has such an affinity for water that it dilutes itself from the moisture in the air about it. The strongest alcohol, therefore, is usually about 180 proof, approximately twice as strong as the strongest distilled drink.

Unlike some foods alcohol does not have to be digested when it is taken into the body. It exerts its action in its original state. The calories given off by oxidation of alcohol — approximately seven calories per gram — are about half-way between the amount given off by carbohydrates and proteins, approximately four and a half calories per gram, and that given off by the fats, approximately nine calories per gram. But unfortunately for those who drink a lot and eat little, alcohol is not a very good food. It cannot be stored by the body and it has several toxic effects, ranging from the mild irritation of the delicate membranes of the stomach caused by any alcohol over about four per cent in strength to changes in the nervous system and cirrhosis of the liver caused by heavy drinking while not eating properly over long periods of time.

The metabolism of alcohol takes place at the rate of between three quarters and one ounce of whisky per hour. So someone could drink as much as 20 ounces of whisky — almost one bottle — gradually over a 24 hour period, at a rate of three-quarters to one ounce of whisky per hour, and experience no effect from the alcohol whatsoever. Not only would they feel no effect but at no time during that period would any alcohol be found in their blood or tissues since the body would be burning or oxidising the alcohol as fast as it was being ingested. By the same token, of course, if this person drank only four ounces of whisky, but all in *one* hour, a fairly high concentration of alcohol would be found in the system.

But the relationship between man and alcohol is of interest to us not only at the level of bodily processes. For while the chemical properties of alcohol provide a necessary base, the behavioural concomitants of drinking alcohol depend as much on ideas of what alcohol does to a person as they do on complex biochemical processes:[4]

> 'When a man lifts a cup, it is not only the kind of drink that is in it, the amount he is likely to take, and the circumstances under which he will do the drinking that are specified in advance for him, but also whether the contents of the cup will cheer or stupify, whether they will induce affection or aggression, guilt or unalloyed pleasure. These and many other cultural definitions attach to the drink even before it touches the lips.'[5]

And intimately related to ideas about the effects of alcohol are ideas about the place of drinking in relation to other activities. From the very earliest times alcohol has been used as an integral part of significant social occasions:

in religious ritual; in rites of passage from birth to funeral; in public happenings; in feasts, agreements, meetings, crownings, warmaking and peacemaking; in magic and in medicine.[6]

A recurrent feature of all literature on the place of alcohol and drinking in any society or group is the conflict between its beneficial and harmful effects. For example, the earliest Indian literary sources, the Vedic hymns, give detailed accounts of the use of Sura in sacrificial ritual but roundly condemn drinking outside the ritual occasions as likely to lead to quarrels and mislead men from the path of virtue.[7] In the Old Testament wine is specified in Numbers for use as a libation in the temple service:

> '28 : 7 The wine for the proper drink-offering shall be a quarter of hin to each ram; you are to pour out this strong drink in the holy place as an offering to the Lord.
> 28 : 8 You shall sacrifice the second ram between dusk and dark, with the same grain-offering as at the morning sacrifice and with the proper drink-offering; it is a food-offering of soothing odour to the Lord'.[8]

By contrast several passages in the Book of Proverbs warn against wine's dangers. In the New Testament wine is mentioned as a festive drink,[9] as a medicament[10] and as a supreme symbol,[11] but again there are many references to inappropriate drinking:

> 'Likewise must the deacons be grave, not double tongued, not given to much wine, not greedly of filthy lucre.'[12]

The field studies of social anthropologists show how cultural practices in relation to drink range from 'avid immersion to total rejection'.[13] Among the Kofyar of Northern Nigeria, for example, 'people make, drink, talk and think about beer', and 'certainly think that man's way to God is with beer in hand'[14] By contrast, the Hopi and other Pueblo Indians of the American South-west so abhorred the use of alcohol that it was successfully banned from their settlements.[15] One of the shortcomings of many anthropological studies which mention drinking is that they have tended to give vivid descriptions of orgiastic tribal drinking sprees while ignoring the prosaic and everyday drinking practices. However, there is now a growing body of anthropological literature which deals with the relationship of drinking to other aspects of social life. Heath,[16] for example, in his study of drinking patterns of the Bolivian Camba gives us a detailed account of the type of alcohol which is drunk: pure cane alcohol which 'is probably the most potent alcoholic drink in customary usage'; of the cost of alcohol and its method of production and sale; of the occasions on which alcohol is drunk, 'only during fiestas, but these are not infrequent'; of the context in which drinking takes place: 'only within a social context, solitary drinking is inconceivable to the Camba', and of the common drinking rituals:

> 'The behavioral patterns associated with drinking are so formalized as to constitute a secular ritual. Members of the group are seated in chairs in an approximate circle in a yard or, occasionally, in a hut. A bottle of *alcohol* and a single water glass rest on a tiny table which forms part of the circle. The "sponsor" of the party pours a glassful (about 300 cc) at the table, turns and walks to stand in front of whomever he wishes, nods, and raises the glass slightly. The person addressed smiles and nods while still seated; the "sponsor" toasts with "*Salud*" (health), or "*A su salud*" (to your health), drinks half of the glassful in a single quick draught, and hands it to the person he has toasted, who then repeats the toast and finishes the glass in one gulp. While the "sponsor" returns to his seat, the recipient of the toast goes to the table to refill the glass and to repeat the ritual.
>
> There are no apparent rules concerning whom one may toast, and in this sense toasts proceed in no discernible sequence. A newcomer is likely to receive a barrage of toasts when he first joins a drinking group, and sometimes an attractive girl may be frequently addressed, but there tends to be a fairly equal distribution of toasts over a period of several hours. To decline a toast is unthinkable to the Camba, although as the party wears on and the inflammation of mouth and throat makes drinking increasingly painful, participants resort to a variety of ruses in order to avoid having to swallow an entire glassful of *alcohol* each time'.

Heath goes on to describe the Camba attitudes toward drink; their comportment when drunk, 'hangovers and hallucinations are unknown among these people . . . A farmhand will "snap out of" intoxication abruptly when the call to breakfast is sounded after a fiesta', and to suggest in summary

> 'that alcohol plays a predominantly integrative role in Camba society, where drinking is an elaborately ritualised group activity and alcoholism is unknown'.

While alcohol may play an integral part in religious and secular ritual so the act of drinking may be seen as serving as a symbolic punctuation mark differentiating one social context from another.[17] Just as the orthodox Jew recites the Havdola blessing over wine, and drinks wine at the end of the Sabbath to mark the division between the sacred day and the rest of the week, so 'the cocktail hour' or the swift half pint in the pub near the office help to separate the life of work from the life of home. This book, however, is not just about people's use of, and attitudes toward, alcohol. It is also about the way people define and handle the problems which they take to be associated with alcohol consumption.

Alcoholism, Other Problems and the Question of Definitions

Once we move from considering patterns of alcohol use to a discussion of alcohol-related problems and alcoholism certain basic questions of definition become important. How much drinking is too much drinking? What is the dividing line between having too much drink and being drunk? When does a drinker become an alcoholic, and who says so? These are not merely academic, philosophical or professional questions but matters of wide practical significance. For, although at one level Mulford[18] is quite right when he says that:

> 'Specific criteria for sorting "real alcoholics" from non-alcoholics are not merely indefinite: they are virtually non-existent'

it is nevertheless the case that both professionals and members of the general population are constantly making that very distinction. What Mulford really means is that there are no universally-agreed-upon criteria.

But before approaching the core question of what counts as alcoholism it would be well to set out some of the problems commonly taken to be associated with alcohol consumption. A special report to the United States Congress on *Alcohol and Health* concluded, in a chapter on alcohol and the central nervous system, that alcohol is implicated as a primary or related causal factor in many pathological conditions including:

> 'Brain disorders such as Wernicke's syndrome, Korsakoff's psychosis, niacin-deficiency encephalopathy, and Marchiafava's disease.
>
> Disorders of the digestive system, such as malabsorption of vital nutrients, gastritis, pancreatitis, fatty liver, hepatitis, and cirrhosis.
>
> Generalized myopathy and cardiomyopathy, numerous nutritional diseases in addition to some of the encephalopathies, including polyneuropathy, beriberi heart, pellagra, scurvy, and anemia.
>
> Atrophy of some endocrine glands, disturbances of metabolism that may aggravate or precipitate such conditions as gout and hypoglycemia, and disturbance of metabolism of other drugs.
>
> Increased risk of accident, injury, and death from intake of other drugs that interact additively or potentiatively with alcohol'.[19]

Just as alcohol consumption may be associated with certain pathological conditions so it may be associated with legal and social problems. In 1973 there were just under 100,000 convictions for drunkenness offences in England and Wales.[20] But, apart from causing public drunkenness, drinking has been shown to be associated with conviction for a whole range of other offences. Edwards,[21] for example, reports that 68 per cent of the prisoners he studied claimed to have been drinking immediately before committing the act for which they were imprisoned, while 55 per cent said they were drunk at the time of the offence. In 1968 almost half of all murder defendants were judged to have had some alcohol in their bodies at the time of the offence.[22] A study of crimes of violence[23] revealed that 20 per cent of such crimes occurred in pubs or cafes where alcohol was served and that the violence was said to have been committed under the influence of alcohol, while a study of sexual offenders showed that 20 per cent had been drinking shortly before the offence was committed.[24] In spite of the well-recognized difficulties of interpreting the statistics of alcohol-related motoring offences[25] the extent of the problem may be judged by the fact that in 1968, the year following the introduction of the 'breathalyser' in Britain, 51,414 tests were administered, of which 26,429 were positive. By 1973 this total had risen to 132,432 tests with 77,206 positive.[26]

Quite apart from its association with pathological conditions and legal misdemeanours, the consumption of alcohol is regularly cited as a contributory factor in the development of a whole range of emotional interpersonal, financial, occupational, marital and family problems[27], and *alcoholism* or *alcohol addiction* is frequently used to describe or explain such situations. It is then that the problems of definition become acute. For what is alcoholism?[28]

Over the past century there has been a discernible and well-documented[29] shift from defining alcoholism as primarily a legal or moral problem:

> '. . . a sin, heinous and soul-wrecking, whose victims shall not possess the Kingdom of Heaven'[30]

to considering it primarily as one of medicine or public health:

> '. . . few would deny that it is a condition which belongs to the sphere of the healing professions'[31]

or more specifically as:

> '. . . a psychological dependence on, or physiological addiction to, ethanol manifested by the inability . . . consistantly to control either the start of drinking or its termination once started . . .'[32]

But despite this broad shift of emphasis the difficulty of defining alcoholism is readily acknowledged by those who work with, study, treat, help, judge or live with people who consider themselves or are considered by others to have some alcohol-related problem. Listen to Kessel and Walton, for example, as they wrestle with 'the question of definition':

> 'What is an alcoholic? Without being adequately defined the term is too readily applied to embrace everybody who drinks abnormally. Not all these are alcoholics. Furthermore, there are many different types of alcoholics and many varied patterns of alcoholism. Some define the alcoholic from the vantage point of the sufferer; they name as an alcoholic the person who recognizes that he has to stop drinking but cannot do so. Others have focused on the observable consequences of

uncontrolled drinking; they define an alcoholic as a person whose drinking has caused increasing problems in his health, his domestic or social life or with his work. Others emphasize the quantity of alcohol consumed and the pattern of the drinking habits; only the man who regularly drinks till he is helpless is an alcoholic from their point of view'.[33]

Having so succinctly posed the problem of definition they then attempt to solve it by constructing a classification which distinguishes teetotallers from social drinkers, excessive drinkers, alcoholics, alcohol addicts and chronic alcoholics:

> 'Some people are *teetotallers.*
> Most people drink moderately, frequently they may from time to time get drunk. These are *social drinkers.*
>
> Some people drink excessively, though not necessarily in their own eyes; their excess may show either by the frequency with which they become intoxicated or by the social, economic, or medical consequences of their continued intake of alcohol.
> These are *excessive drinkers* . . .
>
> *Alcoholics* are people with a disease that can be defined in medical terms and requires a proper regime of treatment. Alcoholics are addicted to alcohol. *Alcohol addicts* are unable spontaneously to give up drinking. Though they may go without a drink for a few days, or sometimes for even longer periods, inevitably they revert. The greater the need to stop drinking, the more difficult do they find it to do so . . .
>
> Most alcoholics proceed to a stage where their brains or their bodies have been so harmed by alcohol that the effects persist even when they are not drinking. This stage may be reached by some excessive drinkers who had not manifested addiction. It is called *chronic alcoholism.* The term should only be applied when the body has been physically damaged by alcohol'.[34]

This classificatory scheme is similar to many others in the academic and professional literature. Some are based on clinical insight and experience[35] and others on systematic abstractions from case histories.[36] But, unfortunately, attempts to construct universally applicable definitions have been rather unsuccessful. This is hardly surprising since any definition or description which purported to incorporate the physiological, biochemical, psychological, legal, moral, religious nature of the phenomenon; the process of its development and likely prognosis; the indications for help or treatment; together with its effects upon the individual and the wider society, is likely to be either totally incomprehensible or of such generality as to bear no meaningful relationship to the social world.[36] Yet, since the many and varied features listed above have all at some time or other been cited as essential components of definitions of alcoholism, the search for a universal, all-purpose definition will no doubt continue. And it is easy to understand why. For clinicians and other helping professionals often feel unable to proceed unless they can match cases to a classification which implies certain therapeutic or helping procedures. As Kessel and Walton put it:

> 'To classify a particular drinker may not be easy, yet it is essential if he is to be helped. We cannot properly proceed until we know whether he is a social drinker, an excessive drinker, an excessive drinker with problems, an alcoholic (i.e. an alcohol addict), or has reached the further stage of chronic alcoholism'.[37]

But the mere construction of general wide-ranging definitions of alcoholism does not really advance our understanding of particular patterns of alcohol consumption or the way in which associated problems are defined or handled. In order to throw light on these questions we must not take for granted at the outset what 'alcoholism', or 'drinking problem', or 'being an alcoholic' is. What is needed instead is an understanding of what these things mean to particular people in particular situations. Such an approach is especially necessary in the discussion of drinking and alcoholism when the medical, psychological, physiological and biochemical bases for regarding someone as an alcoholic are so open to dispute. Given all this, what is the sociologist's contribution to the question of defining alcoholism?

Part of the sociologist's task is to discover and to set out the implications of the fact that people differ, often quite radically, in their assessments of what counts as something. As such, the sociologist does not set out to define 'alcoholism' or 'an alcoholic' so that his definitions can be universally applied to stand for diseases to be cured, studied or consulted about, or people to be treated or helped, or prosecuted, sympathized with or admired. What the sociologist *can* be expected to do, however, is to describe and indicate the social and medical implications of people's differences in their assessment of 'what counts as' alcoholism, being an alcoholic, normal drinking, drinking problem, treatment, help and so on. For despite the lack of any universally accepted definitions people, both professional and lay, do employ the notions 'alcoholism' and 'alcoholic' in the course of their everyday lives, and their action is informed by these definitions and by their assessments of the way other people see the situation.

It is with these everyday definitions of such notions as alcoholism and alcoholic, and with the implications of their use in particular settings, that this book is concerned. Thus, the book does not try to answer the question 'what is alcoholism?', but focuses rather on such intimately related sociological questions as 'what is alcoholism taken to mean by particular people in particular situations?' and 'how do some people get into the position in which they are defined, by themselves or by others, as alcoholics?'. For in any situation the categorization 'he is an alcoholic' is the product of some assessment procedure. It constitutes the outcome of investigations of more or less sophistication, detail, care and interest undertaken by people with more or less concern, skill and practical involvement. In any particular lay or professional setting 'alcoholism' comes to be noticed at certain points and not at others, and whatever the medical bases of its accepted recognition there are many respects in which its most critical features have to do with explicitly *social* considerations.

Sociological Studies of Drinking and Alcoholism

Earlier in the chapter it was noted that wherever alcohol has been known, there have also been social rules and conventions concerning its use. Within any one society, these attitudes toward alcohol may range from those who consider it essential and blessed to those who regard it as destructive and evil, while references to individual and social problems held to be associated with alcohol consumption have been made throughout recorded history. Given the ubiquity of alcohol and its importance not merely for its effect upon the individual but as an integral part of significant social occasions it is not surprising that sociologists and anthropologists have paid attention to it.

However, both 'the problem of alcoholism' and 'the question of definitions' have been tackled quite differently in different types of sociological study. Indeed, some people would feel that certain studies of drinking and alcoholism which call themselves sociological are not 'real' sociology at all: but that merely pushes 'the question of definitions' to a new battlefield which is beyond the scope of this book. Nevertheless, most sociological studies of drinking and alcoholism can broadly speaking be divided into three main types: the societal–cultural, the aetiological–pathological and the ethnographic–processual. All three approaches are concerned with the way in which alcohol is used and responded to, but their major foci and core guiding questions are quite different. The aim of the remainder of this section is not to present an exhaustive review of the sociological literature but rather to use certain studies to exemplify the major themes of broadly sociological work concerned with alcohol, drinking and associated problems.

Societal–Cultural Studies

These are concerned with very broad questions about 'the place of alcohol in society' and with postulating hypotheses about a whole culture of society, or even *all* cultures. The works of Horton, Field and Bales, for example, have the ambitious, 'supra-cultural orientation'[38] of this latter category.

Horton[39] examined the files of the Cross-cultural Survey in the Institute of Human Relations at Yale and extracted information on drinking for 77 different societies. He then constructed a scale of drinking behaviour based on the degree of insobriety commonly reached by adult male drinkers and related this to various indicators of 'subsistence anxiety'. The more primitive a society's food gathering techniques, the greater is the danger of food shortages and the more difficult are life conditions. These conditions, according to Horton, should create a relatively high amount of anxiety. Primitive subsistence techniques were, thus, assumed to be conducive to high anxiety levels and such societies were also found to have a high level of insobriety. The process of acculturation was also assumed to create high levels of anxiety and Horton demonstrated that those societies in which he found evidence of acculturation in progress were also categorized by extremely high levels of insobriety. All this, together with other supporting data, led Horton to conclude that the primary function of alcoholic beverages in *any* society is the reduction of anxiety.

Twenty years later Field[40] re-examined Horton's theory. He used data on 56 of the same tribes, and constructed a new scale of insobriety which measured degree of drunkenness at periodic drinking bouts. While he found no relationship between level of fear — of sorcerers or ghosts — and the extent of drunkenness, he did confirm Horton's finding that tribes with very primitive hunting and gathering economies tend to have more drunkenness than those based on agricultural economies. However, Field suggests that it is differences in the social organization of the tribes which is responsible for the relationship rather than 'subsistence anxiety'. Drunkenness, he claims:

> '. . . is determined less by the level of fear in a society than by an absence of corporate kin groups with stability, permanence, formal structure, and well-defined functions'.

Others concerned with alcohol use at a supra-cultural level have developed classifications of cultural attitudes toward drinking. Pittman,[41] for example, in an 'international overview' of social and and cultural factors in drinking patterns suggests that theoretically:

> ' . . . it is possible to range all cultures on a continuum in reference to their attitudes about drinking. At least four cultural positions can be constructed. These are:
>
> 1. The cultural attitude is negative and prohibitive toward any type of ingestion of alcoholic beverages. This may be referred to as the *Abstinent Culture.*
>
> 2. The cultural attitude toward beverage alcohol usage is one of conflict between co-existing value structures. This may be called the *Ambivalent Culture.*
>
> 3. The cultural attitude toward ingesting beverage alcohol is permissive, but negative toward drunkenness and other drinking pathologies. For labelling, we refer to this as the *Permissive Culture.*
>
> 4. The cultural attitude is permissive toward drinking, to behaviours which occur when intoxicated, and to drinking pathologies. In one sense, this type, the *Over-Permissive Culture,* does not occur completely in societies, but only approximations in certain nonliterate societies, in those

cultures undergoing considerable social change, and those in which there are strong economic vested interests in the production and distribution of alcoholic beverages'.

Pittman then goes on to cite cultures, societies, states, racial groups and religious sects which could be classified in this way. Hindu Indian society, for example, he classifies as an Abstinent Culture in which:

> 'Both custom and tradition . . . established a moral standard which negatively evaluated the drinking of alcoholic beverages. For example, the Indian law-giver, Manu, classed beverage alcohol drinking as one of the greatest antisocial acts or sins and suggested abstention. The principle of total abstinence and Prohibition is reflected in the Indian Constitution . . . written after independence was achieved from Great Britain. (Part IV, Article 47) . . . states: "and in particular, the state shall endeavour to bring about prohibition of consumption, except for medicinal purposes, of intoxicating drinks" '.

Several other writers have developed classifications of various purposes or 'functions' of drinking. In one scheme[42] drinking practices are categorized as either integrative for the individual and society, or anxiety-reducing (particularly for the individual), or as disintegrative for the society and the individual. Bales[43], on the other hand, suggests that alcoholic beverages can serve one or more of the following four functions; religious, ceremonial, hedonistic or utilitarian. Hedonistic or pleasurable usages range from the conviviality engendered by drinking with others to the euphoric feelings of getting high or having 'a glow on',[44] while utilitarian drinking, according to Bales, refers to the use of alcohol to gain some 'relief or satisfaction or self-oriented, self-centred needs'. More specifically alcohol's:

> ' . . . everyday use to begin the day, to get rid of a "hangover", to quiet hunger, to relieve stomach disorder, to get warm, to keep warm, to reward the child . . . to improve the physician's skill, to dispel fatigue and to promote sleep — all of these and more are utilitarian uses . . . '.[45]

While writers such as Horton, Field and Bales attempt to provide supra-cultural analyses of drinking behaviour, others — less ambitious — have concentrated on the place of alcohol in one particular society or one segment of society. Some have concentrated on comparative or interpretive questions such as 'why do the drinking practices of this group or segment of society differ from the practices of others?. Others have focused on basic descriptive questions such as 'what are the drinking practices of this culture, or group, or segment of society?'.

Surprisingly, perhaps, given the wealth of material on clinical, moral and legal aspects of alcohol and associated problems, there has been comparatively little basic descriptive work, particularly on a national scale, on the central phenomenon of all these problems — everyday drinking practices. The most notable exception is the study by Cahalan and his associates entitled *American Drinking Practices.*[46] In his introduction to that book, Selden Bacon identifies its particular contribution:

> '. . . in the area of alcohol phenomena and alcohol-related problems there are studies and books and pamphlets, there are conferences and national organizations and films, there are newspaper reports and laws and handbooks on procedures, but they are often so disparate in language and purpose and target of attack that confusion, evasion and even outright hostility are all too frequent. One is concerned with disease, another with accidents, a third with sales control, a fourth with criminal justice. One is based on biochemistry, another on personality, a third on political art or science and a fourth on community organization and public health. Cahalan, Cisin and Crossley have centred attention on the phenomenon central to all these approaches and central to all the problems no matter what their form, no matter what discipline or language is employed: namely, man using alcoholic beverages. Only as this phenomenon occurs do any of the questions, any of the problems and any of the controversies about cause or about policy for action even have existence. Knowledge about this phenomenon is at the base. The other knowledges, for example, law, psychiatry, metabolism, ethics, may have much to offer this field, but they are not this field itself and they developed their unique theories, methods and assumptions in other settings. Man in society using alcoholic beverages and having attitudes about that use, is the basis of this field. All too frequently this core, this essential and crucial precondition to all questions and answers, has been forgotten'.

The very few studies such as *American Drinking Practices* which are 'concerned with the who, what, when, how much and why of drinking . . . at a particular period of time', provide a broad back-cloth against which to set more specific questions such as why do particular religious,[47] age,[48] sex[49] ethnic,[50] social status[51] or other[52] groups within a particular society have different alcohol consumption patterns. For although there have been very few national studies of everyday drinking practices there have been many studies of how specific segment of a society define and use alcohol. For instance, a great deal of work has been done, particularly in America, on the different drinking patterns of major religious groups.

Three national drinking surveys, conducted since the Second World War, found that among major religious groups Jews contained the highest percentage of adult drinkers. Riley in 1947[53] put the figure at 87 per cent, Mulford in 1963[54] put it at 90 per cent while Cahalan in 1968[55] put it at 92 per cent. By itself, of course, this information is of no great interest. But juxtaposed with another body of material,[56] which suggests that Jews have the lowest rate of alcoholism among all major religious groups, it raises a number of important questions. 'Why do the highest consumers of alcohol have the lowest proportion of alcoholics?', 'is there something about the way Jews use alcohol which prevents them from becoming alcoholic?', 'are Jews less likely to be defined as "alcoholic" than other people with similar drinking habits and problems?'. In short, how does one explain what Keller[57] has called 'the great Jewish drink mystery?'.

Bales,[58] employing his four-fold classification of drinking 'functions', claims that alcoholism rates are low among Jews because of their 'ritual' attitude toward drinking. The frequent use of wine in religious ceremony leads the Jew to reject the use of drink for personal or hedonistic reasons. Hence, according to Bales, the idea of drinking to intoxication for some individual or selfish reason arouses such counter anxiety that few Jews ever become alcoholics. Others have tried to relate Jewish sobriety to the need for Jews to conform to the best standards of society in order to avoid censure and blame,[59] to the use of alcohol for 'instrumental' rather than 'affective' reasons[60] and to Jewish values placed on education, self-control and rational behaviour.[61]

These studies on Jewish drinking, and the studies on other segments of society, all aim to explain why some group drinks in a particular way. Along with all the other studies which were mentioned earlier they attempt to place the use of alcohol in its cultural and social setting; to set out the relationship between alcohol consumption and other familial, religious, occupational, recreational and civic activities; and even, as in the case of writers such as Horton, Field and Bales, to speculate about the role of alcohol in human society as a whole. With a small number of notable exceptions, sociological research into these broad questions of a society's drinking and related practices is not very far advanced. But given the huge investments in time and money which are required to mount and successfully carry through such research this is, perhaps, hardly surprising. Nevertheless, an appreciation of the meaning which drinking has for members of the general population, and of the place it has in their everyday lives is increasingly being recognized as an essential part of any understanding of why particular people develop problems which are in some way connected with alcohol consumption and why those problems are defined and responded to in the way they are. Thus, intimately related to the societal–cultural studies, but different in their core focus and methodology, are the aetiological–pathological studies which compose the second major sociological approach to drinking and alcoholism.

Aetiological-Pathological Studies

These focus directly on the question 'why do some people use alcohol in a way which they, or other people, consider harmful?' or, more simply, 'what are the social causes of "pathological" drinking?'. Two major forms of aetiological–pathological study have developed: the epidemiologic and the case-based.

Epidemiologic studies categorize cross-sections of specific populations in terms of troubles or problems associated with alcohol consumption. 'Problem scores' are assigned to each individual and then explanations are offered, in terms of concomitant or antecedent differences on some 'social' dimensions, for why some people have higher problem scores than other people. Edwards and his associates, for example, conducted just such an epidemiologic study of drinking troubles in a London Suburb.[62] However, a major problem with all epidemiologic studies, from a purely sociological viewpoint, is that the crucial definitional questions have to be answered before the study begins. Problem scores, for example, such as those constructed by Edwards and those discussed in the next chapter, depend upon the researcher deciding at the outset what is to count as 'a drinking problem' of a certain kind and then, in addition, deciding in any particular case whether a specific problem is present or not. There is no way for the respondent, client or patient to define what he takes to be a drinking problem in the light of his everyday circumstances. Nor is there usually any opportunity for additional 'problems' to be accommodated in 'the score'. Another drawback to epidemiological studies, though not built in to them by definition, is that they are usually one-off. As such they identify problems and associated characteristics in individuals and groups but, because the time dimension is missing, can only very tentatively approach the crucial question of cause. The status of the statements which Edwards and his team felt able to make at the end of their research, for example, are honestly signposted in the sub-title of their paper: 'Drinking in a London Suburb: Correlates of trouble with drinking'. Among their conclusions are that:

> 'Younger people are disproportionately likely to experience trouble with their drinking . . .
>
> Demographic correlates of heavier drinking are generally also predictors of higher prevalence of trouble due to drinking . . .
>
> Relative socio-economic privilege does not protect against the likelihood of reported trouble'.

One epidemiologic study, however, which does approach the question of cause is Don Cahalan's study of *Problem Drinkers.*[63] Like Edwards he constructed current problem scores based on the presence of certain predefined problems plus differential scoring for the intensity or severity of the problem within a particular time period. But by conducting the study in two stages he was able to incorporate a change-over-time dimension in terms of which to compute the differential importance of various variables for the onset and development of certain drinking problems. Six key variables were concentrated on:

(1) Attitude toward drinking; he found that highly favoured attitudes toward drinking are strongly correlated with problem drinking.

(2) Environmental support for heavy drinking; the thesis that significant others teach us how and when and how much to drink and also reinforce drinking behaviour by their example and by their own attitudes toward drinking.

(3) Impulsivity and non-conformity; the belief that when heavy drinking is deprecated by society an individual's persistent indulgence in heavy drinking indicates that he is either impulsive or deliberately non-conformist.

(4) Alientation and maladjustment; Cahalan reasoned that those scoring high on this scale would be more likely than others to adopt the use of alcohol to relieve tensions, anxieties and fears of failure.

(5) Unfavourable expectations; the suggestion that those who feel that they can achieve their expectations are less likely than others to drink excessively.

(6) Looseness of social controls; the hypothesis that the greater the number of close primary-group ties a person has, the more likely he will be to live up to a norm of moderation.

The first four of these variables accounted for virtually all the variance in the multiple correlation of the six variables at Stage I with problem scores at Stage II; when problems having occurred in the intervening years were reported. The greatest share of the multiple correlation was accounted for by the 'attitude toward drinking' variable. This variable was built up of various strands such as; would the respondent miss drinking if he had to give it up, did he agree that drinking does more good than harm, did he feel good things could be said about drinking and did he feel that drinking was associated with sociability.

Clearly the range of any possible causal link which epidemiologists can forge is determined by the range of social areas which are built into the investigation before it starts. As a result it is a characteristic of such studies that they usually cover a great deal of ground rather superficially. The second type of aetiological–pathological study avoids this particular difficulty, but faces others.

The second type of aetiological–pathological approach is the case-based study of patients or offenders. Based on alcoholism clinics, hospitals, courts, probation offices, hostels and the like, these studies attempt to discern common social features, situations or events in the individuals' past histories which might suggest why they became 'pathological' drinkers. While case-based studies have, of course, focused on a great many variables such as sex,[64] ethnicity,[65] age of starting to drink,[66] social class,[67] level of education[68] and religion,[69] by far the most attention has been given to the family origins of people who are defined in various institutional settings as 'pathological drinkers'. As Roebuck and Kessler succinctly put it, in their wide ranging discussion of the literature in *The Etiology of Alcoholism:*

'A common assumption . . . is that the individual's family orientation is one of the most important factors in determining behaviour. Given this assumption, it seems logical to examine the families of alcoholics in any attempt to understand the causes of alcoholism'.[70]

Wittman[71], for example, reviewed much early literature on the family of the alcoholic. In the majority of these studies the main aetiological factors in the chronic alcoholic's history were felt to be: a doting mother and a stern father who inspired respect, awe or fear, and who displayed inconsistent tendencies of severity and indulgence thus, the studies claim, producing in the child a feeling of insecurity and helpless dependence. Wittman in her own study of 100 male alcoholics and 100 controls matched for age, education and nationality, substantiated the descriptions she had found in the early literature. However, several other studies have not supported these findings.[72]

Another body of work has concentrated on parental attitudes toward drink. Jackson and Conner,[73] for example, hypothesized that the parents of alcoholics would have different attitudes about drinking from the attitudes of the parents of non-alcoholics. The authors found in their comparison study of 'alcoholics', 'moderate drinkers' and 'non-drinkers' that non-drinkers more frequently came from homes in which neither parent drank and where both parents disapproved of drinking. Moderate drinkers also came frequently from non-drinking homes but almost as often from homes in which both parents drank. Alcoholics, on the other hand, came most frequently from homes in which only one parent, usually the father, drank. Jackson and Conner claim that in this 'ambivalent environment' the individual, who since developed into an alcoholic, was unable to develop a consistent and well-organized attitudinal structure which could restrain him from excessive drinking.

Other writers have focused on the question of whether the children of alcoholics become alcoholics themselves. Kinsey,[74] for example, found that a third of female alcoholics he studied had an alcoholic father while a small proportion had an alcoholic mother. Moore and Ramseur[75] found 35 alcoholic fathers and six alcoholic mothers in the histories of their sample of 100 alcoholics. MacKay[76] analysed the family histories of 20 adolescent problem drinkers referred to an alcoholism clinic. On the bases of this material he constructed five hypotheses about aetiology: (a) alcoholism was a frequent parental trait; (b) the child brought into the first and early drinking situations a high degree of ambivalence, uncertainty and concern based on his observation of effects of alcohol in his own family; (c) in an attempt to demonstrate independence from their parents the children had to prove their ability to drink successfully as compared with the way in which their parents drank, thus they placed value on the use of alcoholic beverages; (d) the family situation produced for these children a feeling of not belonging which was assuaged at least in some part by their drinking associates and (e) their feeling that alcohol had temporarily filled the emptiness physically felt by these children and ameliorated their passive feelings of depression.

Although these and other similar studies were able to cover ground more substantially and in greater detail than the epidemiologic ones mentioned earlier the major problem with them is that they are all retrospective and based on specifically selected populations of already designated alcoholics or problem drinkers. In short, there is no attempt to question why these particular people, among all people who drink in a similar way, are defined by themselves or by others as alcoholics or problem drinkers. There is no information either on how these people actually used alcohol, or how they and professional and lay others intimately involved with them, defined, and responded to drinking problems. The third main type of sociological approach to drinking and alcoholism concentrates on some of these questions.

Ethnographic–Processual Studies

These studies of drinking and alcoholism have focused on particular drinking places, on particular groups of drinkers or alcoholics and on particular helping agencies. In spite of the fact that the majority of people in most societies consume alcohol in some form with greater or lesser regularity there have been few studies of the actual context in which drinking takes place. Clinard's[77] survey of the sociological literature revealed very few published references to the role of public drinking houses in contemporary society and even fewer studies of social interaction in them. In 1897 E. C. Moore attempted to spell out 'the social value of the saloon' in the belief that any institution so widely patronized must supply legitimate needs. He concluded that the saloon:

> ' . . . transforms the individual into a *socius,* where there is no other transforming power. It unites the many ones into a common whole which we call society, and it stands for this union amid conditions which would otherwise render it impossible, and intemperance is but its accident'.[78]

In the three-quarters of a century since that study there have been very few attempts to assess the place of the pub or tavern in the life of those who use it, or even to describe the everyday life and routines in public drinking houses.[79] Two major exceptions are Sherri Cavan's ethnographic account of bar behaviour in San Francisco and the Mass Observation study of The Pub and The People.[80] I have found no sociological studies of drinking behaviour in homes, clubs or other 'private' places.

Clinard, in an attempt to incorporate important institutional factors into his definition of a public drinking house suggests that:

> 'A more complete definition would include these characteristics, (*a*) The serving of alcoholic beverages is an indispensable feature and important source of revenue even if food is served. Because they do not serve alcoholic beverages, such places as soda fountains or milk bars, coffee houses of Greece and the Middle East, or tea houses of the Orient are not public drinking houses as the term is used here. (*b*) As a drinking establishment it is commercial and public in the sense that theoretically the

opportunity to purchase a drink is open to all, whereas the bar of a private club or fraternal organization is restricted to members and their guests. (*c*) The drinking of alcoholic beverages is *group drinking* in the sense that it is done in the company of others in a public place. (*d*) It must have a functionary — a tavern keeper, a bartender, or, as in Europe, a barmaid. This person in addition to serving alcoholic beverages, also acts as a sort of receptionist. (*e*) Finally, it has a physical structure and a set of norms. Patrons are served at a bar, tables or booths, in specially decorated surroundings, with entertainment or recreational facilities like cards, darts and shuffle board available, thus distinguishing it in some way from the customary activities of other similar establishments. Certain norms are also well established, including certain hours of drinking and appropriate drinking behaviour'.[81]

While there have been few studies of drinking places there have been many studies of drinkers — or rather one particular group; the drinkers of Skid Row. This second type of ethnographic–processual research ranges from the general studies of Skid Row,[82] 'Flop Houses',[83] and hobos[84] to those which concentrate on *alcoholic* Skid Row men and women.[85] Some studies focus on the characteristics of the Skid Row alcoholic[86] while others attempt to explain how people are socialized into Skid Row life.[87] Jackson and Conner,[88] for example, discuss the social organization of getting and drinking wine on Skid Row and claim that the small drinking groups which sustain mutual survival and provide emotional support also meet the alcoholic's dependency needs without forcing him to recognize the fact that he is dependent.

In 'The Bottle Gang' Rubington[89] analyses the patterns and significance of salutation, negotiation, procurement, consumption, affirmation and dispersal in an 'East Coast' city. Each of the stages, he claims, has a particular function and manifests certain formalities and rules which are talked about a great deal, but often broken and little enforced. Archard[90] has recently produced an analysis of similar organizational rules in some English bottle gangs.

The third type of ethnographic–processual study focuses on the organizations and agencies which exist to help those who define themselves, or are defined by others, as having some drink-related problem. There are a small number of broadly sociological studies of alcoholism clinics,[91] hostels,[92] Alcoholics Anonymous (A.A.) groups[93] and other facilities.[94]

Bales, for example, in 'The Therapeutic Role of Alcoholics Anonymous as seen by a Sociologist' notes that all spontaneous movements such as A.A. have a tendency through the years to move through a cycle of institutionalization in which 'greater clarification, regularization, and, finally formalization and rigidity' of both structure and function occur. He examines the structure of A.A. and attempts to relate the characteristics of the organization to the major purpose of the group — staying sober. In a concluding paragraph he succinctly describes Alcoholics Anonymous' particular strength:

'In this fund of common experience, and in the particularly intimate friendship it fosters, every member has a resource for helping other alcoholics that can hardly be duplicated by any other type of therapist'.[95]

As well as studying specific organizations a great deal of sociological writing has focused on the implications for an individual of coming into contact with *any* organization or group which attempts to control or deal with illness or some deviance from what the helpers take to be normality. The focus of this work is on the social reaction to that illness or deviant behaviour. As Becker puts it:

'I will be less concerned with the personal and social characteristics of deviants than with the process by which they come to be thought of as outsiders and their reactions to that judgment'.[96]

From this point of view 'mental illness'[97] or 'alcoholism', are, in part, a function of the administrative decisions made by people in positions of power such as lawyers, judges, social workers, or psychiatrists. In short, those who have the power to define some behaviour as deviant and apply sanctions 'create' that deviance. While there has been no major study of the 'labelling process' of alcohol users there has been a good deal of work done on the users of other drugs. Young,[98] for example, builds upon Wilkins'[99] deviancy amplification theory which holds that when a society define a group of people as deviant it tends to react against them so as to isolate and alienate them from the company of 'normal' people. In this situation of isolation and alienation the group tends to develop its own norms and values which society perceives as even more deviant than before. As a consequence of this increase in deviancy, societal reaction increases even further; the group is even more isolated and alienated; it acts even more deviantly; society acts increasingly strongly against it; and a spiral of deviancy amplification occurs. However, it is *not* being suggested that the deviant group is inexorably propelled, as if by magic, along such a path. For, of course, man creates as well as reacts to his circumstances. As Young puts it:

'The drug taking group creates its own circumstances to the extent that it interprets and makes meaningful the reactions of society against it'.

Ethnographic–processual studies are concerned with the social processes involved not only in drinking situations and in the everyday lives of people taken to be alcoholics or problem drinkers, but also in treatment and other helping situations. As such, the psychiatrist, the general practitioner, the social worker and the policeman are every bit as much a subject for study as the barman, the drinker, his family and his friends. Not surprisingly, perhaps, the literature is thinnest in his third major type of sociological approach.

The aim of this chapter has been to identify the kinds of question that the sociologist is particularly concerned with in relation to alcohol, drinking and associated problems. It was suggested that at the heart of any sociological study is the question of definitions and the attempt to describe and trace out the implications of the fact that people, both professional and lay, differ in their assessment of 'what counts as' such things as alcoholism, being an alcoholic, normal drinking, treatment, help and so on. As such, the sociologist does not try to answer the question 'what is alcoholism' but focuses rather on such intimately related questions as 'what do particular people take alcoholism to be?' and 'how do people get into the position of defining themselves or being defined by other people as an alcoholic?'.

In the brief overview of the sociological literature three major approaches to the study of alcohol, drinking and alcoholism have been identified. These range from the ambitious supra-cultural orientation of those who hope to pin down the function or role of alcohol in society as a whole to the small-scale studies of those who attempt to tease out the complex everyday social rules which underpin cocktail bar behaviour or the diagnostic practices in out-patient clinics. But at whatever level, the sociological perspective is concerned with the way in which people understand, interpret, theorize about, anticipate, learn from and make mistakes over, the causes and consequences of their own behaviour and the behaviour of others. In short, it is about how people make their everyday lives work.

Chapter 2

Alcohol Consumption and Alcohol Problems

'Thou swear'st thou'lt drink no more; kind heaven send
Me such a cook or coachman, but no friend'. *Anon.*[1]

It is a truism that alcohol is a socially accepted drug and that drinking is a commonplace activity. Yet the simple question of who drinks what, when and where is often ignored by those who study, treat or try to understand people with drink-related problems. At one level this lack of attention to everyday drinking behaviour is quite understandable. For, given that there are limiteed resources of money, facilities and time, both therapists and researchers usually have more immediately pressing matters to attend to. If it is not the pleas of patients it is the pleas of their families and friends. If it is not the reorganization of services it is changes in the liquor licensing laws, or the setting up of detoxification centres, or the introduction of new laws concerned with drinking and driving, or the need to stress the importance of 'the alcohol problem' to government departments, professional colleagues or the general public. In short, there are enough social, political, legal, medical and administrative problems caused by or closely associated with alcohol consumption for everyday drinking behaviour to be considered as, at best, a peripheral matter.

Nevertheless, any attempt to understand or alleviate a problem will be enhanced by a consideration of the context in which that problem arises or is likely to be handled. If we are interested in alcoholism and drinking problems then the everyday world of drink is very much part of the context in which such problems are initially defined. For, of course, people do not just become alcoholics. The social process begins by someone making the link between everyday drinking and the development of some problem. The link may be based on the quantity which the person consumes, or on that person's behaviour after consuming a certain amount, on their behaviour in other related contexts, or on the importance which they give to drinking in terms of finance, time or precedence over other commitments such as family, marriage or work. In short, a whole range of actions or events in relation to everyday drinking may be seen as significant signs of the development of some alcohol-related problem.

Just as the everyday world of drink has been rather neglected by those who are concerned with alcoholics and problem drinkers, so 'the everyday world of alcohol problems' has been given less attention than it deserves. For although there is a great deal of written material on the alcohol-related problems of people who come into contact with helping agencies we have got much less information about the distribution of such problems in the population at large. Therefore, this chapter, which draws on material from a general population survey conducted in South London, concentrates first on the two simple questions: 'who drinks what, when and where?' and 'what kind of alcohol problems are experienced by members of the general population?'. The final section discusses the complex relationship *between* alcohol consumption and alcohol problems.

Alcohol Consumption

In addition to its importance in relation to the development of a whole range of problems, the question of who drinks what, when and where is well worthy of discussion in its own right since producing, selling, taxing, writing about, or being concerned in some way with alcoholic drinks is a significant feature of contemporary life. In 1970, for example, the Brewers' Society, the principal trade association concerned with the production and distribution of alcoholic drinks within the United Kingdom, calculated that the industry had an invested capital of over £1,700 million — more than three times that invested in the aircraft and aerospace industry, and not far short of the entire capital invested in the manufacture of foodstuffs.[2] The number of men and women employed in the brewing, malting and distilling industry comes to well over 100,000, while the alcohol industry as a whole regularly accounts for more than one third of the total value of United Kingdom exports.[3]

Consumer expenditure on alcohol has risen steadily over the past 15 years in the United Kingdom, the United States and elsewhere. Spending on beer, for example, in the United Kingdom rose from £563 million in 1960 to almost £1,500 million in 1973, and although the average proportion of income spent on alcoholic drinks by all households remains fairly constant at 3·5 per cent, the government's Family Expenditure Surveys[4] show that the greater the income the greater the proportion of all expenditure which goes on drink. However, the exact relationship between household income and expenditure on alcohol is always difficult to assess. For instance the household estimates in the Expenditure Surveys account for little more than half the amount of alcohol which would have been expected from the returns of Her Majesty's Customs and Excise. This is due partly to households under-reporting the amounts actually spent on alcohol and partly because of the difficulty in distinguishing between household and non-household populations.

Estimates of per capita consumption are usually derived from official statistics on production plus imports minus exports. Although Customs and Excise based figures are carefully computed there are three main sources of error in any national per capita consumption figures. First there is the home production of wines and beers which is becoming increasingly popular in Britain, and a major source of alcoholic beverages in many other countries in Africa and South America. Second, there is illegal home distillation. Even in countries where home distillation is legal the amount which is distilled and not declared to the excise department may be as great as the amount which is.[5] A third cause of error in official per capita consumption figures is that in some countries consumption by tourists may not be offset by the amount drunk by nationals when they are abroad.

Although it is difficult to obtain accurate national consumption figures, international comparisons of alcohol consumption are even more difficult to make. The report on *Alcohol and Health* presented to the United States Congress[6] in 1971 contained a league table of 20 nations showing the 'apparent consumption . . . of each major beverage class in U.S. gallons per person in the drinking-age population'. The report is rightly cautious about the value of these data, some of which are reproduced in Table 1.

TABLE 1. Alcohol consumption, in U.S. gallons [a]

	Country	Year	TOTAL Absolute Alcohol
1.	France	1966	6·53
2.	Italy	1968	4·01
3.	Switzerland	1966	3·39
4.	West Germany	1968	3·26
5.	Australia	1966	2·89
6.	Belgium	1967	2·87
7.	U.S.A.	1970	2·61
8.	New Zealand	1964	2·58
9.	Czechoslovakia	1968	2·45
10.	Canada	1967	2·20
11.	Denmark	1968	1·94
12.	United Kingdom	1966	1·90
13.	Sweden	1968	1·74
14.	Japan	1968	1·53
15.	The Netherlands	1968	1·53
16.	Ireland	1966	1·49
17.	Norway	1968	1·13
18.	Finland	1968	1·03
19.	Iceland	1966	0·96
20.	Israel	1968	0·82

[a] Note: Age 15 and over.

'. . . Included are only those countries from which adequate statistics on both alcohol consumption and population are available for recent years . . . Some caution is necessary in evaluating these data: the time period is not the same for all the countries; the assignment of a uniform drinking age of 15 years is surely inaccurate; in some cases, the information about average alcohol content of beverages is not too certain. If the numbers are not treated as absolute but looked on as approximations, however, they are of reasonable use. The more regrettable feature of this table is the absence of many countries from which adequate information could not be obtained'.

National and international figures tend, at best, to generate estimates of average consumption. The 1971 Report to Congress, for instance, after calculating that every drinker in the United States consumed an average of 3·93 U.S. gallons of absolute alcohol in the year 1969–70, pointed out that this

'. . . allows, for one drinker, about 44 fifths of whiskey; or 98 bottles of fortified wine; or 157 bottles of table wine; or 928 bottles of beer . . . or, for a drinker with eclectic tastes, about 12 fifths of whiskey plus 15 bottles of sherry plus 30 bottles of table wines plus 350 bottles of beer. The average may also be calculated as a little over 3 ounces of whiskey a day, or the equivalent in other beverages — for example, one cocktail, one glass of wine, and a bottle of beer a day'

But, as the report went on to emphasize:

'All the preceding calculations have ascribed the alcoholic beverages to an "average" drinker. The average drinker, however, is a myth. The United States probably does not have a single man or woman who consumed exactly 3·93 U.S. gallons of absolute alcohol during 1969–70'.[7]

Clearly, a more realistic picture of everyday drinking would have to take account of the whole range of consumption patterns from those who drink very lightly on rare occasions to those who regularly drink very heavily. Unfortunately the methodological problems involved in conducting realistic drinking behaviour studies are immense, and have taxed the ingenuity of a great many researchers.

The first problem concerns the basic measurement of consumption. Kirsh and associates,[8] in a small-scale study designed to test the validity of self-reporting on alcohol consumption, produce some evidence to suggest that the answers to survey questions may be taken as reasonably accurate while Ira Cisin, one of the authors of *American Drinking Practices*, reminds us that 'detailed accuracy' is not an absolute pre-requisite of useful survey material:

. . . the question of validity ought not to be asked about the *truthfulness* of any individual statements, but about the resultant *summary* classification of each individual . . . the validity question ought to be asked thus: "To what extent will misclassification of drinking behavior result in serious distortion of reported relationships?" '[9]

However, 'the problem of validity' in respect of data on alcohol consumption is not really so easy to accommodate as Cisin suggests. For while it is certainly true that for most practical research purposes it is rarely necessary to do more than place respondents in one of a small number of broad alcohol consumption categories we still need to be satisfied that the readily-acknowledged overall under-reporting is not too unevenly disturbed. Pernanen has recently identified 'the factors responsible for a less than perfect coverage' as 'imperfect sampling frames and cluster effects, non-response, forgetting and lying'.[10]

In most surveys samples are based on one of a variety of official lists or registers and as such certain residences are typically left out. Some, such as hotels, student hostels and military institutions may contain a disproportionate proportion of heavy drinkers while others, such as certain hospitals and old people's homes, may have a concentration of low consumers. In addition, in any large city there are likely to be Skid Row type districts which contain a cluster of unrecorded high consumers, while other low-status low-consumers without fixed addresses will fall outside, the sampling frame. The relative influence of such factors is, of course, difficult to assess but Mäkelä[11] from a 96·7 per cent response rate in a sample based on the Finnish population register got only a 38·0 per cent 'coverage' of consumption. He concluded, however, that the elements not covered in the sample cannot explain the large discrepancy between sales statistics and survey results.

Looking for other explanations for 'under coverage', there is evidence that heavier drinkers are not only harder to locate, but are also more likely to refuse to be interviewed,[12] and while all drinkers tend to remember more drinking occasions in the previous week than in the week before that this 'extinction effect' is more pronounced in frequent rather than infrequent drinkers.[13] A study by Hochstim[14] found more drinkers among women by mail and telephone interviews than by personal interview, while Room found wide regional differences which he attributes to:

> 'greater tendency for respondents to deny or underestimate drinking in milieux where drinking is not publicly accepted'.[15]

The differential coverage of different types of alcoholic beverage also indicates the effect of selective reporting. The low-status drinks such as fortified wines tend to be under-reported to a greater degree than other types of alcoholic beverages,[16] and, as in other areas of social research, the dynamics of the interview situation itself differentially affects reporting rates for certain questions.[17]

On the significance of these and many other methodological points Pernanen concludes that:

'Noncoverage due to incomplete sampling frames, or due to clustering of high consumers into certain areas, or selective nonresponse of high consumers will lead to a biased distribution of consumption and attenuated or perhaps even spurious relationships between drinking variables and other variables . . .

The effects of noncoverage due to forgetting are harder to speculate about. There seems to be no reason to assume that there are subgroups in the population where forgetting (or the drinking patterns that make forgetting more probable) is so significantly different that it would have an effect even on the distribution of consumption. . . .

Selective reporting is the most serious factor affecting coverage. Considering the different norm sets and role definitions applying to different subgroups of the populations as to their drinking and other behavior, it would be surprising if some of these did not under-report to a larger extent than others. . . .

Aggregate coverage figures are still too crude a measure of validity of survey findings to allow any further speculation about the consequences. Studies based on validation of each individual's drinking would be needed, but the practical difficulties are so great that no known attempts have been made. There are no records available that would show an individual's actual alcohol consumption over a period of time. . . .'[18]

Apart from the measurement of alcohol consumption, another major problem is faced by those who wish to group their subjects according to some broad drinking classification. Many workers have assigned people according to a simple quantity–frequency (Q–F) index of the amount of alcohol consumed over a particular period of time.[19] The *American Drinking Practices* survey added a variability dimension and, based on 12 questions, this Q.F.V. index took into account:

'The *quantity* of a beverage consumed at a sitting . . . The *frequency* with which each of the three types of beverage (beer, wine and spirits) was usually drunk; The *variability* of drinking, as shown by a combination of the modal amount consumed and the highest amount drunk at least occasionally'[20]

Cahalan and his associates then assigned their respondents to one of five categories; heavy drinkers, moderate drinkers, light drinkers, infrequent drinkers and abstainers. These categories were the dependent variables for subsequent analysis.

This chapter draws, in part, on material from a very small scale general population study of people aged 18 and over in an area of South London.[21]

Like other general population studies it relies on retrospective accounts of who drank what, when and where. However, unlike the *American Drinking Practices* survey and the study conducted by Edwards and his associates[22] the focus was not on the respondents' notion of their 'usual' drinking behaviour, but rather on their reporting of what they had actually drunk in the preceding seven days. Seven days was felt to be the maximum period over which people could be expected to recall their drinking behaviour with any degree of accuracy. The drawback with this focus on the immediate past is that, as Cahalan and associates say, the procedure is likely to ' . . . catch certain respondents at atypical times and lead to incorrect groupings for average, usual behaviour'.[23]

Before being questioned about their drinking in the previous week, respondents were asked to say when they had *last* had an alcoholic drink of any kind. Three quarters of the sample said that they had had their last drink within the past month while just over 10 per cent said that they had either not had a drink in the past year or that they had never had a drink at all. This proportion of rare or non-drinkers is almost identical to that found by Edwards and his associates in their earlier survey of the same South London area and by the recent survey of Scottish drinking habits,[24] but much lower than the 30 to 35 per cent reported in American[25] and Scandinavian[26] studies. However, these broad 'last drink' categories tended to mask important age, sex and social status differences in everyday drinking behaviour. For example, although just as many women as men had had a drink in the previous month, men were more likely than women to have had a drink in the past week. Similarly, among those who had had a drink in the past week, men were twice as likely as women to have had a drink on more than two of those days.

Alcohol Consumption in the Previous Seven Days

Each of the 286 respondents in the study was questioned about their drinking in the past week. Beginning with the day before the interview the quantity and type of alcohol consumed was recorded in as much detail as possible. The interviewer began by asking whether the subject had had anything to drink at lunch time 'yesterday'. Using this as a focus they then asked about any drinking before lunch, at home, out with friends, in the afternoon, after work and so on. On each drinking occasion the amount and type of drink was noted and then the situation was probed to find out whether the subject had had 'anything else to drink at that time'. This procedure was gone through for each of the previous six days.

Just over 60 per cent of the overall sample had reported having at least one alcoholic drink in the previous seven days, and of these 'drinkers' approximately one in six reported drinking on each of those days. Table 2 shows that men drinkers drank on more days than women drinkers and that 30 per cent of men drinkers aged 35 or over had had a drink on all seven days. These findings are consistent with other survey data on drinking frequency.

TABLE 2. Number of days' drinking in the previous week — x — age and sex

Number of days' drinking in the previous week	Male 'drinkers' under 35	Male 'drinkers' 35+	Female 'drinkers' under 35	Female 'drinkers' 35+	All drinkers
	%	%	%	%	%
1 or 2	50·0	50·0	79·2	77·4	62·4
3 or 4	23·8	13·0	16·7	13·2	15·6
5 or 6	14·3	5·6	4·2	1·9	6·4
7	11·9	31·5	4·2	7·5	15·6
N =	42	54	24	53	173

As a result of the careful probing into what was drunk on each of the seven previous days it was possible to get some idea of *how much* people drank as well as how frequently they drank. The alcohol equivalent for each reported drink was summed to give an overall quantity score. Sixty-two per cent of drinkers were judged to have consumed less than 10 centilitres of absolute alcohol in the previous week, and since 10 centilitres of absolute alcohol is roughly equivalent to five pints of bitter, or eight glasses of table wine, or three quarters of a bottle of sherry, or 11 gins, or a quarter of a pint methylated spirits, the great majority of drinkers could not be said to have drunk very heavily. On the other hand one in four of the male drinkers and one in 10 of the female drinkers reported drinking 10 centilitres or more in a single day.

It is not surprising that more of the drinking men than of the drinking women came into this group of people who had drunk a lot on a particular day, or that 27 out of the 33 people who drank the equivalent of 25 centilitres or over in the previous week were men Interestingly the 4·5 to 1 ratio of males to females in this 'heavy drinking' category is roughly the same as that found in British clinical studies of people with drinking problems. It is not being suggested that these consumption data 'explain' the sex differentials in reported alcoholism prevalence rates but it certainly highlights the importance of attempting to set clinical or organizationally based studies in the context of everyday drinking behaviour. The relationship between consumption and various 'alcohol effects' and 'alcoholism indicators' is discussed in the final section of this chapter.

It was mentioned earlier that nearly all the people who reported drinking *every day* in the previous week were men aged 35 or over. However, Table 3 shows that almost as many young men reported drinking the equivalent of 25 centilitres or more of absolute alcohol in that period. This suggests that young men drink more on any particular drinking occasion than their elders. This appeared to be the case since eight out of the 11 men under 35 reached their 25 or more centilitres of absolute alcohol by drinking on less than six days in the previous week, compared with only four out of the 17 older men. In

TABLE 3. Alcohol consumption in the previous week

Centilitres of absolute alcohol	Male 'drinkers' under 35 %	Male 'drinkers' 35+ %	Female 'drinkers' under 35 %	Female 'drinkers' 35+ %	Total %
1 – <10	42·9	48·1	82·6	83·1	61·4
10 – <15	14·3	13·0	13·0	9·4	12·3
15 – <20	4·8	3·7	0·0	3·4	3·4
20 – <25	11·9	5·6	0·0	0·0	4·5
25 and over	26·2	29·6	4·3	3·8	18·4
N =	42	54	23	53	172

fact, three of the younger men reached the 25 centilitre level but only drank on two out of the seven days. Similarly, while 29 per cent of the older men drinkers had a highest daily consumption equivalent of less than 20 grams of absolute alcohol, equivalent to three tots of whisky, only 15 per cent of the younger men drinkers had such a small 'highest daily consumption' score.

As well as being asked about their recent consumption the respondents were presented with a choice of four terms in which to describe their drinking in the past year: 'none', 'light', 'moderate' or 'heavy'. Thirteen per cent described themselves as non-drinkers and only one per cent as 'heavy' drinkers. It will be seen later that just as people are reluctant to describe themselves as heavy drinkers so people who report having some kind of alcohol-associated problem are reluctant to define themselves as alcoholic. Table 4 shows how those people who had had something to drink in the past week described themselves. All five 'light' drinkers in the 25 centilitres or over category were men. Of the two people who described themselves as non-drinkers in the past year and yet subsequently reported drinking in the past week, one was a middle-aged man who had one glass of sherry and the other was a woman, over 65 years old, who had had one half pint glass of beer.

TABLE 4. Self description and consumption in the previous week

Description of own drinking in the past year	Centilitres of absolute alcohol 1 – <5 N	%	5 – <25 N	%	25 + N	%	TOTAL N	%
No drinking	2	2·7					2	1·1
Light drinking	63	86·3	43	58·1	5	15·6	111	62·0
Moderate drinking	8	11·0	31	41·9	24	75·0	63	35·2
Heavy drinking					3	9·4	3	1·7
N =	73		74		32		179	

The type of drink consumed in the past week was simply classified into beer, wine and spirits. As from 1968 the British Market Research Bureau has published reports on the drinking habits of a national sample of 25,000 people aged 16 and over. Recent figures[27] suggest that approximately 45 per cent of the population had consumed beer in the past year, approximately 40 per cent had consumed some wine and 56 per cent spirits of some kind. In the South London sample men were, not surprisingly, the beer drinkers although 32 per cent of women drinkers had had beer or cider in the previous week. Women drinkers on the other hand were much more likely than men to have had wine to drink in the previous week and also more likely also to have had spirits. One third of all the men drinkers and a quarter of the women drinkers had had more than one type of drink in the previous week but only four people had drunk beer, wine *and* spirit. Table 5 shows that older women drinkers were more likely to drink beer and less likely to drink wine than younger women. It also shows that while beer and wine drinking was quite consistent across all male age categories, spirit drinking was much more frequent among the young men.

TABLE 5. Type of drink consumed in previous week — x — age and sex

Type of drink in previous week	Male 'drinkers'			Female 'drinkers'		
	under 35	35 – 54	55+	under 35	35 – 54	55+
	%	%	%	%	%	%
Beer	78·6	78·3	78·1	16·7	18·2	46·7
Wine	28·6	30·4	21·9	66·7	45·5	33·3
Spirit	47·6	26·1	18·8	33·3	63·6	46·7
N =	42	23	32	24	22	30

The clearest social status distinctions were seen in respect of wine which was consumed by half the drinkers in the non-manual categories and only 20 per cent of those in the manual groups. As can be seen, from Table 6, drinkers in the highest social status category[28] were most likely to drink spirits while people in the skilled manual category were most likely to drink beer.

As well as being asked about what they drank respondents were also asked to say where they usually did their drinking: whether 'at home or out somewhere else'. Almost half of all drinkers said that they usually drank 'out', while three out of 10 said they usually drank 'at home'. The remaining 20 per cent thought that they drank 'at home' and 'out somewhere else' in about equal proportions. Women were twice as likely as men to say that they *usually* drank at home, but there were no major social status category differences. The sharpest contrasts were between the age categories where the younger men and women were most likely to drink 'out', the middle aged most likely to drink out and at home in equal proportion, and the oldest men and women most likely to drink 'at home'.

TABLE 6. Type of drink consumed in previous week — x — social status

	Beer				Wine				Spirit			
	Social status				Social status				Social status			
	1 and 2	3i	3ii	4 and 5	1 and 2	3i	3ii	4 and 5	1 and 2	3i	3ii	4 and 5
	50%	40%	76%	66%	50%	49%	18%	20%	55%	33%	26%	42%
N=	40	48	38	50	40	48	38	50	40	48	38	50

The tendency for younger drinkers to be more likely to drink away from home could not be explained in terms of their having less access to drink in the house, for approximately 70 per cent of respondents in each age–sex category said that there was 'some drink in the house at the moment'. It may well be, of course, that although there was drink available 'in the house' young people were less likely than their elders to have control over it. The availability of drink in the home was not uniform across social status categories and declined steadily from 90 per cent of professional and managerial homes to 62 per cent of the homes of semi- and unskilled manual workers.

One of the signs of a potential problem drinker is often said to be 'drinking alone'. With this in mind each respondent was asked to say how often 'when you drink at home do you drink by yourself. That is, when no one else is drinking here at the same time?' Very few people said that they regularly drank alone and of those who did the great majority were over 55 years old. The greater availability of drink in the homes of those people in the highest social status category has already been noted and they were, in fact, most likely to have drunk alone 'at home' on some occasion. There was little difference between the percentage of men and women who had drunk alone 'at home'. On the other hand while one in three of the men drinkers said that they had drunk 'out' alone on some occasions, only eight per cent of women reported having done so.

The overall picture of who drinks what, when and where in the study area is complex and certainly needs a much more sophisticated study than the present one to describe it. However, certain dominant themes can be picked out from these simple basic data. Although few people reported drinking very heavily it is clear that the great majority of the adult population are regular drinkers, that alcohol is available in a large proportion of homes in the study area, and that almost all drinking, whether at home or elsewhere, is done 'in company'. Young people appeared to be rather more 'social' in their drinking than their elders in that they were more likely to drink away from home and, whether at home or not, were less likely to drink alone. Although there was little difference between the social-status categories in terms of either quantity or frequency of consumption, those in broadly professional and managerial occupations tended to have a more varied association with drink in that they were most likely to have drink available in the home, to have drunk more than one major type of drink in the past week, and to drink in a variety of settings. Finally, although men reported drinking more, and more often, than women their drinking behaviour in other respects was much the same.

Alcohol Problems

Anyone who attempts to estimate the prevalence of alcoholism in any community is faced with two major problems. First, they have to decide what is to count as alcoholism. As was discussed in Chapter 1, this is a major and continuing source of disagreement among both clinicians and researchers. Second, they have to overcome the methodological problem of dealing with a condition which, however it is defined, affects only a small proportion of the population who are themselves reluctant to acknowledge it.

In spite of these difficulties several methods, both indirect and direct, have been developed for estimating prevalence. The most widespread *indirect* method is 'the Jellinek formula' and its variations, based on the assumption of a constant relationship between chronic alcoholism and cirrhosis of the liver.[29] The basic Jellinek formula is:

$$A = \frac{PD}{K}$$

in which A = the total number of alcoholics alive in a given year the prevalence rate which we are seeking. D = the number of reported deaths from liver cirrhosis in a given year and P = the percentage of liver cirrhosis deaths attributable to alcoholism: a presumed constant. The original values of P, 51·5 per cent for males and 17·7 per cent for females, were established by Jellinek on the basis of United States mortality data for the years 1900–1945. Making certain assumptions about the degree of liquor which was available during prohibition and non-prohibition, Jellinek used the differing cirrhosis mortality trends in these periods to determine the part played by alcoholism. The original values were later revised by Jellinek[30] to 62·8 per cent for males and 21·6 per cent for females in line with the sixth revision of the International Lists of Diseases and Causes of Death. K = the percentage of all alcoholics with medical complications who die of cirrhosis of the liver: another presumed constant. This value of K was computed by Jellinek after inspection of autopsy data of approximately 100,000 alcoholics who had experienced various medical complications during their lifetime. Jellinek claimed, on the basis of these data, that the percentage of death from cirrhosis of the liver among all alcoholics with medical complications alive in a given year is 0·694 per cent.

In order to arrive at the *total* number of alcoholics as opposed to the number of living alcoholics *with medical complications* required Jellinek to determine R = the ratio of all alcoholics to those with medical complications. Initially this ratio was set at 4 : 1 but on examination of later data Jellinek was led to conclude that 'the proportion of alcoholics with complications has decreased in America from 25 to 18·75 per cent, which requires an adjustment of R from 4 to 5·3'.[31]

The initial enthusiasm with which the Jellinek formula was received is not difficult to understand. It was relatively easy to use and based on official statistics which are routinely collected in a large number of countries. However, the formula was soon subjected to some heavy criticism. Popham[32] pointed out that P, the proportion of liver cirrhosis deaths attributable to alcoholism, could not be assumed to be constant, and that K, the proportion of alcoholics who die of liver cirrhosis, would almost certainly change with the nutritional status of the population. Nevertheless, in view of the broad agreement of the Jellinek estimates with certain independently derived prevalence rates in a number of countries Popham agreed that the 'Jellinek formula estimates of the prevalence of alcoholism in Canada and the United States in recent years would probably provide reasonably reliable indications of the magnitude of the problem'.

Subsequently Seeley[33] and Brenner[34] presented more detailed criticisms of the constants. Seeley, in fact, felt that estimates based on the formula were so much in error that:

> 'assertions as to the magnitude of the problem are misleading, and scientific studies based on these data, quite probably, invalid'[35]

while Jellinek himself eventually advised against its use:

> 'Generally I would not be in favor of the continued use of my formula, nor any modification of it, as there are too many fluctuating factors present. Much more to be desired is a new basis, and particularly field surveys'.[36]

Nevertheless the use of the Jellinek formula with modifications has continued, and so have the discussions about its adequacy and usefulness. A paper in the *Quarterly Journal of Studies on Alcohol* in 1974 'revisited' the formula and succinctly identified the current state of play:

> 'Comparison of the estimates of the number of male and female alcoholics generated by the simple application of the Jellinek formula . . . and the estimates derived from the method of computation employed by Effron *et al.*, . . . clearly indicates that the latter method provides the more conservative estimates. However, which of the two estimates represents the more accurate approximation . . . remains uncertain'.[37]

Other indirect methods of assessing the prevalence of alcoholism include three discussed by Schmidt and De Lint:[38] the distribution-of-consumption method, the death-from-alcoholism method and the death-from-suicide method. The distribution of consumption method is discussed in the next section of this chapter but the other two are based, like the death from cirrhosis method, on certain assumptions about constant relationships between the indirect indicator and alcoholism. Each method is subject to the same questions about the universality of the constants and the criteria upon which the raw official data concerning death classifications and consumption are constructed. Nevertheless Schmidt and De Lint produced very similar estimates of alcoholism prevalence in Ontario from all four methods. Clearly the discussion about indirect methods is far from concluded.

Jellinek, in his statement of dissatisfaction with his own formula, called for the use of 'field surveys' to measure the prevalence of alcoholism. Field surveys, however, are expensive to mount and present several major methodological problems. Nevertheless there have been several attempts to assess the prevalence of alcoholism in the United Kingdom and elsewhere using these more *direct* methods.

Parr,[39] for example, approached the problem by asking a sample of general practitioners to estimate how many alcoholics they had on their lists. Alcoholics were defined, according to the World Health Organization definition,[40] as

> 'Excessive drinkers whose dependence upon alcohol has attained such a degree that they show a noticeable mental disturbance or an interference with bodily or mental health, interpersonal relations, smooth economic and social functioning; or the prodromal signs of such development; they therefore require treatment'.

Weighting his figures in the light of differential reporting according to list size, Parr calculated that there were 40,000 alcoholics in England and Wales. This figure is only just over one tenth of that arrived at by the Jellinek formula.[41] Prys-Williams[42] felt that the pressure of time on general practitioners with larger lists resulted in their failure to identify patients with drinking problems. Basing his calculation, therefore, on the estimate given by the G.Ps with smaller lists in Parr's study he revised the prevalence figure to 60,000, and then revised it again to 70,000 on the grounds that Parr's figures excluded those alcoholics who did not consult general practitioners. It is unlikely that these rough and ready guesses by general practitioners are the kind of 'direct surveys' which Jellinek had in mind.

A much more detailed study was conducted in the county of Cambridgeshire by Moss and Beresford-Davies.[43] They based their prevalence estimate on the results of detailed questioning of 13 social agencies in the study area who were asked to report on all clients who had:

(1) Consulted for or been admitted to hospital on account of a specific drinking problem or for a medical or psychiatric condition attributable without doubt to excessive drinking over a prolonged period *or*
(2) Been prosecuted more than once for drunkenness *or*
(3) Drunk methylated or surgical spirits or similar substances *or*
(4) Experienced at least two of a long list of social, familial, occupational consequences of excessive drinking.

On the basis of these data Moss and Beresford-Davies concluded that in Cambridgeshire there was an alcoholism rate of 6·2 per thousand males and 1·4 per thousand females. The Office of Health Economics[44] estimated a national prevalence rate of 220,000 by weighting these Cambridgeshire figures by Parr's regional differentials. However, this figure like Parr's is well below the 1948 W.H.O. estimate of 350,000 based on the Jellinek formulation.

The weakness of 'direct surveys' such as those by Parr, Prys-Williams and Moss and Beresford-Davies is that, since they are based on those 'alcoholics' who have been recognized as such by official helping agencies, they are really not 'direct' enough. The implication of such studies is that the rest of the population from which such people are drawn are experiencing very few problems associated with alcohol. Furthermore, treatment facilities may be geared to a certain number of people with particular problems or sets of problems which may, in fact, be experienced by a significant proportion of the population at large. In order to overcome this major problem of the representativeness of treated or identified alcoholics it is necessary to undertake studies of the general population.

To date there have been very few general population studies of drinking problems. The most notable is Cahalan's national study of *Problem Drinkers in America*.[45] In this he devised a 'current problem score' from combining the results on 11 specific types of problem; with the individual problems being scored differently according to their presumed frequency and severity. The prevalence of the 11 specific types of problem, which ranged from the physiological to the legal, marital and occupational, was measured in terms of their occurrence within a three-year period 1965 to 1967. Fifty-seven per cent of the men and 79 per cent of the women reported that they had not experienced any of the 11 types of problem during the three-year period. Cahalan disclosed that the major drinking-related problems for men were frequent intoxication, a pattern of drinking which was taken to be symptomatic of possible addiction, problems with spouse or relations and psychological dependency upon alcohol. The major problem reported by women was 'that a physician had advised them to reduce their drinking for health reasons'. The peak of prevalence for almost all types of drinking problems was among men in their twenties, while for all ages the frequency of the problem was higher among lower-status men than among higher-status men when all other variables were held constant.

Cahalan's study is called *Problem Drinkers*. It was not his intention to discover the 'alcoholics' in the American community, but rather to identify the relationships between particular types of alcohol-related problems and certain social and psychological variables which he took to be important in the development of problem drinking. This approach was also adopted by Edwards and his team in their study of drinking in a London suburb.[46] In the course of that survey 25 possible 'troubles connected with drinking' during the previous 12 months were enquired about. These ranged from being 'under the influence', which was reported by 25 per cent of the total sample, to having 'lost a job through drinking' which had happened to less than one per cent.

As part of the present study of the general population of a South London borough, everyone who had reported drinking any alcohol at all in the past year was asked to fill in a self-completion questionnaire. The first part of the questionnaire contained eight questions focused on a broad spectrum of 'alcohol effects': ranging from alcohol making the person 'feel dizzy' to being 'unable to think clearly' and 'sick'. The overall percentage of drinkers reporting each of the eight 'alcohol effects' is shown in Table 7 together with a breakdown in terms of age and sex.

TABLE 7. Percentage of drinkers reporting each 'effect of alcohol'—x—age and sex

Question: 'In the past 12 months has drinking alcohol ever made you . . .	Total	Males under 35	Males 35+	Females under 35	Females 35+
	%	%	%	%	%
. . . feel sleepy?'	56·1	83·3	56·6	61·3	39·6
. . . feel dizzy?	36·2	77·1	22·4	51·6	20·9
. . . noisier than usual?	33·3	61·5	28·9	32·2	22·2
. . . unsteady on your feet?	30·1	60·4	27·6	32·2	15·4
. . . sick?	26·8	54·2	18·4	25·8	19·8
. . . drunk?	26·0	64·4	27·6	16·1	7·7
. . . unable to think clearly?	22·0	45·8	30·3	12·9	5·5
. . . slur your speech?	18·3	41·7	23·7	9·7	4·4
N =	246	48	76	31	91

Although the percentage of the population sample reporting any particular effect varied from the 56 per cent who said that alcohol had made them 'feel sleepy' to the 18 per cent who reported that alcohol had made them slur their speech, there were very consistent age and sex differences. Younger people were more likely to report each effect than their elders and men were more likely to report each effect than women. The differences in proportion on specific effects ranged up to the 9 : 1 ratio of young men to old women reporting being drunk, being unable to think clearly and alcohol having made them slur their speech.

Table 8 sets out the total number of 'effects' for the four age–sex categories. It shows that three quarters of the men under 35 reported four or more of the eight effects in the previous year as opposed to nine per cent of women aged 35 or over. One in six of the young male drinkers reported all eight effects.

TABLE 8. Number of 'alcohol effects' reported — x — age and sex

Number of effects in the past year	Total	Males		Females	
		under 35	35+	under 35	35+
	%	%	%	%	%
0	30·1	6·3	30·3	22·6	45·1
1	16·7	2·1	19·7	19·4	20·9
2	11·4	8·3	10·5	16·1	12·2
3	11·0	8·3	10·5	9·7	13·2
4	5·7	10·4	5·3	9·7	2·2
5	10·2	25·0	9·2	12·9	2·2
6	7·3	14·5	7·8	9·7	2·2
7	3·3	8·3	2·6	0·0	2·2
8	4·5	16·7	3·9	0·0	0·0
N =	246	48	76	31	91
At least 1 effect	69·9	93·7	69·7	77·4	54·9
4 or more effects	30·9	74·9	29·0	32·3	8·8

As well as being asked about the immediate effects of drinking, respondents were asked a series of 15 questions about alcohol problems. Taken directly, or adapted slightly, from the Edwards 'troubles with drinking' schedule,[47] these are all questions which clients are traditionally asked by therapists and other workers in the field of alcoholism in any attempt to assess the impact which drinking is having on their client's life. It is upon the answers to such questions that diagnoses of alcoholism are in practice made.

TABLE 9. Percentage of drinkers reporting each 'alcoholism indicator' —x— age and sex

Question: 'In the past 12 months have you . . .	Total %	Males under 35 %	Males 35+ %	Females under 35 %	Females 35+ %
. . . been aware of drinking more quickly than most people you were with?'	11·0	27·7	11·8	6·5	3·3
. . . ever had a drink before going to a party in case you would not get enough there?'	10·2	14·9	9·2	16·1	6·6
. . . been criticized for your drinking?'	9·4	23·4	13·1	3·2	1·1
. . . ever been unable to do things you should have done in the morning because of a hangover?'	8·6	19·1	7·8	9·7	3·3
. . . ever been in arguments with family or friends after drinking?'	8·2	27·7	7·8	3·2	0·0
. . . ever found that you could not remember the night before after drinking?'	7·8	21·3	5·3	3·2	4·4
. . . deliberately decided never to drink again?'	7·3	10·6	9·2	6·5	4·4
. . . been advised to cut down the amount you drink?'	6·1	12·8	9·2	0·0	2·2
. . . ever concealed from someone the amount you were drinking?'	4·9	6·4	10·5	0·0	1·1
. . . on any occasion felt unable to stop drinking?'	4·5	4·3	6·6	6·5	2·2
. . . ever found that your hands were shaky in the morning after drinking?'	4·5	6·4	6·6	3·2	2·2
. . . ever been in a fight with family or friends after drinking?'	4·5	17·0	3·9	0·0	0·0
. . . ever had a drink first thing in the morning to steady your nerves?'	3·3	4·3	6·6	0·0	1·1
. . . ever been unable to do your work or housework because of drinking?'	1·6	6·4	1·3	0·0	0·0
. . . neglected your family at all because of drinking?'	0·4	2·1	0·0	0·0	0·0
N =	245	47	76	31	91

Table 9 shows how frequently such 'problems' are reported by a sample of the general population. As with the 'alcohol effects' questions young male drinkers are, with a few significant exceptions, *most* likely and older female drinkers *least* likely to report having had these problems in the past 12 months.

Table 10 displays the number of 'alcoholism indicators' reported by each age–sex category.

TABLE 10. Number of 'alcoholism indicators' reported — x — age and sex

Number of 'alcoholism indicators' in the past year	Total	Males		Females	
		under 35	35+	under 35	35+
	%	%	%	%	%
0	63·3	27·7	60·5	67·7	82·4
1	15·9	21·3	18·4	19·4	9·9
2	8·6	23·4	5·3	6·5	4·4
3	3·7	8·5	3·9	3·2	1·1
4	3·7	8·5	3·9	0·0	2·2
5	3·7	0·0	2·6	3·2	0·0
6	1·2	4·3	0·0	0·0	0·0
7	0·8	4·3	2·6	0·0	0·0
8	1·6	0·0	1·3	0·0	0·0
9	0·4	0·0	1·3	0·0	0·0
12	0·4	2·1	0·0	0·0	0·0
N =	245	47	76	31	91
It least 1 indicator	36·7	62·3	39·5	32·3	17·6
2 or more indicators	19·2	51·1	21·1	12·9	7·7

The exceptions to the overall trend of young men drinkers being most likely to report problems in the past year are of particular interest. Table 10 showed that older men were slightly more likely than young men to agree to three questions: 'In the past 12 months have you . . .

. . . ever concealed from someone the amount you were drinking?

. . . on any occasion felt unable to stop drinking?

. . . ever had a drink first thing in the morning to steady your nerves?

and almost equally likely to agree to two questions: 'have you . . .

. . . deliberately decided never to drink again?'

. . . ever found that your hands were shaky in the morning after drinking?'

Three of these five dimensions; feeling unable to stop drinking, early morning drinking and morning shakes are classical indicators of alcoholism. The overall figure of approximately six per cent for these dimensions accords with

American[48] and British[49] data. The other two features; concealing the amount drunk and deciding never to drink again are significant pointers to people who may feel that they are drinking too much or that they have some kind of 'problem'. The implication of this material is that while the 'alcoholism indicators' which are based on social disapproval or are defined in terms of interference with normal daily routines may decline with age, other *core* features which have traditionally been associated with the definition of alcoholism or alcohol dependence remain or increase.

Kay Fillmore recently attempted[50] to 'understand the dynamics involved in the aetiology of problem drinking in alcoholism' by seeing whether original data on respondents in the Straus and Bacon student drinking survey[51] were predictive of their drinking problems and behaviour 20 years later. She concluded that

> 'At least 50% of the drinkers at both measurement points who were problem drinkers in their late 30s and early 40s showed signs of problem drinking early in life. The remainder developed problems in the intervening period. Of equal interest were those who showed signs of problems at Time 1 but did not at Time 2 although they were still drinkers at Time 2. The remission of drinking problems in the aging process is an area worth investigating'.

It certainly is worth investigating. But unfortunately a 'problem drinker' was defined as

> 'A person who received a cumulative score of 7 or more, based on the scores in the areas of drinking-related problems on the job or at school, with friends–neighbors or spouse–relatives, health and financial problems, binge drinking, behavior symptomatic of alcoholism, psychological dependence on alcohol, problems with the law, police or accidents, and belligerence associated with drinking. It also includes an index of frequent intoxication based on quantity and frequency of drinking so that the possibility exists that the problem-drinking score could be artificially correlated with quantity and frequency'.

Thus, there is no way of knowing which *type* of problems persisted from Time 1 to Time 2 or appeared or disappeared in the intervening period.

As well as being asked to report on their own drinking and associated problems the South London respondents were asked to say how they felt 'about people having a drink' and also how they felt 'about people being drunk'. While very few people said that they disapproved of people having a drink almost four out of five said that they disapproved of people being drunk. Women were less likely than men to approve of people having a drink but they were much more likely than men to strongly disapprove of drunkenness. There was very little difference between the various social

TABLE 11. Feelings about people 'being drunk' — x — age and sex

Feelings about people 'being drunk'	Males under 35 %	Males 35–54 %	Males 55+ %	Females under 35 %	Females 35–54 %	Females 55+ %
Approve or indifferent	48	24	20	12	15	6
Disapprove	32	50	47	68	55	35
Strongly disapprove	20	26	33	20	30	59
N =	50	39	45	34	45	63

status categories on these two issues. However, older respondents both men and women, were more likely than younger ones to disapprove of drinking and particularly, as Table 11 shows, to disapprove of people being drunk.

General attitudes, however, may very rarely inform day-to-day decisions or actions. In order to get some idea of how involved people had actually been with someone who they felt had been drinking 'too much' they were presented with five typical situations. Although older people were much more likely than younger people to strongly disapprove of people being drunk, Table 12 shows that younger people of both sexes were more likely than their elders to have actually felt critical toward someone in the past year 'because of their behaviour while drunk. However, people in the under 35 age group were much more likely to have been involved with drink and drinking situations. They drank more and more frequently than their elders and were more likely

TABLE 12. Involvement in problem drinking situations in past year — x — age and sex

'Problem drinking situation' in the past year	Male under 35 %	Male 35+ %	Female under 35 %	Female 35+ %
Felt critical of someone's behaviour when drunk	38·0	21·4	30·6	14·8
Taken care of someone who was drunk	38·0	23·8	16·7	6·5
Been in car when driver had drunk too much	38·0	15·5	19·4	8·3
Argument with someone who was drunk	32·0	6·0	22·3	7·4
Fight with someone who was drunk	16·0	8·3	8·3	0·0
N =	50	84	36	108

to do their drinking in public places rather than at home. Thus, it is not surprising to find also that they were more likely than their elders to have been involved in each one of the situations in which someone else's drinking was felt to be causing a problem.

There were very few social status differences on these issues apart from the fact that people in the lower social status categories were more likely to have been involved in a fight than people in the higher status categories and also more likely than them to have had to take control of someone who was 'too drunk to manage on their own'.

Epidemiological studies such as those reported on in this section go some way toward identifying the prevalence of certain alcohol associated problems in the general population. 'Problem' in these studies is simply defined, in Knupfer's[52] terms, as 'a problem — any problem — connected fairly closely with drinking'. Although such studies take us away from the retrospective accounts of those who have already been defined as alcoholic, there are two major developments which need to supplement the epidemiologic method. First, we need to attempt to tease out what is the precise relationships between alcohol consumption and those 'problems' which are taken to be associated with it. This question is discussed in more detail in the next section. Second, we need to be able to follow in some detail the drinking careers of a cohort of the general population. To date no one has done this. It is, of course, not surprising since 'problems' take a long time to develop and the demands of both research careers and governmental control over finance make the likelihood of such longitudinal work being set up remote. Similarly, as was pointed out at the beginning of this chapter, there are unfortunately always enough people with problems *now* or people who can be reasonably assumed to be 'at risk' for all therapists, researchers and funding agencies to have something more immediately pressing to do with their time and money.

Alcohol Consumption and Alcohol Problems

Attempts to relate the consumption of alcohol to the problems taken to be associated with it have, by and large, concentrated on the covariation of national or regional rates and statistics. There has been a great deal of attention paid, for example, to the relationship between consumption and death from cirrhosis of the liver. Jolliffe and Jellinek pointed out in 1941[53] that the rapid decline in the cirrhosis death rate in the United States from 1916 to 1920 corresponded with the period of most effective state and wartime prohibition, that the plateau from 1920 to 1933 coincided with the period in which the Eighteenth Amendment was in effect, and that the graduaal increase from 1933 to 1940 occurred after national prohibition was repealed. They considered it reasonable to conclude that a significant association exists between changes in the death rate from cirrhosis of the liver and changes in the consumption of alcoholic beverages. This view was challenged by Lilenfeld and Korns[54] in 1950, but a great deal of later work has shown the cirrhosis of the liver–alcohol consumption relationship to hold in many different countries.[55] Terris, for example, evaluated:

> ' . . . national mortality data for cirrhosis of the liver with regard to a number of parameters: long term trends, age, sex and race, urban–rural differences, social class and occupation, and alcohol consumption. The evidence strongly supports the conclusion that cirrhosis mortality is directly related to per capita consumption of alcohol . . . '.[56]

Subsequently similar relationships have also been shown between alcohol consumption and the rates for certain other causes of death.[57]

Another body of related work has focused on the distribution of alcohol consumption in a population and in particular on the relationships between distribution and per capita consumption, and between per capita consumption and excessive drinking or drinking which can indicate alcoholism.[58] The Ledermann model is an attempt both to describe and predict the consumption of alcoholic beverages in homogeneous populations. The three major implications of the model concern the number of heavy drinkers, the amount of alcohol consumed by heavy drinkers and the number of alcoholics. Because Ledermann wanted to find a general formula which could be applied to any population of drinkers he rejected, on logical grounds, the idea that alcohol drinking would be normally distributed. In Sweden, for example, the average amount of alcohol consumed each year is about 4·5 litres. Thus, if drinking is normally distributed in Sweden, and since the left-hand tail of the distribution is zero because there cannot be negative consumption, there could not be anyone drinking more than about nine litres per year. In fact a portion of the population does drink more than this amount.

After examining data from several countries Ledermann concluded that the frequency distribution of alcohol consumption in a homogeneous population could be estimated with a log normal[60] rather than a normal curve — this means that the natural logarithms of consumption rather than raw consumption data are normally distributed. The assumption that alcohol consumption is log normally distributed implies that most drinkers consume a small amount while a few drink large quantities. If Ledermann's conclusions are valid then the frequency distribution of alcohol use can be calculated from estimates of the mean annual consumption of alcohol for any homogeneous population. Similarly predictions about the number of heavy drinkers following changes in mean consumption can also be made, which in turn may have preventive policy implications. This is discussed further in Chapter 5. Some investigators, such as de Lint and Schmidt,[61] argue that the best way to reduce the number of heavy drinkers is to reduce the mean consumption of the population, possibly by taxation or pricing policy. Room points out, however, that

> 'The existence of the log normal distribution as an approximation of cross-sectional empirical realities does not demand that prevention

> measures, to be effective, must apply to all consumers, as for instance a rise in price does'.[62]

Room draws the analogy with incomes where attempts are made to redistribute incomes among individuals rather than altering all incomes with a uniform change in taxation.

Not surprisingly the greatest interest in the Ledermann model of alcohol consumption has been shown by those concerned with policy. And in spite of the fact that the adequacy of the model, both as a descriptive device and as one which has predictive value, has been seriously questioned,[63] it is likely to play a major role in preventive strategy. A recent World Health Organization working group concerned with Alcohol Control Policy and Public Health, for example, outlined its position as follows:

> 'Provision of appropriate treatment and rehabilitation services is vital, but with a health problem of such large dimensions, and one where response to treatment is by no means always certain, it is clear that the institution of effective preventive policies should receive urgent public health attention . . .
>
> The most helpful lead which has (re-) emerged in recent years . . . is the notion that the rate of any alcohol related problems in a population is related to the *per capita* level of alcohol consumption in that population, with the corollary that any measures which diminish total alcohol consumption will decrease the alcoholism rate. Such an argument may at first seem contrary to common sense . . .
>
> . . . The empirical evidence, however, clearly suggests otherwise. Both as estimated over time within a single country (as has now been shown for a large number of countries), and as shown by comparison between countries, population consumption averages appear to be fairly closely related to alcoholism rates. Although alcoholism in these studies is usually measured on the basis of cirrhosis of the liver mortality rates, these may be seen as a reflection of a larger phenomenon, the theoretical basis of which lies in the distribution of consumption.
>
> It therefore becomes relevant to public health to identify factors potentially within society's grasp which may influence overall consumption rates, for the manipulation of these factors might form a basis for the practical public health approach now urgently required'.[64]

While there has been a great deal of discussion about the relationship between alcohol consumption and alcohol problems almost none of it has focused on particular people with particular problems. Thus, the South London survey presented an opportunity to move away from national consumption data and global assessments of what constitutes or indicates alcoholism to a brief consideration of the relationship between alcohol consumption and a whole range of alcohol problems in a local population.

The limitations of the survey design are fully acknowledged and have been discussed earlier in the chapter. Nevertheless it was possible to see whether there was, in fact, any relationship between the self-reporting of various problems and the amount of alcohol which respondents said they had consumed in the past week. This represents a preliminary move toward testing the largely unquestioned assumption that those who consume the most alcohol have the largest number of alcohol problems. Alcohol problems are represented by the 'alcohol effects' and 'alcoholism indicators' which respondents reported in the self-completion section at the end of the interview schedule.

Table 13 shows the number of alcohol effects for four broad levels of consumption categories. Half of those who had had a drink in the previous year but not in the past week did not report any alcohol effects, whereas only six per cent of those who drank more than the equivalent of 25 centilitres of absolute alcohol in the past week were 'effect' free. Twenty-five centilitres of absolute alcohol are equivalent to approximately 12 pints of beer or 20 glasses of table wine or three quarters of a bottle of whisky. The mean number of reported alcohol effects rose steadily with each consumption category.

TABLE 13. Alcohol consumption and number of alcohol effects

Number of alcohol effects	Drank in last year but not in past week	Drank in the past week (centilitres of absolute alcohol)		
		1 – <10	10 – <25	25 and over
	%	%	%	%
0	50·0	30·8	8·9	6·5
1	18·1	17·3	17·6	12·9
2	9·7	15·0	5·9	9·7
3	6·9	10·6	11·8	19·5
4	2·8	6·7	11·8	3·2
5	4·2	7·7	23·5	19·5
6	4·2	7·7	8·9	12·9
7	2·8	1·9	2·9	0·0
8	1·4	2·9	8·9	16·1
N =	72	104	34	31
Mean number of effects	1·5	2·3	3·7	4·1

In just the same way, Table 14 shows that the mean number of alcoholism indicators increases with each consumption category.

In addition to setting out the overall alcohol consumption and alcohol problem data it was important to know whether there was any indication that the relationship was more pronounced in particular sections of the population.

TABLE 14. Alcohol consumption and number of alcohol indicators

Number of alcoholism indicators	Drank in past year but not in past week	Drank in the past week (centilitres of absolute alcohol)		
		1 – <10	10 – <25	25 and over
	%	%	%	%
0	74·6	71·8	55·6	19·4
1	14·1	15·3	14·7	26·8
2	4·2	7·8	14·7	12·9
3	2·8	1·0	8·8	7·3
4	1·4	1·0	0·0	12·2
5	0·0	1·0	0·0	4·9
6	1·4	0·0	0·0	2·3
7	0·0	1·0	2·9	4·9
8	1·4	0·0	0·0	0·0
9	0·0	1·0	0·0	0·0
12	0·0	0·0	2·9	0·0
N =	71	103	34	41
Mean number of indicators	0·6	0·6	1·3	2·4

Table 15, therefore, sets out the mean alcohol effects score for the four broad age–sex categories while Table 16 sets out the alcoholism indicator and consumption data. Since, the numbers were so small the two higher consumption categories for females have been combined.

TABLE 15. Mean number of alcohol effects — x — consumption, age and sex

Age–sex categories and mean number of effects	Drank in past year but not in past week	Drank in the past week (centilitres of absolute alcohol)		
		1 – <10	10 – <25	25 and over
Males under 35				
mean effects	4·5	4·1	5·3	6·0
(N = 46)	(6)	(17)	(12)	(11)
Males 35 +				
mean effects	1·6	2·1	3·0	3·1
(N = 73)	(20)	(25)	(12)	(16)
Females under 35			10 and over	
mean effect	2·0	2·4	2·7	
(N = 31)	(7)	(19)	(5)	
Females 35 +				
mean effects	0·8	1·6	2·4	
(N = 91)	(39)	(43)	(9)	

TABLE 16. Mean number of alcoholism indicators — x — consumption, age and sex

<table>
<tr><th rowspan="2">Age–sex categories and mean number of indicators</th><th rowspan="2">Drank in past year but not in past week</th><th colspan="3">Drank in the past week (centilitres of absolute alcohol)</th></tr>
<tr><th>1 – <10</th><th>10 – <25</th><th>25 and over</th></tr>
<tr><td>Males under 35</td><td></td><td></td><td></td><td></td></tr>
<tr><td>mean indicators</td><td>2·8</td><td>1·8</td><td>2·7</td><td>2·2</td></tr>
<tr><td>(N = 45)</td><td>(5)</td><td>(17)</td><td>(12)</td><td>(11)</td></tr>
<tr><td>Males 35 +</td><td></td><td></td><td></td><td></td></tr>
<tr><td>mean indicators</td><td>0·8</td><td>0·6</td><td>0·3</td><td>2·8</td></tr>
<tr><td>(N = 73)</td><td>(20)</td><td>(25)</td><td>(12)</td><td>(16)</td></tr>
<tr><td>Females under 35</td><td></td><td></td><td colspan="2">10 and over</td></tr>
<tr><td>mean indicators</td><td>0·4</td><td>0·4</td><td colspan="2">1·4</td></tr>
<tr><td>(N = 31)</td><td>(7)</td><td>(19)</td><td colspan="2">(5)</td></tr>
<tr><td>Females 35 +</td><td></td><td></td><td colspan="2"></td></tr>
<tr><td>mean indicators</td><td>0·2</td><td>0·4</td><td colspan="2">0·6</td></tr>
<tr><td>(N = 90)</td><td>(39)</td><td>(42)</td><td colspan="2">(9)</td></tr>
</table>

From both tables it appears that the relationship between consumption and problems is more noticeable in the older age groups. Among the younger men the mean number of alcoholism indicators is actually higher for those who had not had a drink in the past week than it is for those who had consumed the equivalent of 25 centilitres or more of absolute alcohol. It is also clear that at each level of alcohol consumption the younger people of both sexes reported more alcohol effects and alcoholism indicators than their elders, and that males reported more than females.

Those apparently differential relationships between alcohol consumption and alcohol problems may be due to systematically selective reporting of consumption, effects or indicators, or due to differential tolerance to alcohol, or due to some of the effects or indicators being differentially important to people in different age–sex categories, or due to methodological weakness in the study design. However, the data highlight the complex questions which need to be answered before making any claim to understand the nature of the relationship between alcohol consumption and alcohol problems.

Similarly, we need to know much more about the kind of problems which appear to be most strongly related to different levels or patterns of alcohol consumption by different categories of people before preventive strategies based on the manipulation of overall population consumption are designed or implemented.

Chapter 3

Causes of Drinking Problems

'As is general in the diagnosis of social problems, it is difficult and often impossible to disentangle the intricate web of causes and effects. Even in relation to disease the consumption of drink may be effect as well as cause . . . '. *Levy.*[1]

The question of what *causes* alcoholism is obviously complex, and has exercised a vast number of people concerned about their own or other people's drinking problems. The aim of this chapter, however, is not to construct yet another causal theory, but rather to look at the kind of causal theories with which other people, both professional and lay, tend to operate. For causal theories are not merely things which 'scientists' or 'theorists' construct. Causal theories are part of that stock of everyday knowledge in terms of which each of us makes our way around the social world as we see it. Any attempt to understand the way in which people behave in relation to alcohol or in relation to people with some 'alcohol problem' will be enhanced, therefore, by a consideration of the causal theories with which those individuals appear to be operating.

That 'alcoholism is a disease' is one familiar way of thinking about alcohol and its associated problems; and various implications of such an approach for drinkers, therapists and the wider society are discussed in the next chapter. However, it is not the only approach. In an attempt to avoid some of the most obvious drawbacks to calling a person 'an alcoholic' and terming his problem 'a disease' there have been many attempts to shift the focus of academic and professional attention from 'alcoholism' to 'problem drinking'. Robert Plaut, for example, in the report of the Cooperative Commission on the Studies of Alcoholism[2] defines problem drinking as

' . . . a repetitive use of beverage alcohol causing physical, psychological, or social harm to the drinker or to others'.

while Genevieve Knupfer[3] states simply that

'... a problem connected fairly closely with drinking — any problem — constitutes a drinking problem'.

The generality of these formulations not only avoids some of the unhelpful implications of a disease theory of alcoholism but opens up the possibility of developing causal theories based on the analysis of a whole range of problems associated with alcohol.

However, epidemiologic studies of drinking problems, such as those reported on in the previous chapter,[4] demand that crucial definitions are made before the study begins. It is necessary to have decided what is to count, in operational terms, as 'a problem' of a particular type in order to say anything about its incidence or prevalence. Similarly particular ideas about cause will draw the attention of researchers to certain types of drinking activity, certain types of person and certain types of situation. For the world is full of 'theories of alcoholism' which inform the everyday lives of researchers, alcohologists, planners, drinkers and their intimates. Thus, the causal theories which people hold are very much a matter of study.

The aim of this chapter is to give some indication of the range of causal theories with which people are operating in relation to drinking problems: first, the types of theory offered in the scientific–professional literature, second the theories of those called upon professionally to handle drinking problems and third the theories of causation held by members of the general population. The 'professional' and 'everyday' theories are based on material collected as part of the South London study.

'Scientific' Theories

The simple question which any theory of alcoholism or problem drinking is attempting to throw light on is 'Why do some people drink alcohol in a manner which appears to cause or exacerbate some problem for them or for others'? The amount of scientific writing addressed to this question is immense. So is the range of different sciences and disciplines attempting to provide answers. In fact, the authors of one major review of *Alcohol and Health*,[5] were so overwhelmed, that they concluded that the

'... causes of alcoholism are unknown ... Most probably, the condition reflects a form, or response to an interactive combination, of physiological, psychological, and sociological factors in an individual and his environment'.

Although it is difficult to think of many things which could not be said to be 'an interactive combination, of physiological, psychological, and sociological factors in an individual and his environment' the authors' conclusion does identify for us the three major areas in which alcohologists have worked in their attempt to answer the deceptively simple causal question which was posed at the head of this paragraph.

Biochemical Theories

The first set of 'scientific' theories are those which attempt to explain heavy regular alcohol intake in terms of physiological or biochemical mechanisms. In the last century there was a great deal of concern about the possibility of alcohol consumption adversely affecting hereditary material itself. Morel,[6] for example, in addition to suspecting alcohol of being injurious to the 'germ plasma' regarded alcoholism, criminality, insanity, epilepsy and feeblemindness as all part of a single syndrome of *hereditary degeneration*, while Tredgold in his treatise on amentia wrote:

> 'I believe that there are certain diseases which bring about a deterioration of the germ plasma. The chief of these are alcoholism and consumption, although it is probable that other poisons, sexual excesses, and many factors of modern life, may, by lowering the general vitality, produce a similar effect'.[7]

Edwards[8] and McClearn[9] have reviewed the more recent thinking on possible *genetic* links to alcoholism. Much of this work is based on animal reasearch, particularly on mice and rats, and McClearn offers an elegant rebuke to those who reject such work out of hand as irrelevant to the human condition of alcoholism.

> 'The opinion is sometimes encountered that alcoholism is uniquely a human disorder, and that research on infrahuman animals has no relevance whatsoever. This position begs the question in suggesting that an important part of the problem is already solved, at least at the general level: it presumes that the roots of alcoholism have been shown to lie in experiential factors that are exclusively human, and that no useful animal primordia or anlagen exist for these experiences. This type of anthropocentric vanity is increasingly difficult to defend in the face of the accumulating knowledge of animal behaviour. . . . The utility of the comparative method in the study of alcohol problems will depend upon whether the crucial etiological factors are those we share with the mouse and rat as fellow mammals or whether they are those that differentiate us as members of different genera. Only time will tell, and, in the meantime, we must employ the comparative method with an appropriate degree of humility, avoiding both the error of rejecting the possible relevance of animal data and the equally indefensible error of premature and uncritical generalization from animal research to the human condition'.[10]

Work on inbred and selectively bred mice has revealed striking differences between strains in alcohol preference,[11] which were demonstrable in representatives of the strains from several laboratories and by various techniques.[12] Other work has demonstrated differential sensitivity to alcohol among inbred strains,[13] and linked different alcohol preference rates to differences in the activity of enzymes involved in alcohol metabolism.[14] Such animal studies have, as McClearn puts it; 'contributed greatly to the credibility of a model of alcoholism that includes genetic parameters'. Unfortunately, as McClearn also notes, the research on man himself is less conclusive.

Family studies have naturally formed the core of work designed to test genetic theories of alcoholism in humans, since if genes influence the condition then those who have part of their hereditary material in common with known alcoholics should be more likely to suffer from the condition. Åmark,[15] on the basis of extensive and detailed studies of the family histories of several large samples of alcoholics from the Swedish population suggests a clear familial component to alcoholism. He computed that the likelihood of alcoholism among brothers of known alcoholics was 21 per cent, among sisters 0·9 per cent, among fathers 26 per cent and among mothers 2 per cent, compared with general population frequencies of 3·4 per cent for males and 0·11 per cent for females.

It is often claimed that these data may as easily be explained by shared cultural and other environmental factors as by shared genes. However McClearn notes that in one respect a genetic model can provide a more systematic explanation than a sociocultural one:

> 'By no means all, in fact a minority, of the siblings of alcoholics also become alcoholics in spite of sharing with their alcoholic sib many of the environmental factors featured in most sociocultural explanations. On the other hand, on the basis of elementary genetic principles, one would expect to find both affected and nonaffected ones within most sibships'.[16]

Again, McClearn feels that while the explanations of sex differences in alcoholism incidence in terms of sex roles and other cultural influences 'undoubtedly have considerable merit' mention should also be made of two genetic situations that are, in general, pertinent to conditions in which the incidence in males exceeds females, namely: sex linkage and sex limitation.

One way of attempting to separate out the genetic and environmental factors in the development of alcoholism has been to study adopted children, since an adopted child shares the environmental factors provided by a family but not its genetic lineage. A persisting resemblance of a child to its biological parents may then be taken to suggest genetic factors. Unfortunately this hypothetically elegant design is confounded, in practice, by such things as the time a child lives with its biological parents prior to adoption, the 'matching' policies of adoption agencies and, at a self-fulfilling prophecy level, the knowledge by children or adopting parents of any alcoholism of the biological parents and their own belief in a genetic theory of alcoholism. The first major study to use this 'adoption' design[17] showed no significant difference between the drinking behaviour of the adopted sons whose biological fathers were alcoholic and those whose biological parents were non or light drinkers. However recent work by Goodwin and associates[18] throws doubt on this finding and suggests further that the severity of the parent's alcoholism is positively related to alcoholism in the offspring irrespective of whether they were reared by the alcoholic parent or adopted by non-relatives soon after birth.

The comparison of monozygotic and dizygotic twins has recently been used in alcoholism research. Studies suggest that in the case of both drinking behaviour and ethanol metabolism rate[19] monozygotic or identical twins resemble each other substantially more than dizygotic or fraternal twins. While many of the core assumptions underlying twin research are open to dispute[20] this material provides support for those who stress the importance of considering a genetic component in any causal model of alcoholism. Additional support comes from recent work attempting to relate alcoholism to known single genes. Most of these studies have focused on blood groups[21] and on the incidence of colour vision defects.[22] Smith and Brinton,[23] however, have cast doubt on this latter body of work when they found colour vision defects in alcoholics when they first tested them but not after detoxification and dietary treatment. They suggest, therefore, that the defects are secondary to alcoholism and caused by vitamin depletion.

The key feature of most of the genetic work, which distinguishes it from the searches for other causal components of alcoholism, is the constant attempt to design studies which will enable statements to be made about the *relative weight* of genetic as opposed to environmental influences. Workers in other disciplines have tended to assume that the factors or parameters in which they were interested were of *exclusive* importance. As McClearn sums up:

> 'The dichotomous view that a trait must be due either to heredity *or* to environment has also permitted the development of a curious prejudice with respect to theories of the etiology of alcoholism. The burden of proof seems to fall on the proponent of a hereditary role. Environmental factors are assumed to be relevant unless demonstrated not to be; genetic factors are assumed, a priori, to be irrelevant, and can be admitted only after rigorous demonstration. For example, in reports of the incidence of alcoholism within families, one frequently finds a statement to the effect that, because there is no positive proof for the direct inheritance of a tendency toward alcoholism, the statistics must be interpreted as revealing the adverse effects of family environment. Another aspect of this same type of bias is the willingness of many investigators to conclude that the demonstration of the influence of some particular environmental factor confirms the importance of environmental factors as a class, and negates the influence of genetic variables as a class'.[24]

Psychological Theories

The second main set of 'scientific' causal theories are those which take alcoholism to be a symptom of some underlying personality or emotional disorder. The three main approaches made by psychologists to understanding alcoholism have focused on personality trait analyses, learning theory and psychoanalytic theory.

Many attempts have been made to identify an *alcoholic personality* in the hope that it would enable people with a pre-disposition to alcoholism in terms of some personality pattern or characteristic, to be approached, warned or helped at a pre-alcoholic stage.[25] Blane,[26] for example, has set out some of the personality characteristics which are commonly reported in studies of alcoholics and suggests that they are relevant to any consideration of treatment or rehabilitation. These characteristics include low frustration tolerance, sociability, feelings of inferiority combined with attitudes of superiority, fearfulness and dependency. Unfortunately, Orford reminds us that, as with so many areas of alcoholism research:

> 'Without much exaggeration it could be said that for every statement to be found in the literature concerning the relationship between alcoholism and personality, a contradictory statement could be found elsewhere'.[27]

However, among those personality traits which have been linked with alcoholism more frequently than most are oral dependence,[28] the wish for suicide,[29] immature over-dependence,[30] low self-esteem[31] and over-sensitivity.[32]

With some significant exceptions, which will be mentioned later, the majority of the early 'personality and alcoholism' studies were methodologically inadequate to the task of throwing any real light on the causes of alcoholism. A major weakness was the unstructured, uncontrolled nature of many studies based as they were on personal or clinical impressions with no attempt to match the 'personality traits' of 'alcoholics' against the wider population from which the alcoholics were drawn. Not surprisingly many of the 'characteristic personality traits of alcoholics' became much less characteristic when standardized personality tests were used in studies with adequate control populations. Syme[33] in his review of later well-designed studies concludes that

> '. . . no reliable findings emerge to indicate that alcoholics as a group can be distinguished from other groups of people on the basis of any single investigated personality dimension'.

The search for '*an* alcoholic personality' has, by and large, been abandoned in favour of rather more modest goals, such as setting out the range of personality types found in particular populations and sub-populations of alcoholics.[34] As well as moving away from the idea of *an* alcoholic personality there has been a move away from the assumption of the homogeneity of the condition of alcoholism. These parallel moves have led to a much more fruitful search for the linking of individual differences in both symptomatology and personality factors. It also allows attention to focus on people other than those who have been formally defined as 'alcoholic'; and it is only after this has been done can significant aetiological theories relating personality to alcoholism begin to be constructed. For underlying all simple cross-sectional studies of the relationship between personality and alcoholism is the core problem of teasing out whether particular personality traits are the cause of or the effect of the alcoholism.

Clearly, the only way of satisfactorily resolving this dilemma is by detailed longitudinal study of a large number of persons from a time prior to any sign of alcoholism until such time as they were agreed to be suffering from the condition. No such study exists. However, two major retrospective case-history-based studies have identified a small number of children who had attended social work[35] and child psychiatric[36] clinics and who were then found to have developed alcoholism later in life. Those who became alcoholic were more likely than other children to have displayed such characteristics as 'unrestrained aggression', 'hyperactivity', 'denial of childhood fear' and generally 'anti-social symptoms'. Although similar findings come from Jones' Oakland Growth Study, Orford again strikes the right cautionary note when he says that:

> 'Although there would appear to be a certain consistency amongst the findings of these three studies, it has to be pointed out that they are all based upon small numbers of people who eventually developed alcoholism, all were carried out in the USA, and the first two larger studies were based upon groups of adolescents who had already been defined as problems or potential problems. Once again, generalisations should be made only with the utmost caution. . . . (S)imple generalisations about personality and alcoholism are always unwarranted. . . . Potentially the most fruitful research to pursue in this area is that of establishing connections between individual differences in personality, in motivation for drinking, and in drinking patterns and symptomatology'.[37]

Learning theories of various types have been invoked not only in the attempt to explain why some people become alcoholics, but to explain why people drink at all.[38] Some theorists see alcohol consumption as a reflex to certain kinds of stimulus or as a way of reducing anxiety or fear. Operating on the pleasure–pain principle, such theories hold that people are drawn to pleasant situations and repelled by unpleasant or anxiety arousing ones. The basic assumption of a reinforcement theory of learning is that the learning of an association between a stimulus and a response requires the presence of some sort of reward or reinforcement. Dollard and Miller,[39] for example, suggest that alcohol is reinforcing because it results in a reduction of fear, conflict and anxiety, while Bandura[40] maintains that excessive alcohol consumption is maintained through positive reinforcement resulting from the central depressant and anaesthetic properties of alcohol. Individuals who are repeatedly subjected to environmental stress are consequently more prone to drink anaesthetic qualities of alcohol than those individuals who experience less stress and for whom, therefore, alcohol has only a weak reinforcing value.

However, once we move from drinking to alcoholism it has to be explained why the obvious and admitted pain, discomfort and distress caused by regular excess drinking does not serve to deter further drinking.[41] Learning theorists tend to accommodate this problem by suggesting that the anxieties, guilt, or physiological symptoms induced by excessive drinking may themselves become a signal for another bout of alcohol consumption. 'The learning paradigm, therefore, favours the establishment and repetition of the resort to alcohol'.[42] A 'gradient of reinforcement' is then postulated to underpin this process. According to this principle, immediate reinforcements are more effective than delayed ones.

Other questions which learning theorists have to answer is why do not all social drinkers who suffer stressful experiences not recognize the anxiety reduction and other positive reinforcement qualities of alcohol and, if they do, why do not they all go on to become alcoholics? These questions are often answered in terms of a principle of differential reinforcement,[43] and stimulus generalization[44] according to which alcoholics are people who have acquired, through differential reinforcement and modelling experiences, alcohol consumption as a widely generalized dominant response to aversive stimulation. Attempts at more sophisticated learning theories employing 'decision pay off matrices'[45] or 'avoidance-approach conflict systems of unstable equilibrium'[46] often have at their base some notion of the drinker either not *really* knowing what he is doing or eventually making a mistake: 'finding himself accidentally beyond the equilibrium point and consequently having a tendency to approach more closely to the goal . . . a state of high blood alcohol'.[47]

The third main type of basically psychological theory is concerned with offering *psychodynamic* interpretations of alcoholism and problem drinking. McCord and McCord[48] set out the three basic positions upon which such an approach rests. First there is the Freudian view that alcoholism results from one or more unconscious tendencies, including self-destruction, oral fixation and latent homosexuality. Menninger,[49] for example, maintains that alcoholics have a powerful urge to destroy themselves because of guilt and a need for punishment caused by personally unacceptable aggressive wishes. Such an approach is clearly one way of accommodating the basic learning theory dilemma which was mentioned earlier. For alcoholism can be seen as self-destruction through an attack on the body purporting to be a relief of pain.

Many psychoanalytic writers have associated alcoholism with oral fixation. Fenichel,[50] in his review of psychoanalytic works, classed alcoholics with 'other drug addicts' because of their apparent basic personality similarities and suggests that all addicts use the effects of the drugs 'to satisfy the archaic oral longing which is a sexual longing, a need for security, and a need for the maintenance of self-esteem simultaneously'. The difficult family settings from which alcoholics come create specific oral frustrations in childhood and it is these frustrations which, according to these particular theorists, lead to oral fixations.

A number of writers have attempted to link alcoholism with latent homosexuality.[51] Fenichel,[52] for example, saw latent homosexuality as a concomitant result of the oral frustration conducive to alcoholism. Machover and his associates[53] saw the relationships between alcoholism, infantile experiences and homosexuality in terms of an overindulgent mother who 'stimulates an intense oral libidinization whose demands cannot be met'. Traumatic weaning then forces the child to seek supplies from its father. The father's emotional coldness impels him to force the child into independence which is experienced as rejection and deprecation. The child, according to this theory, is left with intense needs for oral indulgence and with deep feelings of inferiority in his envy of masculine potency as exemplified by his father. Compulsive drinking is seen as an effort to allay anxiety over masculine inadequacy and as a means of masculine assertion. The alcoholic's homosexuality is latent, residing in drives toward overcoming it through submission to strong father figures.

The other two basic psychoanalytic positions set out by McCord and McCord are the Alderian view that alcoholism represents a struggle for power[54] and the view that alcoholism develops in responses to an inner conflict between dependency drives and aggressive impulses.[55] Summing up a brief discussion of psychoanalytic theories the authors of a recent report felt that:

> '(E)vidence to support the psychoanalytic views is necessarily inconclusive, since it is difficult to devise experimental tests of these theories. . . . Nevertheless, the application of psychoanalytic ideas in the treatment of alcoholism has been reported to give successful results'.[56]

Sociological Theories

The third major set of 'scientific' theories are those which postulate a causal relationship between the development of some kind of alcohol problem and the sociocultural setting in which that problem is located. The range of broadly sociological studies of drinking and alcoholism was discussed in Chapter 1. In this section, therefore, there is only need to repeat, in brief outline, the three main types of aetiological theory.

Sociological theories of cause range from, on the one hand, those which see alcohol use as functional for society as a whole[57] and likely to lead to a high level of associated problems in those societies which do not permit emotional outlets through ceremonies and rituals;[58] via those 'sub-structural' theories[59] which build upon empirical findings that alcoholics are over-represented in specific age, religious, sex, ethnic, class categories or specific family, marital, employment situations; to the labelling or societal-reaction theories which see the alcoholics or problem drinkers as people who for whatever reason become publicly designated as deviant and then reinforced in their deviant role by public reaction.[60]

These sociological theories of alcoholism, no less than the genetic and psychological ones discussed earlier, have their crucial weaknesses. The global, supra-cultural theories are, of necessity, speculative, imprecise and virtually impossible to refute or test. Sub-structural theories, by contrast, are invariably based upon studies with glaring methodological weaknesses. Studies of the 'family background of alcoholics', for example, have been given a great deal of attention, but we rarely know whether the families which are included are representative of all alcoholics, and we are even less likely to know what similarity there is between the families of alcoholics and the families of non-alcoholics. Many of the studies are based on alcoholics' memories of their families. All this is very unfortunate since a long-term study of developing alcohol problems within the context of, familial, marital, occupational and other day-to-day relationships is vital to any sociological theory of the causes of alcoholism. To date, because of the obvious difficulties involved, no such study has been carried out.

It is clear that a large number of well-developed 'scientific' theories of alcoholism are available. However, if we are interested in why people do what they do in relation to both alcohol and drinkers we need to have access to the 'professional' and 'everyday' theories of alcoholism in terms of which people actually operate in particular situations.

'Professional' Theories

As part of the South London study, 31 general practitioners (G.P.s), 28 social workers (S.W.s) and 23 probation officers (P.O.s) were interviewed. These represented half the general practitioners and probation officers and a quarter of the social workers in the study area. At the end of the semi-structured interview, which had focused for the most part on a particular case, all the professionals were presented with a self-completion questionnaire and asked to indicate how strongly they agreed or disagreed with a series of statements about alcohol, alcoholics, alcoholism, treatment and helping organizations.

Some of these statements dealt with ideas about cause, and two focused on the first type of 'scientific' theory outlined in the previous section; namely the idea that alcoholism is hereditary or is the result of some biochemical predisposition. Table 1 shows that, apart from approximately one in four general practitioners, there was little 'professional' support for either of the statements.

TABLE 1. 'Professional' theories: heredity and biochemical predisposition

		G.P.s %	S.W.s %	P.O.s %
'Alcoholism is hereditary'	Strongly agree	3·3	0·0	0·0
	Agree	16·7	0·0	0·0
	Uncertain	23·3	11·5	36·4
	Disagree	50·0	53·8	59·1
	Strongly disagree	6·6	34·6	4·5
	N =	30	26	22

		G.P.s %	S.W.s %	P.O.s %
'The alcoholic has some chemical in his make-up which makes him drink'	Strongly agree	4·0	0·0	5·6
	Agree	20·0	4·0	0·0
	Uncertain	32·0	48·0	55·6
	Disagree	36·0	36·0	27·8
	Strongly disagree	8·0	12·0	11·1
	N =	25	25	18

The notion that becoming an alcoholic was merely a question of how much alcohol people consumed found almost no support either. As Table 2 shows, only three people, all general practitioners, agreed with the statement that 'the only difference between an alcoholic and a heavy drinker is the amount they drink'. The distinction between being the alcoholic and the heavy drinker appeared to be accounted for in other ways; one of which was the idea of addiction. Approximately half of all the professionals, as Table 2 shows, thought that 'only people who are addicted to alcohol are alcoholics' and also that 'anyone who drinks too much may become addicted to alcohol'.

Two of the other statements on the self-completion schedule focused on the broadly psychological theories which were discussed in the previous section. The idea that 'only people with special types of personality become alcoholics' received some support, particularly from general practitioners, while, as Table 3 shows, 40 per cent of probation officers agreed with the statement that 'alcoholics drink in order to relieve conflicts which started in childhood'. However, a majority of each profession was uncertain on this question.

The final two statements which could be classed as broadly causal touched on the third, more sociological, areas discussed in the previous section. The first contains the suggestion that drinking patterns are learned from those with whom the drinker is in close contact, such as family and friends. This notion received support from each profession, but particularly from general practitioners. However, it still has to be explained, of course, why this 'learned' pattern of drinking gets out of hand, or leads to alcoholism for some people and not others. One answer to this question is offered in the causal statement which, as Table 4 shows, found greatest 'professional' support; namely the one which claimed that 'alcoholics drink in order to cope with difficult life situations'. The strength of agreement with this statement could be due to the fact that it contains within it implications of several causal notions, such as the idea of people 'learning' that drinking relieves stress, anxiety or worry; the idea of 'escape' drinking; and the idea that any satisfactory theory of alcoholism must take into account the features of the social situation in which the drinking takes place, and the meaning of the drinking for the various people involved.

TABLE 2. 'Professional' theories: consumption, addiction and alcoholism

		G.P.s %	S.W.s %	P.O.s %
'The only difference between an alcoholic and a heavy drinker is the amount they drink'	Strongly agree	3·2	0·0	0·0
	Agree	6·5	0·0	0·0
	Uncertain	9·7	11·1	8·7
	Disagree	61·3	66·7	65·2
	Strongly disagree	19·5	22·2	26·1
	N =	31	27	23

		G.P.s %	S.W.s %	P.O.s %
'Only people who are addicted to alcohol are alcoholics'	Strongly agree	10·3	3·8	13·6
	Agree	51·9	42·3	40·9
	Uncertain	17·2	15·4	18·2
	Disagree	17·2	23·1	27·3
	Strongly disagree	3·4	15·4	0·0
	N =	29	26	22

		G.P.s %	S.W.s %	P.O.s %
'Anyone who drinks too much may become addicted to alcohol'	Strongly agree	6·7	3·7	10·0
	Agree	53·3	44·4	40·0
	Uncertain	13·3	14·8	20·0
	Disagree	23·3	33·3	30·0
	Strongly disagree	3·3	3·7	0·0
	N =	30	27	20

TABLE 3. 'Professional' theories: personality and childhood conflict

		G.P.s %	S.W.s %	P.O.s %
'Only people with special types of personality become alcoholics'	Strongly agree	13·8	8·3	5·0
	Agree	34·5	25·0	20·0
	Uncertain	31·0	45·8	35·0
	Disagree	17·2	16·7	35·0
	Strongly disagree	3·4	4·2	5·0
	N =	29	24	20

		G.P.s %	S.W.s %	P.O.s %
'Alcoholics drink in order to relieve conflicts which started in childhood'	Strongly agree	3·4	0·0	4·5
	Agree	20·7	8·7	36·4
	Uncertain	58·6	65·2	54·5
	Disagree	17·2	26·1	4·5
	Strongly disagree	0·0	0·0	0·0
	N =	29	23	22

TABLE 4. 'Professional' theories: social learning and coping

		G.P.s %	S.W.s %	P.O.s %
'Many alcoholics learn their drinking pattern from friends and relatives'	Strongly agree	7·7	0·0	4·5
	Agree	77·0	33·3	40·9
	Uncertain	7·7	48·1	31·8
	Disagree	7·7	18·5	22·7
	Strongly disagree	0·0	0·0	0·0
	N =	26	27	22

		G.P.s %	S.W.s %	P.O.s %
'Alcoholics drink in order to cope with difficult life situations'	Strongly agree	20·0	0·0	8·7
	Agree	63·3	60·7	73·9
	Uncertain	13·3	35·7	8·7
	Disagree	3·3	3·6	8·7
	Strongly disagree	0·0	0·0	0·0
	N =	30	28	23

This material from the self-completion schedule is, of course, superficial and in need of qualification. The very fact of presenting a wide range of statements which correspondents felt obliged to have an opinion on, means that the resultant data are unlikely to create a tight, logically consistent picture. There was really no possibility of 'pure' causal theories emerging. However, the material is interesting for what it does tell us. First, there was little support from any of the professional groups for the basic biochemical or genetic theories of alcoholism, and only moderate support for the basic psychological theories. The 'professionals' were clearly much more likely to think of alcoholism in terms of social learning and to see alcoholics as people who drink in order to cope with the difficulties of everyday life.

Fortunately, the self-completion material was not the only access to the professional's ideas about cause. As part of the main interview each professional was asked to identify a recent client or patient who had some alcohol-related problem. This case then served as a focus for a series of questions about definitions, life situations, referral, professional practice, quality of services, and, in addition, causation. All professionals, who were able to identify a recent case about which they could talk fully, were asked to say what they thought caused the particular drinking problem. Table 5 sets out the broad categories of cause mentioned by each professional group in relation to their 'problems' cases. As with the self-completion material no pure 'scientific' theories emerged. Several of the respondents, particularly social workers and probation officers, made statements which came into more than one broad causal category.

TABLE 5. 'Professional' ideas about the cause of specific drinking problems

	G.P.s	S.W.s	P.O.s	All Professionals	
	%[a]	%[a]	%[a]	N	%[a]
Individual weakness	20·7	44·4	57·8	21	36·9
Childhood / social deprivation	0·0	44·4	57·8	15	26·3
Social pressure to drink	41·4	11·1	10·6	15	26·3
Depression, anxiety, worry	31·0	11·1	15·8	13	22·9
To escape, cover up	0·0	55·5	38·8	12	21·1
Response to life problems	17·2	22·2	21·1	11	19·3
Loneliness, boredom	20·7	0·0	15·8	9	15·8
Habit	3·4	0·0	0·0	1	1·8
Don't know	3·4	0·0	0·0	1	1·8
N =	29	9	19	57	
No answer	1	0	0	1	
No case	1	19	4	24	
Total	31	28	23	82	

[a] Total per cent = More than 100 per cent since several professionals mentioned more than one cause

General Practitioners

Thirty of the 31 general practitioners in the sample were able to identify someone with a drinking problem whose case they knew well. Twenty-nine of these 30 made some statement about the cause of the problem under discussion. The most frequently mentioned cause (N = 12) was that the drinking was done in response to social pressures of various kinds, but in particular to the pressure of being in a job in which there is either the opportunity or the expectation to drink: 'Job opportunity, whole family in catering'; 'Journalist — major factor'; 'Journalism': ' . . . part-time in a bar': 'R.A.F. when young'; 'ex-Naval officer'; 'Docker, it's like being a publican', and:

> 'Served in the Fleet Air Arm. Was a pilot and young and probably had a devil may care attitude. Could be dead tomorrow and trying to keep up with the others'.

Other explanations for the problem drinking were that it was in response to anxiety, illness or depression (9), a result of an individual weakness of some kind (6):

> 'Definitely psychologically vulnerable'.
> 'Inadequate personality'.

a response to loneliness or boredom (6) or a reaction to certain life problems (5) such as 'fear of losing his job', or 'an unhappy marriage'. One general practitioner said that he did not know what caused his patient's drinking problems, while another thought that he had just 'got into the habit of drinking'.

This last respondent was the only one of all the professionals to make a statement which could in any way be said to imply that the patient's problem was one of addiction. Clearly when general practitioners considered the cause of a particular person's drinking problem they were rarely thinking in terms of the grand 'scientific' theories which fill the academic and professional literature. They were thinking, rather, in terms of individual susceptibilities, triggering events or drink-encouraging situations.

Social Workers

Only nine out of the 28 social workers who were interviewed in the study locality identified a particular case from their list in which a drinking problem was involved. The question of how cases were recognized is discussed in Chapter 6. However, in spite of the small number it was possible to see clear differences between social workers and the general practitioners on the question of cause. Only one of the social workers offered explanations in terms of response to anxiety or depression. One mentioned social pressure to drink as a contributory factor, while only two identified significant life events:

> 'Drinking was a reaction to the illness and death of her husband'.
>
> 'He was a good soldier but invalided out with a back injury'.

The main categories of cause given by social workers were, first, childhood or social deprivation (4):

> 'Being a product of a large disorganized family where father is alcoholic and mother is emotionally very deprived, he never got any care or attention'.
>
> 'She's had a rough life — homeless for a while. Rejection by family probably made it worse'.

and, second, the use of alcohol to cover up some personal weakness or 'to forget' (5):

> 'She has little confidence and no motivation to help herself. She needs some sort of prop'.
>
> 'Enjoys drinking to forget about responsibilities'.

This tendency to consider cause in terms of childhood experience or inherent personal weakness, and thus by definition out of current reach, may either be a cause of or a justification for why so few social workers identified people on their lists as having a drinking problem. In any event cases were, perhaps, more likely to be recognized and categorized in terms of problems which the workers took to be more amenable to alleviation if not solution.

Probation Officers

Nineteen out of the 23 probation officers said that they had a person on their case load with some kind of drinking problem. Not only did a larger proportion of probation officers than social workers identify cases with drinking problems but they also made more detailed and complex statements about cause. However, in spite of this complexity, it was possible to draw out certain dominant themes.

First, like some of the social workers, several probation officers (11) stressed adverse early life influences, such as heavy parental or family drinking:

> 'His father drank heavily, so as a child he identified with a male figure who drank heavily'.

'Brought up in a family of drink abusers. Mother died in a drunken brawl'.

Emphasis was also placed on personal weaknesses of various forms (11):

'His feelings of inadequacy'.

'Tied up with his view of himself — low feeling of self worth'.

And intimately related to this was the third major theme of drinking to cover up, bolster or escape (7):

'This led to him drinking to escape and cover up his inadequacy'.

'I would conjecture that it has been a way of bolstering himself socially'.

In addition, probation officers also thought that their clients drank in response to anxiety or depression (3), loneliness (3) and particular life problems (4). Several of the accounts contained statements from more than one of the causal categories. One, in fact, mentioned almost every one of them:

'His father drank heavily, so as a child he identified with a male figure who drank heavily. Also suffered childhood deprivation, so has poor self-image and feelings of rejection. Has nervous temperament accentuated by war-time tremor drinking in isolation, release from depression. It glosses over all the problems temporarily at least. Also marital situation — his wife not on the whole a warm person. Drinking could be seen as regression — the oral thing'.

From the self-completion statements and the discussion of particular cases certain differences between the professional groups emerged. By and large the general practitioners tended to see the drinking problems with which they were confronted as either a result of everyday social pressures to drink in a harmful way, or as a coping response to loneliness and other life problems. There was little evidence that general practitioners saw problem drinkers or alcoholics as inherently different from other people. Social workers and probation officers, on the other hand, while acknowledging the importance of the idea that people may drink in order to cope with everyday problems, were, in addition, inclined to look for childhood deprivations or individual weaknesses which might explain why these particular people resorted to drink to cope with life stresses.

It is also clear that when professionals are called upon to talk about the causes of the particular problem cases which they have had to handle, that they do not do so in terms of pure 'scientific' theories such as those discussed in the first section. Roebuck and Kessler in their book *The Etiology of Alcoholism* attempt to:

'... pave the way for hoped-for interdisciplinary articulation of several levels of analysis in the etiological study of alcoholism and/or problem drinking'.[61]

It seems as though professionals who actually have to deal with alcohol-related problems have no difficulty in handling a wide range of causal notions in relation to any particular case.

'Everyday' Theories

One of the main reasons for conducting the general population study was to get some idea of whether the general population's views on alcohol-related problems, their causes and their consequences were very different from the views of the helping professionals in the same locality. In relation to actual drinking problems the overall general population sample was broken down into three categories The first category was a small group of eight people who said that they felt that they had definitely had a drinking problem at some time in the past or felt that they had one at present. Second, there were 36 people who knew someone else with a current drinking problem well enough to be able to answer detailed questions about the development, effects and handling of the problem. Finally, there were the remaining 242 people who said that they had never had a drinking problem themselves and did not know enough about anyone with one, to answer detailed questions.

TABLE 6. 'Everyday' and 'professional' theories: coping and special personality

		Self-defined problem drinkers %	People who knew problem drinkers %	Remainder of population sample %	The professionals %
'Alcoholics	Strongly agree	75·0	31·4	22·0	9·8
drink in order	Agree	0·0	48·6	53·5	65·4
to cope with	Undecided	12·5	11·4	14·9	19·8
difficult life	Disagree	12·5	5·7	8·7	4·9
situations'	Strongly disagree	0·0	2·9	0·8	0·0
	N =	8	35	241	73
'Only people	Strongly agree	25·0	2·9	2·1	9·6
with special types	Agree	12·5	20·0	14·2	27·4
of personality	Undecided	0·0	25·7	32·9	37·0
become	Disagree	62·5	37·1	40·8	21·9
alcoholics'	Strongly disagree	0·0	14·3	10·0	4·1
	N =	8	35	240	73

Since the interviews with members of the general population sample were quite long and detailed, particularly for those who had themselves got a drinking problem or who knew someone with one, the self-completion section of the questionnaire was shorter than that for the professionals. As a result only two of the causal statements were included; the one which suggested that alcoholics were people with 'special types of personality' and the one which suggested that alcoholics drink in order 'to cope with different life situations'. Table 6 shows that the general population groups were even more likely to strongly support the 'coping' theory than were the professionals. However, apart from the small group of people who said that they themselves had had a drinking problem, the general population were rather less likely than the professionals to see the alcoholic as a person with a particular type of personality.

Since several of the general population sample identified themselves as having had a drinking problem or said that they knew a lot about someone else with a problem it was possible, as with the professionals, to ask questions about the cause of a *specific* problem. The remainder of the general population were merely asked a hypothetical question about why they thought people drank 'in a way which causes them problems'. Table 7 sets out the broad categories of the general population's ideas about cause.

TABLE 7. 'Everyday' theories of cause

Cause	Self-defined problem drinkers	People who knew problem drinkers	Remainder of population sample	Total general population sample	
	%[a]	%[a]	%[a]	N	%[a]
Depression, anxiety, worry	12·5	0·0	44·6	109	38·2
Response to life problems	12·5	30·5	30·2	85	29·6
Social pressure to drink	75·0	22·2	15·3	51	18·0
Loneliness, boredom	0·0	8·3	19·8	48	16·8
'Trouble' (unspecified)	0·0	2·8	18·6	46	16·1
To escape, cover up	12·5	0·0	16·9	42	14·6
Habit, loss of control	0·0	0·0	16·5	40	14·0
Individual weakness	0·0	0·0	7·0	17	5·9
Childhood/social deprivation	12·5	11·1	0·8	7	2·4
Don't know and reason	12·5	19·4	2·8	15	5·2
Don't know	0·0	19·4	2·8	14	4·9
Total	8	36	242	286	

[a] Total per cent = More than 100 per cent since several respondents mentioned more than one cause

Self-defined Problem Drinkers

The reason given by five of the eight people who said that they were, or had been, having some kind of difficulty with drink was that the problem drinking was in response to social pressure or particular social circumstances:

> 'All my friends drank a lot, played darts. There was no other entertainment'

> 'It was the social thing to do during the war. We were all away from home and husband abroad'.

The other three people all gave different reasons for why they had some drink-related problem. One said that he drank in response to 'nerves, depression, ill health', and another because of 'a combination of heredity and some very unpleasant personal and family problems going back a long time'. The third was rather less certain: 'Um. I don't know. Adventurous spirit, just to enjoy the sensation of drink'. However, later in the interview this young man said that 'it's very hard when your friends drink and its very nice to get completely and utterly inebriated. It's better than suicide'. So here again there is the mention of social pressure to drink, and also the suggestion of drinking to escape.

People who Knew Problem Drinkers

In addition to the eight people who had themselves experienced some problem associated with drink there were 36 other people in the general population sample who had been closely involved with, or knew a lot about, someone else's drinking problem. But although these people were all talking about someone they 'personally know well' their ideas about cause were much more uncertain than the eight people with problems. In fact seven out of the 36 said that they just did not know what caused the person to drink in that way, while a further seven who did offer a reason concluded that they did not *really* have any idea:

> 'His marriage broke up, *but I don't really know*'.

> 'Maybe it was caused by the fact that one of her boy friends let her down years ago, *but I don't really know*'.

> '*Don't know*. Maladjusted life at home. That could be it. Comes from good stock. Salvation Army I think. *No I don't know*'.

Among those who were more positive about cause 10 spoke of the person's problem drinking being a response to particular life problems and pressures:

> 'A marriage that went wrong. Children to bring up on her own'.

'Probably the "rat race". The pace of life in the business world and outside too. Great deal of worry with business'.

'Loss of his wife'.

while eight others focused on the social pressure to drink, and of being in situations where drinking is usual or expected:

'He's Irish. Social background, drinking is more acceptable in Ireland. Especially excessive drinking which seemed fairly commonplace years ago'.

'He drinks to be sociable. Reps come in and they go out together to the pub'.

Four people mentioned that the parents of the person with the problem were heavy drinkers, while others spoke of the drinking being a response to loneliness, and 'personal problems'. Other reasons ranged from 'Giving up smoking' and 'Just likes the taste' to one young lady who felt that her husband's friend drank because 'He's got a high blood count which gives him a thirst'.

Remainder of the General Population

Those members of the general population who had had least experience of alcohol-associated problems were also least restrained and tentative about the question of cause. Whereas about 40 per cent of those who actually knew well someone with a drinking problem said that they did not know what caused it, only five per cent of those who had no close experience of drinking problems had any reservation about why people develop drinking problems. The cause most commonly given, by nearly half of the group, was that drinking is in response to the person's unhappiness, depression or worry. However, not everyone was so convinced by this argument:

'Some say too much worry, family problems. I had family trouble and it didn't drive me to drink, so I don't know. Perhaps they are highly strung'.

This idea of personal weakness or inability to cope was mentioned by several other respondents (17):

'Weak character, things happen out of the blue and they can't cope with it'.

'A general personality weakness. Their insecurity drives them to seek comfort and companionship, particularly in the pub'.

'Weakness I think. I think a person should know when they've had enough. I've been to parties but I've never been drunk. I've known when to stop'.

Just as the respondents who knew someone with a drinking problem felt that the person may have drunk in response to particular life problems, so this was given as a reason by one in three of the main general population sample. Mention was also made of drinking in response to unspecified 'problems' or 'troubles' (45), and of people being under social pressure to drink (37):

'Lots of jobs nowadays require them to drink more than they want to from a business point of view'.
'They get in with a crowd and they have one drink and then it's their turn to stand a round and so it goes on'.

Two other main categories of cause were boredom or loneliness (48) and drinking to escape from problems or 'to drown one's sorrows' (41):

'If they've got any problems on their mind they have to drink to forget them'.

'Things get on top of them. Take to drink as a form of escape'.

'If a man's had a row with the wife he finds solace in a drink and if the rows continue he can become an alcoholic'.

This last respondent was the only one to mention either 'alcoholism' or 'alcoholic' in response to the question about cause. However, whereas none of those who had experienced a drinking problem themselves or knew someone well who had, and only one of the 57 professionals who were interviewed about particular cases spoke of addiction or dependence, one in six of the general population either mentioned drinking becoming a habit:

'It's habit, one drink leads to another'.

'Habit, like smoking'.

'Some go out in the first place just for a social life and then the drink becomes a habit'.

or people 'losing control over' their drinking:

'I don't think they just start drinking it grows. You start with half. Maybe they find company in the pub, then they start to drink. They then go on if the company isn't there'.

'It gradually grows on them. They just can't stop'.

'They've let it get hold of them'.

'It just becomes a habit, they have to. They let the drink take charge. They can't control themselves'.

This chapter has outlined the major scientific approaches to the causes of alcoholism and also the types of causal statement made both by those professionals who are called upon to handle alcohol-related problems and by members of the general population. It is clear first; that professionals are tending to operate with broadly social rather than biochemical or psychodynamic theories in relation to particular cases and second; that both the professionals and those members of the general population who have had most experience of drinking problems, whether their own or other people's, differ in their ideas about cause from the large bulk of the general population. These latter people, approximately 85 per cent of the general population, were much more likely to talk in the traditional terms of addiction, habit and loss of control.

The question now arises of what are the social implications of these general ideas about the nature of alcoholism, and what is the relationship between them and such things as, the kind of help which can or should be given, and how particular problems are recognized and handled in particular situations. The next four chapters focus on these and other more detailed questions.

Chapter 4

Alcoholism and Disease

'. . . any label or definition is only a matter of convenience and convention'.
Jellinek[1]

Attempts to spell out the nature of the relationship between alcoholism and disease have formed a well-established and lively debate. Jellinek's classic discussion,[2] for example, placed the debate in its historical and cultural context while, at a more day-to-day level, Griffith Edwards reminds us that:

> '. . . when all the relevant information on the causes of abnormal drinking has been gathered in, the decision as to alcoholism being a disease will still rest very much on the definition of "alcoholism" on the one hand and of "disease" on the other'.[3]

Edwards thus directs our attention to the crucial question for the sociologist, namely, the question of what counts as something for particular people in particular social situations and what are the implications of those definitions for social behaviour. In some quarters, however, the question of alcoholism and disease is not taken to be one of debate or definition but one of decree or declaration. Moser, in a recent World Health Organization survey of *Problems and Programmes Related to Alcohol and Drug Dependence in 33 Countries,* reports that:

> '. . . almost all the respondents affirmed that dependence on alcohol and other drugs is recognized as illness in their country . . .

and, as an example, cites:

> 'Costa Rica, where alcoholism was officially declared as a disease according to presidential decree issued in 1954'.[4]

Gitlow, a physician, also takes the matter to be settled and beyond debate on the grounds that:

> 'The American Medical Association, American Psychiatric Association, American Public Health Association, American Hospital Association, American Psychological Association, National Association of Social Workers, World Health Organisation and the National College of Physicians have now each and all officially pronounced alcoholism a disease'.[5]

In the light of this formidable array of official pronouncements that alcoholism *is* a disease he feels that 'the rest of us can do no less'. In fact he goes further and suggests that 'we must now question the motives of those who would strip the alcoholic of his "disease" label'. However, it is not only South American presidents and certain medical professionals who assume that the matter has been decided. John N. Mitchell, the then Attorney-General, in an address at the testimonial dinner honouring R. Brinkley Smithers for outstanding leadership and dedication to the conquest of alcoholism, spoke at length of:

> ' . . . *the fact, acknowledged now by all the professionals in the field* that alcoholism as such is not a legal problem — it is a health problem. More especially simple drunkenness per se should not be handled as an offense subject to the process of justice. It should be handled as an illness, subject to medical treatment . . . (I)n most of the cases that come to public attention, a major disease is not being treated by doctors, therapists or medical technicians. The disease is being treated by policemen, judges, and jailors'.[6]

The purpose of this chapter is neither to settle the debate, nor to support or oppose the decrees and declarations. The aim is, rather, to look at three particular aspects of the complex question of the relationship between alcoholism and disease. The first section concentrates on the 'scientific' debate about whether alcoholism is a disease and, in particular, on the seminal contribution of E. M. Jellinek. The second section looks at how widespread the idea that 'alcoholism is a disease' really is. The third section is concerned with certain social purposes and consequences of operating with a disease theory of alcoholism.

Jellinek and Aspects of the Disease Conception of Alcoholism

The question of what counts as alcoholism and of what is the nature of its relationship to disease is constantly under review. There has been a discernible and well documented shift over the past century from considering alcoholism as primarily a legal or moral problem to considering it primarily as one of medicine or public health:

'Our Victorian ancestors . . . put people appearing intoxicated in public places in gaol. That the more times a person was arrested and incarcerated, the more likely he was to appear intoxicated again did not diminish the zeal of the persecutors. Against this mindless, purely punitive approach, the concept of "alcoholism as a disease" arose'.[7]

But while there has been this general shift of emphasis the alcoholic father is still likely to be morally condemned and the habitual public drunkard is still likely to be arrested, fined or jailed. Just as the Victorians made their distinction between the deserving and undeserving poor so we have our punished and treated alcoholics. This is discussed further in the next section.

Jellinek, in a series of papers, attempted to tease out the nature of the relationships between alcoholism and disease, and he played a major role in focusing attention on the core question of what it means to say that alcoholism is a disease. It is not being suggested that Jellinek somehow changed the world's ideas about the nature of alcoholism. Nor is Jellinek to be blamed for the way in which his ideas have been selectively plundered and unhelpfully interpreted. However, since Jellinek has, with justification, been referred to as 'primarily responsible for the great progress made in the understanding of and approach to alcoholism',[8] he must stand as at least representing a major body of thought on the nature of the relationship between alcohol consumption, alcoholism and disease and, as such, must be held partially responsible for the way in which 'the disease concept of alcoholism' is now applied. How happy he would be with the various manifestations of its application is a quite separate question upon which we can merely speculate.

In his much quoted 1952 article Jellinek[9] restricted the application of the disease conception to 'addictive drinking' —

'The disease concept of alcohol addiction, does not apply to the excessive drinking, but solely to the loss of control which occurs in only one group of alcoholics and then only after many years of excessive drinking . . . the loss of control is a disease condition per se'.

Not only was Jellinek clear about the precise nature of the disease conception of alcoholism but he was also clear about the need for a restricted definition of alcoholism itself and clear about the harmful consequences which would follow from the 'unwarranted extension' of the conception to all excessive drinking. For 'sooner or later', he believed, such a misapplication would 'reflect on the legitimate use too and, more important, will tend to weaken the ethical basis of social sanctions against drunkenness'. Later, in *The World and its Bottle*,[10] Jellinek again denied the usefulness of defining as 'alcoholism' everything which, in any culture, is given that label:

'The extension of the term alcoholism to cover all forms of drinking which may occasion damage is not impossible', but 'while such a broad connotation would perhaps eliminate much conflict in international communication on this subject, it would hardly be a useful means'.

Perhaps because of his increasing involvement with organizations committed to 'international communication', Jellinek later reneged on this position and in *The Disease Concept of Alcoholism* used the term alcoholism to refer to 'any use of alcoholic beverage that causes any damage to the individual or to society'. The utility of such a wide-ranging definition of alcoholism, claimed Jellinek, was that it 'forces us to single out species of alcoholism and to speak of them in stringent terms'. While such a strategy might have helped to solve some of Jellinek's problems in 'international communication' it tended to cloud rather than illuminate other related issues. For instance, the five species of the genus alcoholism which Jellinek outlined do not in fact cover the whole range of alcoholism as he defined it:

> 'The definition of alcoholism, namely that alcoholism is any drinking that leads to any damage, does not permit of designating as alcoholic all those who occasion some kind of damage through their use of alcoholic beverages. I would call alcoholics only those who manifest the alpha, beta, gamma, delta, and epsilon varieties of alcoholism'.

Because of the wide-ranging definition of alcoholism and the concomitant fact that 'we cannot say that alcoholics are those who suffer from alcoholism' Jellinek concentrated his attention upon only certain of the alcoholisms when he addressed himself to the question of in what way alcoholism is a disease. His answer to this question was that only gamma 'loss of control' and delta 'inability to abstain' alcoholisms qualify as diseases, because only they are addictions in the pharmacological sense.

Having come to this conclusion Jellinek felt that the next challenging question should concern the pharmacological nature of addiction to which 'the newer techniques in pharmacology, physiopathology and biochemistry should be addressed'. He considered it was the case that 'if any physiological or biochemical anomaly — which in itself may not seem grave — can strip nervous tissue of its resistance to adaptation of its metabolism to a noxious substance then that adaption with all its concomitant behavioral changes may be designated as a disease'. This, then, was what Jellinek postulated as the disease nature of alcoholism.

Over the whole body of his writing Jellinek was quite consistent about the distinction which should be maintained between 'alcoholism' as broadly defined and 'the disease nature of alcoholism' restrictively defined as addictive alcoholism. Unfortunately his discussion of the topic made him appear less clear on intimately related points. The apparent lack of clarity was probably due to the fact that, in addition to setting out his own position in *The Disease Concept of Alcoholism,* he was also endeavouring to produce a short history and extensive contemporary description of how various countries, groups and associations defined alcoholism and how they saw the relationship between alcoholism and disease. On the latter point Jellinek maintained that, while ideas about the nature of the relationship between alcoholism and disease varied from group to group, 'the indications for the great majority are that the accepted version is merely that "alcoholism *is* a disease" '.

This is the crux of the problem. For if, as Jellinek pointed out, a steadily increasing majority of medical professionals, governments, voluntary associations and members of the general public accepted 'merely that alcoholism *is* a disease' how helpful was it for him to extend his own definition of the broader term 'alcoholism' to include 'any use of alcoholic beverage that causes any damage to the individual or to society'? His justification for adopting the wide-ranging definition of alcoholism is acceptable in that it might force a careful scrutiny of the alcoholic. However, since he was readily recognized as an authority on alcohol-related problems and since so many people were, as he himself reported, unable to understand or at least maintain the distinction between alcoholism and the disease nature of alcoholism, Jellinek must be said to have contributed to the designation of an ever-widening set of conditions and behaviours as symptoms or diseases when, in fact, his *own* conception of the disease nature of alcoholism was just as restricted and clearly defined as ever.

Certain consequences result from the adoption of a wide-ranging definition of alcoholism and a concomitant acceptance merely that 'alcoholism *is* a disease. The third section of this chapter is devoted to the identification and discussion of such consequences. However, if all this is to be of any social relevance, as opposed to being *merely* of academic interest, it must be shown that a significant number of people, both professional and lay, do actually take alcoholism to be a disease.

Alcoholism and Disease: 'Legal', 'Professional' and 'Everyday' Perspectives

Whether or not alcoholism is in practice taken to be a disease is not a matter to be decided by academic debate or presidential decree but by examination of the way in which alcohol-associated problems are actually handled. Evidence at the broadest level can be found in such things as government acts, court decisions, medical regulations and insurance rules. The W.H.O. survey of *Problems and Programmes Related to Alcohol* gives instances of such formal manifestations of the assumption that alcoholism is a disease.[11] In Sweden, for example, alcoholism and drug dependence are 'recognised as illnesses by the Psychiatric Care Act of 1966', while the legal status of intoxication and alcoholism in America has changed dramatically in the years since 1966:

> 'For over 350 years public intoxication had been handled exclusively under the criminal law. About 25 years ago alcoholism began to be recognised as a medical problem under treatment statutes enacted in some States.

These laws, however, had remained largely ignored or poorly implemented. . . . (F)ollowing the landmark decisions in 1966 more progress has been made toward the medical and rehabilitative handling of intoxication and alcoholism under State and Federal law than in the previous 350 years'.[12]

The legal challenge to the public intoxication statutes relied on the core principle of criminal responsibility — that criminal sanctions may be applied only to voluntary action. It was successfully argued in the Easter v District of Columbia appeal case in 1966 that as a result of his disease an alcoholic drinks involuntarily and therefore cannot be criminally punished for his intoxication. However, the implications of the 1966 decisions were complex and both State and National Supreme Courts were deeply divided on the issue. The following extended extract from the report to Congress on *Alcohol and Health* gives a clear idea of the issues involved. It deals with the celebrated case of Powell v Texas (1968).

'Leroy Powell, an uneducated laborer who earned about $12 per week, also had an extensive arrest record for nothing other than public drunkenness. On December 19, 1966, Powell was arrested for public intoxication in Austin, Tex. On December 20 he was found guilty and fined $20. His conviction was appealed to the Travis County Court, where the judge found that he was an alcoholic but nevertheless affirmed his conviction. Since he had no other right of appeal within the State court system, he appealed directly to the United States Supreme Court.

In June 1968, the Supreme Court handed down its judgment, affirming Powell's conviction. A full appreciation of the implications of that case, however, requires analysis of the opinions written by members of the Court, none of which represented a majority view

An opinion by Mr. Justice Marshall, in which Justices Warren, Black, and Harlan concurred, commented that:

The picture of the penniless drunk propelled aimlessly and endlessly through the law's "revolving door" of arrest, incarceration, release, and rearrest is not a pretty one,

and noted the urgent need for some clear promise of a better world for these unfortunate people. These four Justices nonetheless concluded that the development of common law principles of criminal responsibility, and their application to new medical knowledge, should be left to the States and should not be hardened into rigid constitutional principles.

An opinion written by Mr. Justice Fortas, in which Justices Brennan, Douglas, and Stewart concurred, concluded that imposing criminal penalties upon an alcoholic for his public intoxication would violate the eighth amendment, because criminal penalties may not be inflicted upon a person for being in a condition he is powerless to change. This opinion accepted the argument that alcoholism is a disease which renders its victims powerless to avoid intoxication.

Thus, the deciding vote was cast by Mr. Justice White. In a separate opinion, he concurred both with the reasoning expressed in the opinion of Mr. Justice Fortas, and with the disposition of the case expressed in the opinion of Mr. Justice Marshall. In Justice White's view, the controlling issue was whether Powell could avoid being intoxicated *in public*. Because there was no evidence that Powell could not avoid being in public on the occasion on which he was arrested, Mr. Justice White voted to affirm the conviction. At the same time, however, he recognized that homeless derelict alcoholics suffer from a disease and could not properly be convicted for their public intoxication:

> The fact remains that some chronic alcoholics must drink and hence must drink *somewhere*. Although many chronics have homes, many others do not. For some of these alcoholics I would think a showing could be made that resisting drunkenness is impossible and that avoiding public places when intoxicated is also impossible. As applied to them this statute is in effect a law which bans a single act for which they may not be convicted under the eighth amendment — the act of getting drunk.
>
> It is also possible that the chronic alcoholic who begins drinking in private at some point becomes so drunk that he loses the power to control his movements and for that reason appears in public. The eighth amendment might also forbid conviction in such circumstances, but only on a record satisfactorily showing that it was not feasible for him to have made arrangements to prevent his being in public when drunk and that his extreme drunkenness sufficiently deprived him of his faculties on the occasion in issue.

A careful reading of the case therefore demonstrates that the Supreme Court, by a vote of five to four, agreed with the earlier rulings in *Easter* and *Driver* that a homeless derelict alcoholic may not constitutionally be punished for his public intoxication. As was recently stated in the Senate Report on the Comprehensive Alcohol Abuse and Alcoholism Prevention, Treatment, and Rehabilitation Act of 1970:[13]

> . . . five of the nine Justices agreed that alcoholism is a disease, that an alcoholic drinks involuntarily as a result of his illness, and that an alcoholic who was either homeless or who could not confine his drunkenness to a private place for some other reason could not be convicted for his public intoxication. Powell's conviction was upheld by a 5-to-4 vote, however, because the record failed to show that he was homeless or otherwise unable to avoid public places when intoxicated

As the law now stands, therefore, a homeless alcoholic cannot constitutionally be punished for his public intoxication.

Unfortunately, the case had not been as widely understood and applied as it should have been.

The Supreme Court of Pennsylvania, after a close analysis of the *Powell* opinions, expressed the same understanding as the Senate report:[14]

> As a result, *Powell v State of Texas* unequivocally holds that to the extent certain behavior is a "characteristic part" of a disease, to the extent it is an actual symptom of the disease, such behavior cannot be criminally proscribed

In the District of Columbia, the United States Court of Appeals ruled after the *Powell* decision not only that *Easter* remained the controlling law in that jurisdiction, but that alcoholism might properly be a defense to any criminal act caused by the condition.[15] The Supreme Court of Minnesota ruled, in 1969 that alcoholism is a defense to a charge of public intoxication,[16] but the Supreme Court of Alaska and the Georgia Court of Appeals have ruled that an alcoholic is criminally responsible for his public intoxication'.[17]

Growing official awareness of the futility of criminal sanctions against intoxication and alcoholism is not, of course, confined to the United States. Non-criminal detoxification centres were set up in Prague in 1951 and in Warsaw in 1956 to provide emergency care and treatment for the large number of people who had previously gone through the courts. By 1959 the Polish experiment was considered to be so successful that legislation was introduced requiring detoxification facilities in every city with a population over 100,000. More than 30 such centres now exist in Poland and over 50 in Czechoslovakia. Britain, Mexico and Finland, among others, have just begun to set up similar facilities.

Judicial decisions, legislation and the reports of eminent organizations and individuals do not ensure, by themselves, that those considered to have some alcohol-related problem will receive social or medical help rather than punishment for it. If the broad framework of enabling legislation and official pronouncements is to be translated into a helping system it has first to be made to work by people who share its general basic assumptions and second it has to be considered appropriate by those it is designed to help.

Three of the statements in the self-completion section of the interviews with general practitioners, social workers and probation officers in South London dealt with alcoholism and illness. Table 1 shows that general practitioners were the most likely to agree with the statement that alcoholism is a disease, the most likely to say that it is a mental illness and the most likely also to *disagree* that it is a physical illness.

The general population sample was presented with only one of these three statements: 'alcoholism is a disease'. Table 2 shows that overall there was a slightly higher percentage of the general population who agreed with the statement than of the professionals. Table 2 also shows that those who were

TABLE 1. Professionals' views on alcoholism as a disease, as a mental illness and as a physical illness

		G.P.s %	S.W.s %	P.O.s %
'Alcoholism is a disease'	Strongly agree	23·3	3·7	10·5
	Agree	56·7	44·4	42·1
	Uncertain	10·0	18·5	31·6
	Disagree	10·0	18·5	15·8
	Strongly disagree	0·0	14·8	0·0
	N =	30	27	19
		G.P.s %	**S.W.s %**	**P.O.s %**
'Alcoholism is a mental illness'	Strongly agree	16·1	3·8	9·5
	Agree	38·7	23·7	23·8
	Uncertain	22·6	34·0	23·8
	Disagree	19·4	30·8	38·2
	Strongly disagree	3·2	7·7	4·8
	N =	31	26	21
		G.P.s %	**S.W.s %**	**P.O.s %**
'Alcoholism is a physical illness'	Strongly agree	0·0	0·0	5·6
	Agree	17·9	25·9	22·2
	Uncertain	17·9	37·0	38·9
	Disagree	53·6	22·2	27·8
	Strongly disagree	10·7	14·8	5·6
	N =	28	27	18

most likely to agree were those who had had closest contact with alcohol problems, either their own or someone else's. It is impossible to say, of course, whether the belief that alcoholism is a disease preceded the recognition of the problem, was a result of the way in which some helping professional responded to the problem or was a way of coping subsequently with the fact *of* the problem. Such questions can only be approached by detailed long-term study.

One implication of the widespread acceptance of the notion that alcoholism is an illness or a disease is that medical and other professionals will be willing and able to help those who have some kind of alcohol problem. In fact, as far as the professionals themselves are concerned Table 3 shows that

TABLE 2. Alcoholism and disease, 'professional' and 'everyday' perspectives

		Self-defined problem drinkers	People who knew problem drinkers	Remainder of general population	Professionals
		%	%	%	%
'Alcoholism is a disease'	Strongly agree	12·5	47·2	23·3	13·2
	Agree	87·5	44·4	46·9	48·7
	Uncertain	0·0	0·0	15·4	18·4
	Disagree	0·0	5·6	12·4	14·5
	Strongly disagree	0·0	2·8	2·1	5·3
	N =	8	36	241	76

only 40 per cent of them felt that they had much to offer the alcoholic. Not only that but those who agreed that alcoholism is a disease or that alcoholism is a mental illness were no more likely than other professionals to feel that they had something to offer.

TABLE 3. Feeling of having something to offer alcoholics

		G.P.s	S.W.s	P.O.s
		%	%	%
'I feel that I personally do not have much to offer alcoholics'	Strongly agree	3·4	0·0	0·0
	Agree	24·1	20·8	26·1
	Uncertain	24·1	37·5	34·8
	Disagree	41·4	41·7	34·8
	Strongly disagree	6·9	0·0	4·3
	N =	29	24	23

Helping alcoholics was felt by most professionals, as Table 4 shows, to be something for which specialized training is required. However, none of the general practitioners had actually received any. Four of the social workers and seven of the probation officers had attended a short two-day course organized by the local Council on Alcoholism but most of them felt that it had not been very helpful.

Just as the professionals felt that specialized training was required so, as Table 5 also shows, they felt that the various helping organizations should have particular workers known to be specially responsible for dealing with people with alcohol problems. But throughout the interviews it was clear that the professionals were most ready for *other* organizations to have the specialists rather than their own. Reasons for not having specialists in their

TABLE 4. Professionals' view on specialization

		G.P.s %	S.W.s %	P.O.s %
'To effectively help alcoholics requires specialized training'	Strongly agree	22·6	22·2	18·2
	Agree	38·1	40·7	54·5
	Uncertain	9·7	7·4	4·5
	Disagree	29·7	29·6	22·7
	Strongly disagree	0·0	0·0	0·0
	N =	31	27	22

		G.P.s %	S.W.s %	P.O.s %
'Organizations should have workers who have specialized responsibility for alcoholics'	Strongly agree	30·0	17·9	26·1
	Agree	56·7	53·6	47·8
	Uncertain	10·0	21·4	17·4
	Disagree	3·3	7·1	8·7
	Strongly disagree	0·0	0·0	0·0
	N =	30	28	23

own organizations ranged from 'impractical' to a fear that the specialists would lose their range of skills. One probation officer felt that specializing in alcoholics' problems would be 'unrewarding', while another that 'officers would leave the service'. As Table 5 shows, there was a clear unwillingness by most of the professionals to consider taking on the job themselves of specializing in alcoholism.

So while most professionals agree that alcoholism is a disease and that alcoholism is a mental illness very few of them are willing to accept that either they personally or their own organizations are the appropriate people to provide the specialist assistance which they feel is necessary.

TABLE 5. Professionals' willingness to specialize in 'alcoholism' themselves

		G.P.s %	S.W.s %	P.O.s %
'I would like to be a worker with special responsibility for alcoholics in my organization/profession'	Strongly agree	0·0	0·0	8·7
	Agree	13·8	3·6	8·7
	Uncertain	17·2	21·4	30·4
	Disagree	51·7	64·3	43·5
	Strongly disagree	17·2	10·7	8·7
	N =	29	28	23

It was also seen earlier that a large majority of the general population agreed with the statement that alcoholism is a disease. If this general feeling is to be translated into action they will also have to feel that medical professionals, for example, are actually able to help alcoholics. All the general population sample were presented with a list of 10 helping individuals and organizations and asked to say which they felt would be most helpful and the second most helpful 'for someone whose drinking is causing them problems'. Two of the people on the list were a 'general practitioner' and a 'psychiatrist'. However, those who agreed that alcoholism is a disease were no more likely than other members of the general population to say that general practitioners and psychiatrists were the most helpful for alcoholics. Ideas about help are discussed more fully in Chapter 5.

From the data in this section it appears that neither the professionals nor the general public make the direct link between a general belief that alcoholism is a disease and a particular belief about the appropriateness of seeking medical help for some drinking problem. However, there are other purposes and consequences of operating with the notion that alcoholism is a disease quite apart from as a simple indication of medical professional action.

Some Purposes and Consequences of Operating with a Disease Conception of Alcoholism

The lack of a direct link between a belief that alcoholism is a disease and a belief that medical professionals are the appropriate people to deal with people whose drinking is causing them problems does not mean that the disease conception of alcoholism is irrelevant to everyday action in relation to alcohol and associated problems. For the belief that alcoholism is a disease can stand for other more general ideas about the nature of the problem under discussion and can, for instance, be used as a statement about individual responsibility in some overall therapeutic or helping strategy. As Room[18] puts it:

> 'The necessities that nurtured the disease conception . . . were practical rather than theoretical . . . The promulgation of disease concepts of alcoholism has been brought about essentially as a means of getting a better deal for the "alcoholic" rather than as a logical consequence of scholarly work and scientific discoveries'.

The logical conclusion to this use of the disease conception as an administrative or therapeutic strategy is the position of 'humane cynicism'[19] exemplified by Pattison:[20]

> 'The major advantage of defining alcoholism as a disease is social. It legitimates social support for rehabilitation of the alcoholic rather than

punishment. To say that alcoholism is an illness should not be construed as a statement about the aetiology or treatment of alcoholism'.

Unfortunately, it is not possible to legislate for what people in general will take words and phrases to 'really' mean. Although Pattison may be quite clear in his own mind that, for example, 'to say that alcoholism is an illness should not be construed as a statement about the aetiology and treatment of alcoholism' it certainly may *not* be so clear to members of the general population who are constantly being persuaded by health education campaigns merely that alcoholism is a disease. Davies, also accepting the basically strategic nature of the statement that alcoholism is a disease, recently suggested that it should be abandoned.

> 'The concept of alcoholism as "a disease" has outlived its usefulness. By employing it, alcoholics are missed, and those who are recognised because they have developed the "symptoms" and shown "the sign" are well advanced in the condition . . . '.

Unfortunately, again, the general population may not be either ready or willing to abandon the simple idea that alcoholism is a disease. And if, in fact, as was suggested earlier, an increasing number of people are coming to accept as axiomatic that 'alcoholism *is* a disease' and perhaps, along with Jellinek, are also defining as alcoholism 'any use of alcoholic beverage that causes any damage to the individual or to society' then this is likely to have certain social consequences.

These consequences, which have clear implications for those whose concern is with prevention, education and treatment, or with the provision of medical and social services associated with alcohol related problems, are briefly discussed below. To an extent the consequences stem from the acceptance of *any* disease concept of alcoholism but clearly become more problematic and assume greater significance as a more wide-ranging disease conception is adopted.

Consequence 1: *People may define their condition and behaviour as a medical matter, when the medical profession does not define the situation in that way, and vice versa.*

Whether the self-defined alcoholic's definition of himself is accepted as appropriate by the medical profession as a whole, or by the particular member of the profession to whom the matter is presented, will depend upon how inclusive *their* disease conception of alcoholism is and whether they operate with similar criteria of what counts as alcoholism. If members of the medical profession operate with a restricted definition of alcoholism and a stereotype of the alcoholic as a 'down and out', recognizable by appearance, manners or loss of social position, then this has clear consequences for diagnosis and for their willingness to treat as legitimate the self-defined alcoholic's presented complaint. Blane, Overton and Chafetz[22] have demonstrated that people not conforming to the popular Skid Row stereotype are missed diagnostically, while Pattison[23] reports than many doctors will not define as 'an alcoholic' person who is working and retaining his social and economic standards.

However, even if the medical profession's definition is less inclusive than that of a presenting 'alcoholic', certain processes are likely to operate *in effect* to widen the disease conception in any particular case. These processes are inevitable given that doctors have a commitment and a general readiness to conceive of any presented complaint as an illness to be treated, or at least as an appeal to them as doctors to be of 'help' in some way. A member of the medical profession may thus be drawn as a medical expert into an area which he may feel 'in his bones' does not come within his competence to be expert about. However, the process does not stop here, for any intervention, however reluctant, will tend to reinforce the lay conception of the disease nature of alcoholism. For if, as Jellinek wrote,[24] 'a disease is what the medical profession recognizes as such', then from the layman's point of view it is perfectly reasonable to define as a disease 'anything which the medical profession is seen to be willing to deal with in some way'.

When the medical profession accepts a more inclusive definition of alcoholism than does the alcoholic this also has implications for diagnosis and treatment. In such a situation the patient is likely to resist any attempts to persuade him that he is an alcoholic, or is exhibiting early symptoms of the condition, if his behaviour does not match up to *his* stereotype of an alcoholic. Thus if, for example, the patient's definition of the alcoholic is restricted to the Skid Row or down-and-out stereotype, then clearly a successful preventive or early treatment programme will only be initiated with extreme difficulty, while the chances of obtaining help at what the medical profession might see as an early stage in the disease process will be remote.

Consequence 2: *A person defined as an alcoholic by the medical profession may not be treatable because of the way he conceptualizes his responsibility for his condition.*

Both the general public and the medical profession tend to share certain assumptions about the relationship between disease and individual responsibility. These are that while the individual may have intentionally exposed himself to disease conditions, or behaved in some way which increased his likelihood of contracting a disease, it is not possible once the disease is contracted to get rid of it by will power. Parsons' discussion of the sick role[25] still informs much of the sociological work in this field and has been shown to accurately reflect widespread beliefs about the nature of 'being ill'.[26] Briefly, Parsons pointed out that whenever a person's illness condition is legitimized by the authority of the medical profession, his intimates or other people having influence over him, he assumes a special role. This role, the sick role, replaces or modifies his usual occupational, familial and other roles. It permits him special rights such as freedom from usual obligatory duties, requires him to observe certain rules such as cooperating with the doctor, and imposes special requirements on other people near to him, such as his family, friends and medical personnel.

On the crucial question of responsibility for the disease or illness condition Parsons has this to say in a section in which he discusses the relationship between illness and deviance:

> 'If being sick is to be regarded as "deviant", as certainly in important respects it must, it is . . . distinguished from other deviant roles precisely by the fact that the sick person is not regarded as "responsible" for his condition, "he can't help it" '.

Such assumptions are certainly appropriate when applied to a *restricted* definition of the alcoholism 'disease'. For, implied in the notion of 'the addictive drinker' is the idea that once the disease has been contracted it can be arrested or cured only by outside intervention. However, in the situation where the disease conception has been widened to cover other alcoholisms there are immediate implications for the alcoholic, the medical profession and, thus, for treatment.

Let us assume that both the doctor and non-addictive drinker accept a wide-ranging definition of alcoholism along the lines of that set out by Jellinek, and also accept that alcoholism is a disease. Any attempt by the doctor to persuade the alcoholic to change his drinking habits is likely to fail since he will, by definition, believe himself incapable of doing so. In fact, if the doctor suggests any course of action for the alcoholic which is based upon expectations about the alcoholic's 'will power' or the alcoholic having the right 'motivation', then such a course of action is likely to be unsuccessful if the alcoholic defines out of court the notion of individual responsibility for his condition. Even in the event of the doctor and an addictive drinker sharing a restricted definition of alcoholism the problems for treatment are no less acute. As well as the patient being likely to define out of court the responsibility for his condition and drinking behaviour, the expectation that will power is not sufficient to change drinking behaviour is built in to the very notion of 'loss of control' or 'inability to abstain' addictive drinking.

Siegler, Osmond and Newell[27] in their delineation of eight 'models of alcoholism' stress the importance of the question of differing conceptualizations of individual responsibility for illness conditions. A belief in individual responsibility for a condition is one of the key distinctions between the 'old' and the 'new' medical models, while a major component of the Alcoholics Anonymous model, as they present it, is that it 'lifts the burden of personal responsibility from the shoulders of the alcoholic by persuading him that alcoholism is bigger than he is'. Nevertheless, many of those who attempt to treat addictive drinkers appear to demand that 'the alcoholic' display the 'correct motivation' prior to being allowed to embark on a treatment programme, while a change in 'motivation' is presented as an essential prerequisite to starting on an upward path to recovery, according to certain diagrammatic representations of alcohol addiction and recovery.[28]

Consequence 3: *Different diseases might serve as models for different people's conception of the disease nature of alcoholism. Thus a disease which may appropriately serve as a model for addictive alcoholisms may be inappropriate as a model for a wider conception of the disease nature of alcoholism and vice versa.*

Just as both laymen and professionals may differ in their beliefs about individual responsibility for some illness condition and thus about the nature of appropriate treatment, so they may also differ in their ideas about what other disease alcoholism approximates to and in what ways. Some people may operate with a quite inappropriate particular disease analogy and thus prejudice the likelihood, or outcome, of treatment or the possibility of recovery. It is quite reasonable, particularly in relation to such an ill-defined notion as alcoholism, for people to structure their experience in alcohol-related situations by reference to those diseases and disease features which they find manageable, understandable and which have served them adequately in previous experiences with illness and disease. It is not possible or necessary to set out the implications of operating with every known disease as a model for alcoholism, or to identify the range of particular disease models which implicitly or explicitly underlie the main body of medical and lay thought on alcoholism. Such challenging enterprises are quite beyond the scope of this chapter. It *is* possible, however, to indicate, quite briefly, some of the incompatible notions about 'alcoholism' and 'the alcoholic' which could stem from the widespread use of specific disease models.

If, for instance, a common infectious disease was adopted as a model it would be reasonable to expect immunity from further attacks after one self-limiting bout of 'alcoholism'. If such a view were held, it would have definite implications for the alcoholic's readiness to consult initially, and also his readiness to give up drinking as part of any treatment or recovery progremme. For what would be the point of abstaining if immunity to the disease had been obtained? If, on the other hand, the alcoholic conceived of alcoholism as an illness like bronchitis, then an acute attack, possibly culminating in a period of detoxification, might be thought to have weakened the tissues in some way and made the body more susceptible to subsequent acute attack. Similarly, it is reasonable in the bronchitis case to assume that in the interval between acute attacks the person is free from the condition. This latter notion, however, is strictly at variance with a basic tenet of, for example, the Alcoholics Anonymous philosophy which encourages its members and the general public to believe that alcoholism is a disease which, once contracted, can never be cured. The most that can be hoped for is that the condition is arrested. As the subjects of a popular newspaper article usually put it; 'I'm still an alcoholic but it doesn't matter because I don't drink'. It appears that Alcoholics Anonymous operates with the conception of alcoholism as a disease rather like cancer or diabetes which it is not in the individual's power to get rid of. Yet there is also the belief that if the individual acts in a particular way — takes a drink — then the disease will *inevitably* remanifest itself. While this view is lagely consistent with the diabetes model it neither accords with the cancer conception of disease nor with the evidence concerning the many 'alcoholics' who have returned to 'normal drinking'.[29] The only way to square the latter incompatibility is to argue that such people were not *really* alcoholics in the first place.

Consequence 4: *An ever-increasing range of conditions and behaviours may be conceptualized as related to stages in a disease process.*

If a member of the general public accepts that alcoholism, widely defined, is a disease then it will be perfectly reasonable for him to be on the lookout for signs or symptoms of early stages in an assumed disease process. Such a strategy is encouraged by charts like Jellinek's and Glatt's which foster the notion of alcoholism as a 'developmental process'[30] marked by 'phases and sequences of symptoms'.[31] A member of the general public, thus bolstered in his strategy, is likely to assume that one stage in the 'developmental process' follows inevitably after another. This assumption is reasonable since it is consistent with the way in which many people conceptualize disease processes; for instance, 'once you've got it it's got to run its course'. Consequently, if one stage is believed to follow another and if, for example, 'heavy habitual social drinking' is felt to be a symptom of one stage of the disease process — as it might be if a wide-ranging definition of alcoholism is accepted — then it is reasonable for the drinker to believe that there is no way of preventing his progression through the subsequent stages of the process until 'rock bottom' is reached This again is reasonable since 'it has to get worse before it gets better' is a familiar and appropriate notion when applied to certain other diseases. It is hardly surprising, therefore, that a heavy social drinker should continue to drink if, first, he has been led to believe that an alcoholic cannot stop because he is addicted and if, second, he believes that he is an alcoholic and has a disease in which stages inevitably follow one another until rock bottom is reached. There is no reason to suppose that such a self-fulfilling prophecy should not apply in respect of alcoholism in the same way as it has been so clearly demonstrated to operate in relation to streaming and scholastic attainment in the field of education'.[32]

It may certainly be the case that by operating with, and encouraging the general public to accept, a *disease* conception of alcoholism the medical profession and Alcoholics Anonymous vitally aid the 'rock bottom' alcoholic's progress toward the goal of an 'interesting, happy, useful way of life'.[33] On the other hand if an alcoholic who accepts that alcoholism is a disease and a concomitant need for total abstinence, actually has a drink, it would be perfectly reasonable for him to continue drinking. It would be reasonable first, because it would follow that he would believe himself to be, by definition, 'lost' and unable to stop drinking even if he wanted to, and reasonable second, because believing himself to be inevitably lost would be reason enough for him to drink himself to oblivion as quickly as possible. Unfortunately, since ideas cannot be locked away like drugs in a cupboard, a disease conception of alcoholism cannot be kept in a bottle until it is deemed fit to dispense it as a handy therapeutic tool. Significantly, on Glatt's chart 'learns alcoholism is a disease' comes after the 'rock bottom' stage.

Consequence 5: *The medical profession will be considered to have competence in an ever-widening sphere of everyday life.*

Once a disease conception of alcoholism is extended to include the behaviour concomitant with the addiction or with the physical damage caused by alcohol consumption then there will be an inevitable extension of medical competence into an ever-widening sphere of life. This will take place under the heading of 'preventive medicine'. It is implicit in such a phrase that the medical profession will treat not only disease entities but behaviour considered to be part of a causal chain leading to the development of disease entities. The medical profession is then obliged to advise about, or intervene in relation to, any behaviour which falls into such a category. In the case of alcoholism, the medical profession would consider themselves, and be considered by the general public, as the relevant authority to decide upon, for example, licensing laws or alcohol pricing policy if it was shown that a rise in the price of alcohol or shorter licensing hours were associated with a drop in alcohol consumption. The idea that a time might come when a public health official would decide upon the licensing hours in a particular area should not be thought of as impossible or even extremely unlikely. For the idea that anything which is considered to affect in some way the working of the body or mind is 'a medical problem' and thus within the jurisdiction of the medical profession is happily applied in other spheres. Medicine is readily seen to be a legitimate arbiter in cases of clashes of values or political principle; witness the abortion controversy or the history of the fluoridation campaigns in the United States.[34]

Medical authorities do not actually have to make decisions in the political or educational arena, or even lend their weight to one side or the other, for decisions to be taken in their name. For there is nothing like the phrase 'for health reasons' for enhancing any proposal. The response to the 'clacker' craze which swept Britain in 1971 was a fine example of the use of such a manoeuvre. In the autumn of that year thousands of children plagued their parents and schoolteachers with the awful row produced by knocking two small plastic balls together at great speed. The problem which faced school authorities was how to justify the banning of these noisy and irritating toys from school premises. There was, of course, no reasonable justification. Until, that is, someone reported that clackers had broken the wristbones of a number of children. Overnight the 'irritating toys' turned into 'harmful and dangerous objects' and were banned on 'health grounds' from schools in several areas. That other much more 'harmful and dangerous' pastimes such as inter-school football matches should also be banned was not proposed!

This chapter has focused on the relationship between alcoholism and disease. Clearly, the question of whether or not alcoholism is a disease is not merely a matter of subtle academic debate, nor is it a matter to be decided by presidential decree or by medical professionals, health educators or administrators as part of some grand therapeutic strategy. Although these are all important social phenomena which may help to create or change a general climate of opinion the question of whether or not alcoholism is a disease is always problematic at ground level. It is always a matter to be teased out in particular situations if we are to gain any understanding of why people, both professional and lay, do what they do in relation to alcohol, drinking and what they take to be associated problems. As Edwards succinctly put it:

> '. . . the decision as to alcoholism being a disease will still rest . . . on the definition of "alcoholism" on the one hand and of "disease" on the other'.[35]

Chapter 5

Help and the Helpers

> 'In the past alcoholics have been neglected, punished, committed to mental institutions, and a few have been treated in private sanitariums. (A)lcoholics who could afford it were sent to private hospitals "to take the cure" . . . Other . . . alcoholics . . . have spent most of their lives in jails'. *Root.*[1]

The range of facilities and types of treatment for those who consider themselves or are considered by others to have some alcohol-associated problem is immense. The first section of this chapter outlines briefly the main kinds of help which are currently available. However, if we are to increase our understanding of why people do what they do in response to the alcohol problems which they perceive it is not sufficient to know merely what kind of helping facilities are available. We need to know, in addition, what the potential consumers of services believe to be the *most* appropriate forms of help and why. The second section of the chapter, therefore, deals with this question and also outlines the views of members of the general population on why certain agencies are *least* helpful for someone whose drinking is causing them problems.

Types of Help

The various methods and techniques for helping alcoholics can be categorized in many ways: in terms of the professional or theoretical orientation of the helper, or the organizational structure of the facility in which the help is given, or the main aim or goal of the treatment procedure, or the particular characteristics of the people for whom the help is designed, or the form, severity or point in the development of the problem to be alleviated, and many more.

Increasingly, however, the response to the multi-faceted nature of alcoholism is not to attempt to match particular people with particular problems to particular helpers with particular skills, but rather to employ a grapeshot or 'total treatment approach'. As Catanzaro puts it:

'Another important principal in treating the alcoholic is to pool the available sources of help, making a "community treatment team" for the alcoholic. Members of this treatment team include Alcoholics Anonymous, Al-Anon, Alateen, outpatient alcoholic clinics, the general hospital, the local Council on Alcoholism, alcoholic halfway houses, The Salvation Army, interested clergymen, social agencies, the state alcoholism program, the community mental health center, and, of course, the family physician. Naturally not all of the resources will be utilized in any one case. But utilizing as many of them as possible in each case will help the therapist to dilute his own share of the demanding task of successfully treating an alcoholic and will, in addition, make the treatment more successful'.[2]

Catanzaro claims that the utilization of as many resources as possible makes 'the treatment more successful'. The question of treatment success, and in particular the implications of operating, as Catanzaro does, with 'total abstinence from the use of alcohol' as one of the key goals of treatment is discussed in Chapter 8. This section, however, is concerned to set out the main types of help which are currently available for those who have some kind of drinking problem, irrespective of the goals in terms of which such treatments are employed.

Although it is not possible to produce a set of mutually exclusive categories, the many and various therapeutic strategies employed in relation to alcoholism can be grouped for purposes of discussion under three simple headings: those 'treatments' which focus on particular individuals with some alcohol-related problem, those which focus on groups of individuals with similar or inter-related problems and those which focus on communities as a whole.

Focus on the Individual

Treatment and helping strategies which focus on the individual drinker can be conveniently subdivided into those which are designed to alleviate acute withdrawal and associated complications, and those which attempt to solve the problems which are considered to have caused, or been caused by, excessive alcohol consumption. As the progress is made from acute withdrawal to those everyday life-problems taken to have been caused by excessive drinking so the balance of treatments naturally changes from the physical to the predominantly psycho-social.

Many alcoholics when coming into first contact with treatment agencies may be more or less intoxicated, in a poor state of general health, and possibly injured. The first stage of treatment, therefore, is often detoxification and first aid. Glatt succinctly summarizes the position as follows:

'When first seen, the alcoholic is generally starved, not only of food — in particular, vitamins, minerals and proteins — but also of fluids, rest and sleep. Malnutrition, dehydration, salt depletion, restlessness and insomnia, may thus require first-aid measures'.[3]

Anticonvulsant drugs and tranquillizers may be administered prophylactically in order to combat the possibility, in a small minority of cases, of severe withdrawal problems such as extreme tremulousness, hallucinosis, convulsions, and the most serious of all, delirium tremens:

> 'With delirium tremens there is profound confusion, vivid hallucinations (both auditory and visual) delusions, tremor, agitations, and sleeplessness, as well as a tremendous amount of increased activity. There is fever, tachy-cardia, and profuse perspiration . . . some of these cases can end fatally. The danger . . . is an associated injury or infection'.[4]

Tranquillizers, however, when administered in adequate dosage make the full-blown picture of florid delirium tremens much less frequent now than in the past, while even if the condition has been allowed to develop these drugs are capable of terminating it within a few hours.

Once the acute withdrawal and general health first aid stage is passed a wide range of treatments and investigations can be brought to bear on those weaknesses, defects, troubles and complications which are taken to have led to, exacerbated, or been caused by the individual's excessive alcohol consumption.

Apart from the withdrawal phase there may be a host of other physical complications which need attending to, such as acute gastritis and enteritis, which require gastric sedatives and bland diet. Varices of the esophagus and cardiac end of the stomach present the possibility of acute haemorrhage while one of the most common complications is cirrhosis of the liver. Administration of the necessary vitamins and minerals and an adequate diet will usually result in the recovery of the liver to its normal function. However, in extreme cases, and in cirrhosis of long duration, the destruction may be so severe that recovery is impossible, while in some cases surgery is necessary to establish increased circulation through the liver in an effort to relieve the portal system.

Once the focus shifts from withdrawal and the physical complications of excessive consumption to the question of associated psycho-social problems the range of possible therapeutic involvements increases. The first section of Chapter 3 outlined the main approaches to the question of the cause of drinking problems. Genetic and broadly socio-cultural causal theories provide few direct therapeutic indications, and tend to lead little further than the general proposition that alcoholics are 'not as other men' and are, therefore, for some reason — rarely specified — not able to handle alcohol. Treatment is then geared to achieving and maintaining abstinence. Several abstinence-maintaining regimes are basically physical. The regular use of implantation of alcohol sensitizing drugs, if followed by drinking within a certain period, may produce very severe, unpleasant and 'even life-threatening'[5] symptoms. Strong emetics, and electric shocks have been administered in conjunction with the consumption of alcohol as part of an aversive conditioning strategy. Covert sensitization utilizing aversive images has also been used.[6]

A common criticism of all such conditioning therapy is that it is purely a symptomatic treatment which makes no attempt to deal with the underlying cause of the alcohol-related problems. Quite apart from the difficulty of identifying 'underlying causes' exponents of aversive therapy would say that while past events may be of importance in so far as they may have initiated the excessive drinking they may now be irrelevant. The drinking itself, they claim, now constitutes the primary problem and further drinking only serves to compound it. The first step in treatment, therefore, is to interrupt the ingrained pattern of drinking by whatever methods are most suitable to the individual case. The counter argument is that any 'real' success can only be effected by psychotherapy directed toward the underlying psychopathology.[7]

Once the focus shifts from withdrawal and the establishment of abstinence to rehabilitation other helpers assume an increasing importance. The pastoral counsellor,[8] the probation officer and the social worker may all have a part to play in helping the alcoholic to create, as Root puts it, 'a new design for living':

> 'He wants things to do. He must be helped to set up realistic goals. For example, he must be helped to assume his rightful role within his family milieu if he is fortunate enough to be living with his family . . . he must be helped with his employment situation . . . He will need continued support and encouragement. He must also be assisted in trying to rebuild his life in the community . . . '.[9]

Focus on Groups

Milieu therapy, group psychotherapy and some of the core activities of Alcoholics Anonymous, all shift the focus of attention from the patient-therapist, client-helper diads to groups of individuals who have similar or related problems.

Milieu therapy or the therapeutic community approach[10] is the most highly structured of these group approaches. It is based on the assumption that personality disorders are in great part the result of adverse environmental circumstances which prevent or hinder personality development. The purpose of milieu therapy, therefore, as Cumming and Cumming put it, is:

> ' . . . a scientific manipulation of the environment aimed at producing changes in the personality of a patient'.[11]

Thus an attempt is made to utilize every patient-staff and patient-patient transaction for therapeutic purposes. Not only that but:

'. . . the following aspects must be considered and actively manipulated before one may clearly . . . (be said to be) . . . utilizing a therapeutic milieu approach: the physical setting, authority and control, roles and role relationships, culture, and, finally, communication'.[12]

Not surprisingly, given their number, the proportion of people with some kind of alcohol-related problem who have experienced or are likely to experience a full-blown milieu therapeutic regime is extremely small. A much larger proportion, however, are likely to take part in other forms of group-therapeutic activity. For some therapists the attraction of 'group therapy' has been a matter of simple statistics. As Glatt explains:

'The large number of alcoholics requiring treatment make it impossible in practice to treat by individual psychotherapy all those who may be in need of psychotherapeutic help. Partly for this reason . . . group psychotherapy has found increasing recognition as a very valuable tool in the treatment of alcoholism'.[13]

The real value of group therapy is seen to derive from the core principle that the group itself provides things for the alcoholic which even limitless access to an individual therapist cannot. Thomas succinctly identifies some of these benefits:

'. . . the group has something to offer that the individual counselor cannot match. In a group, the alcoholic has several people to talk to, several people to upset him, and several people to show him ways to do something about his problem. It would be asking a lot of an individual therapist to do all that — to give the patient all of the different views that might come up in a group.

One of the principles of therapy is consensual validation, meaning that the people involved must reach a mutual agreement (consensus) about the nature of the problem (validity) before progress is made. The group provides a sample population to test one's ideas. The individual counselor is but one person. The alcoholic, for example, might say to the therapist— seeing him alone, "You and I agree on this, but how do I know you're right. I'd like some different ideas".

Also, it has been recognized that the alcoholic is difficult to treat by single individuals. Many physicians, clergymen, and others have been disillusioned by this situation. Perhaps it is because the therapist is an authority figure — a kind of father image — and the alcoholic has probably had difficulties with authority figures. With the group, it is different. The alcoholic must look at others like himself. He must look at his own image'.[14]

There are many types of therapeutic group structure and form with many general and detailed objectives. In practice groups usually operate with a multiplicity of aims and with several different techniques and approaches being utilized from time to time as therapists and group members see fit. A distinction can be made, however, between broadly didactic and broadly non-directive groups or group sessions. The didactic or teaching group is based on a leader or series of leaders who perform to an audience of patients whose contribution is usually limited to question and answer sessions. It becomes more of an interacting group if patients are encouraged to answer each other's questions and to present personal accounts to illustrate, question and justify particular points of view. But whatever the level of patient contribution the therapist in the didactic group is in a clearly dominant and controlling position.

In so-called non-directive groups the patients are the deciding (directing) people; deciding what to talk about or, indeed, whether to talk at all. The role of the therapist is essentially to facilitate a situation in which 'there is always an air of dignity surrounding the patient's views, whatever they are . . . by simply adopting an understanding and a warm attitude which is sensed by the patient'.[15] The work of Carl Rogers[16] has had a great impact on the development of non-directive group therapy, in spite of the bastardization of some of his views. For:

> ' "Nondirective" in many cases had been taken for "nonactive" or "non-interested" Rogers would probably say "far from it", and continue to spell out the active nature of the therapist's concern for the client — not in telling him what to do, but in setting up the conditions whereby he could do it himself'.[17]

In addition to the basic forms of intra-group relationship and leadership style and function, there are a variety of special techniques such as psychodrama[18] and role playing which may be used as adjuncts to group therapy or as the focus of special groups themselves. As well as having the attraction of novelty, which makes them particularly useful with alcoholics who may have been struggling unsuccessfully with their drinking problem for a long time, these techniques are all designed to encourage and facilitate the process whereby the alcoholic becomes an

> ' . . . accepted member of a group of people who all "speak the same language", he gets the feeling of "belonging", he learns the need to contribute and to give just as well as to take, he participates in a striving for a common goal, he helps others by, and whilst, trying to help himself'.[19]

Group sessions are not, of course, confined to special treatment units. They are often a feature of other settings where groups of people with a particular problem are gathered together, such as residential hostels or half-way houses. These facilities, as their name implies, provide residence, a home base and a bridge between penal, medical and other large institutions and the wider community. It is considered that satisfactory rehabilitation can best be achieved if the return to the community is gradual rather than abrupt. Having a small number of residents at any one time enables attention to be given to particular medical, personal and social needs, while the small-group living arrangements encourage the alcoholic:

> '. . . to learn how to live a . . . more constructive life. . . . (T)he half-way house environment can be characterized as a group-living experience which reconstitutes the protective and supportive elements of a good family, while encouraging and providing opportunities for independent growth'.[20]

The other significant gathering of people with alcohol-related problems is, of course, the Alcoholics Anonymous group. Founded by two active Oxford Group members it rests on the principles of open self-scrutiny, admission of defects, aid to others and making reparations for harm done in the past. Based originally on the idea that alcoholism is, in essence, an allergy to alcohol[21] this led naturally to the core A.A. position which identifies drinking itself as the disease process. Stopping drinking and remaining abstinent are, thus, the key goals of A.A. members.

The A.A. programme is built on the Twelve Steps which identify the problem as firmly located within the individual, but which the individual alone is incapable of curing:

'We —

1. Admitted we were powerless over alcohol — that our lives had become unmanageable.
2. Came to believe that a Power greater than ourselves could restore us to sanity.
3. Made a decision to turn our will and our lives to the care of God as we understood Him.
4. Made a searching and fearless moral inventory of ourselves.
5. Admitted to God, to ourselves, and to another human being, the exact nature of our wrongs.
6. Were entirely ready to have God remove all these defects of character.
7. Humbly asked Him to remove our shortcomings.
8. Made a list of all persons we had harmed and became willing to make amends to them all.
9. Made direct amends to such people wherever possible, except when to do so would injure them or others.
10. Continued to take a personal inventory and when we were wrong promptly admitted it.

11. Sought through power of prayer and meditation to improve our conscious contact with God as we understood Him, praying only for knowledge of His will for us and the power to carry that out.
12. Having had a spiritual experience as a result of these steps, tried to carry this message to alcoholics and to practise these principles in all our affairs'.[22]

These 12 steps are supplemented by the Twelve Traditions which deal with the cohesion and management of the groups.

> 'The "12 Traditions" of Alcoholics Anonymous are, we A.A.'s believe, the best answers that our experience has yet given to those ever urgent questions "How can A.A. best function?" and "How can A.A. best stay whole and so survive?" '[23]

The first tradition identifies the common welfare as paramount:

> 'Each member of Alcoholics Anonymous is but a small part of a great whole. A.A. must continue to live or most of us will surely die. Hence our common welfare comes first. But individual welfare follows close afterward'

while others deal with the sole justification for membership 'a desire to stop drinking', the need for autonomy, anonymity, minimum organization, self-sufficiency 'declining outside contributions' and both personal and group single-mindedness 'no A.A. group or member should ever, in such a way as to implicate A.A., express any opinion on outside controversial issues'.

Almost from its inception A.A. has received some of the most fulsome praise which any therapeutic regime has ever received:

> ' . . . the remarkable success of Alcoholics Anonymous . . . perhaps without parallel in our society today'.[24]
>
> ' . . . our most important resource'.[25]
>
> ' . . . wonderful, inspiring and ubiquitous'.[26]
>
> ' . . . generally agreed that the most successful therapeutic program for the treatment of alcoholism has been formulated and established by Alcoholics Anonymous'.[27]

while the editor of a recent special volume of the Annals of the New York Academy of Sciences devoted to the Person with Alcoholism suggested that

> ' . . . the success of A.A. in helping alcoholics to achieve a continued sobriety has been one of the major phenomena of the century'.[28]

Yet despite such claims it was not until very recently that any serious attempt was made to document or verify the real extent of A.A.'s success either in its own terms or in comparison or conjunction with other systems of help. A clear discussion of these issues, by Leach[29] under the heading 'Does Alcoholics Anonymous Really Work?', draws on the very small number of loosely evaluative studies which have been conducted[30] plus the 1968 A.A. General Service Board Survey of members in the United States and Canada. Leach concluded that

> '. . . A.A. merits more understanding than the current state of knowledge about it affords . . . (and that) . . . the answer to the heading of this chapter is yes, Alcoholics Anonymous really does work'.

But even if we accept Leach's conclusion there are supplementary and no less important questions to be considered, such as: 'for whom does A.A. "really work", and how?'. Some writers have suggested that A.A. merely replaces addiction to alcohol with addiction to A.A. which, although not physically damaging like 'being an alcoholic', is just as disruptive of everyday family relationships and distressing to the ex-drinker's intimates.[31]

Focus on the Community

Certain legislative measures, such as those concerned with public inebriates or drunken drivers, focus on specific sections of the drinking population. While these laws may have some deterrent effect on the development of new problem cases, legislation aimed at *whole communities* is intended to make less likely the development of alcohol problems through the regulation of the amount or character of alcohol consumption. The principal measures are those which control the number of places in which alcoholic beverages may be purchased, the type and location of outlets, the age at which persons may consume and purchase alcoholic beverage, the hours and days of sale, differential taxation and price control and state control of production.[32]

The arguments advanced for and against the efficacy of any or all of these control measures are many and various. However, Popham, Schmidt and de Lint have recently distilled three 'models of prevention', which appear to underpin a great deal of the research, controversy and policy proposals. These are:

> 'The Bimodal Model. The heavy alcohol consumption of problem drinkers and alcoholics is considered to be symptomatic of some disorder peculiar to them. Therefore, by implication, the distribution of consumption in a population will be bimodal in character, and factors which may cause a change in the consumption level of normal drinkers will have little or no effect on that of pathological drinkers. Accordingly, legal measures which seek to control the prevalence of alcoholism by restraining overall consumption are held to be misdirected and ineffective . . .

The Integration Model. It is believed that to eradicate or even substantially reduce the prevalence of alcoholism would require fundamental changes in the social and mental health status of the population. However, it is also believed that more problems result from the mysticism associated with alcohol, and the guilt attendant upon its use than would occur if drinking were an integrated part of everyday life. . . . Thus, it is argued that young people should be introduced to alcoholic beverages at an early age so that they may learn to drink moderately, and come to regard the activity as of no greater significance than eating. Restrictive control measures are seen both as reinforcers of an unhealthy ambivalence towards drinking, and as impediments to the adoption of healthy drinking styles. . . .

The Single Distribution Model. Proponents argue that the frequency distribution of alcohol consumption per drinker in any given population is continuous, unimodal and positively skewed . . . , the variance is constant and only the mean differs from one group to another. Under these circumstances, the relative frequency of high level consumers . . . depends upon the mean per drinker consumption in a population, and factors which alter the latter may be expected to alter the former. Since the same distribution is found to obtain in populations which differ greatly in attitudes towards drinking, beverage preferences, drinking customs, and in the educational and legal measures employed to combat the problems of alcohol, it is concluded that there is as yet no way to modify the prevalence of heavy consumers without altering the average consumption of other drinkers'.[33]

The arguments in support of and opposition to each of these positions range far and wide. But the weight of evidence seems currently to favour the simple conclusion that relaxing the legal controls on alcohol availability and consumption 'leads to an increase in consumption, and an increase in consumption adds to the complications'.[34] In the light of the Prohibition experience in the United States and other examples of drastic controls in liquor availability it seems clear that highly restrictive controls on accessibility do lead to lower consumption and fewer alcohol problems. However, tight control is only likely to be achieved if there is substantial public support, while the controls themselves are apt to involve costs which may be seen to outweigh their benefits.[35] Such costs include resentment of the system by self-defined non-problem drinkers, increase in the production of illicit liquor and attendant criminality, difficulties of law enforcement with the attendant loss of respect for and confidence in the law which this entails, a loss of tax revenues and the reduction in the personal and social enjoyment which alcohol consumption provides.

The possibility of such costs resulting from drastic controls is often invoked as a reason for rejecting any form of legal restraint in alcohol production, availability or consumption. However, increased attention is currently being given to the possibility of gradual overall consumption control. As Edwards elegantly puts it:

> 'Since we are not able to manipulate personality and produce a race with no neurosis, the only realistic method of exerting a benign influence on the prevalence of alcohol addiction is by control of the environmental conditions of drinking, and it is the availability element that remains the prime candidate for control'.[36]

The Helpfulness of Particular Agencies

If we are to gain some kind of understanding of why people do what they do in response to the alcohol-related problems which they consider themselves to be confronted with, it is essential to gain some idea of who they think will be helpful in such situations. It would have been unrealistic to have questioned the general population sample about *particular* treatments, such as those outlined in the previous section. The focus of the questioning, therefore, was on familiar agencies, professionals and helpers.

Respondents were shown a card on which was a list of 10 occupations and agencies, and asked to say which of them they thought ' . . . would be the most helpful for people whose drinking is causing them problems'. They were then asked to indicate the second most helpful and the least helpful. Table 1 shows that Alcoholics Anonymous and general practitioners were each considered by half the sample as either the *most* or the second most helpful, while employers, priests/clergymen and probation officers were felt to be the *least* helpful. There were very few age, sex or social status differences on either of these two issues. Younger respondents under 35 were more likely, 26·4 per cent, than their elders, 14·2 per cent, to see priests/clergymen as least helpful. People in the highest social status category[37] were more likely, 42·3 per cent, than other people, 23·8 per cent, to see the general practitioner as most helpful, and less likely, 45·3 per cent, than other people, 58·3 per cent, to see employers as least helpful, while men were slightly less likely than women to see employers as least helpful. In short, the similarities between the age, sex and social status categories were more noteworthy than the differences.

Perhaps the most interesting feature of the material in Table 1 is that two organizations which do not exist in the study locality; the Alcoholism Advice Centre and the Drinking Advice Centre, were considered by almost 50 per cent of respondents to be either the *most* or the *second most* helpful agency for people whose drinking is causing them problems. It is clear that people do not need to have had any personal contact with an organization or to have any detailed knowledge of its day-to-day workings to make a judgement about its potential usefulness in some hypothetical situation.

TABLE 1. Sources of help 'for people whose drinking is causing them problems'

Most or 2nd most helpful	N	%	Least helpful	N	%
1. Alcoholics Anonymous	134	46 9	1. Employer	137	47·9
2. Family Doctor	132	46·2	2. Priest/Clergyman	49	17·1
3. Alcoholism Advice Centre	93	32·5	3. Probation officer	31	10·8
4. Psychiatrist	47	16·4	4. Social worker	16	5·6
5. Drinking Advice Centre	42	14·7	5. Family Doctor	11	3·8
6. Social worker	30	10·5	6. Psychiatrist	9	3·1
7. Priest/Clergyman	26	9·1	7. Samaritans	4	1·4
8. Samaritans	26	9·1	8. Drinking Advice Centre	4	1·4
9. Probation officer	6	2·1	9. Alcoholism Advice Centre	3	1·0
10. Employer	6	2·1	10. Alcoholics Anonymous	1	0·3
Don't know	30		Don't know	21	
Total	286		Total	286	

TABLE 2. Reasons why agencies are *most* helpful

Reasons[a]	N	%[b]
A. Expertise or personal experience in relation to the problem		
(i) It's their job, they know about it	60	21·7
(ii) They know about causes or consequences of drinking	33	11·9
(iii) They have experienced the problem themselves	19	6·9
B. Things which the agency can do about the problem		
(i) They can give advice/talk about the problem	64	23·1
(ii) They can refer on/to experts	39	14·1
(iii) They can get people to cut down/stop their drinking	25	9·0
(iv) They can cure/treat the problem	13	4·7
(v) They have group meetings/therapy	9	3·2
C. Qualities of the agency, unconnected with the specific problem		
(i) General/unspecific approval of the agents or agencies	31	11·2
(ii) They have a good relationship with their patients/clients	24	8·7
(iii) They are immediately available	8	2·9
(iv) They are friendly	5	1·8
(v) They are anonymous	3	1·1
	277[c]	

[a] In addition 19 'other' reasons were given ranging from 'they are very good with juveniles' to 'prayer' and 'they listen'.

[b] Total per cent = more than 100 per cent because some respondents gave more than one reason.

[c] Nine respondents did not know which of the 10 agencies would be *most* helpful.

Reasons Why Agencies are Most Helpful

Table 2 sets out the broad categories of help which respondents expected the *most* helpful agencies could provide, irrespective of what those agencies were. Details of what people felt *particular* agencies could offer are presented later in the section.

Three broad categories of reasons were given. First were those people who felt that a particular agency was the *most* helpful because of their *expertise or experience.* Some people spoke of this in only the most general terms:

> 'They would know how to deal with it. It's their job'.
>
> 'They have more experience. As to their methods I don't know'.

while others picked out the agent's particular expertise in relation to understanding the cause or consequence of the problem:

> 'Well he would know what makes these people do the things they do and why they do it'
>
> 'They could warn you of the consequences'.

The second broad category of reasons were based on the *things which the most helpful agency could actually do* for the person with the drink-related problem. These ranged from giving advice, which was mentioned by about a quarter of all respondents, referral, getting people to cut down on their drinking or to stop altogether, general statements about being able to treat or cure the patient, and the fact that the agency could offer group therapy and group meetings:

> 'It's the group therapy that helps them to give it up I think. I've seen programmes on T.V. and read about it'.

The third broad category of reasons were those concerned with *qualities of the agent or agency* which the respondent felt would be helpful. Some just made a very general statement of approval:

> 'They've got good name'.

while others mentioned the agency's friendliness, anonymity;

> '. . . they don't advertise who or what you are'.

and being immediately available in times of crisis:

> '. . . with them you can get in touch with them right away, where anyone else you have to make an appointment'.

Not all agencies were felt to be helpful in the same way, of course. In order to gain a better understanding of the way in which the general population perceives the value of specific agencies it is necessary to see why particular agencies were felt to be the *most* helpful and the *least* helpful.

The Most Helpful Agencies

TABLE 3. The *most* helpful agencies

Agency	N	%
1. Alcoholics Anonymous	98	35·3
2. Family Doctor	75	27·1
3. Alcoholism Advice Centre	46	16·7
4. Drinking Advice Centre	16	5·8
5. Psychiatrist	13	4·7
6. Social worker	12	4·3
7. Priest/Clergyman	9	3·2
8. Samaritan	5	1·8
9. Probation officer	3	1·1
10. Employer	2	0·8
	277	
Don't know	9	
Total	285	

The three agencies which accounted for approximately 80 per cent of answers are discussed in detail; beginning with Alcoholics Anonymous.

ALCOHOLICS ANONYMOUS (N = 98)

TABLE 4. Reasons why A.A. is the 'most' helpful

	N	%
Shared experience of the problem	19	19·4
General approval of A.A.	5	5·1
Don't know, heard that they are the people	11	11·2
It's their job. They know, have the training, experience	27	27·6
Give advice, talk to people	16	16·3
Get people to stop or cut down on their drinking	10	10·2
Meetings and group therapy	9	9·2
'Immediate' link with someone	7	7·1
Cure or treatment	4	4·1
Anonymity	3	3·1
Total	98	113·3[a]

[a] Total per cent = more than 100 per cent since some respondents gave more than one reason.

Clearly, the main distinguishing feature between Alcoholics Anonymous and the other organizations mentioned in the list is, as Bales puts it:

'. . . the things the members have in common which hold them together . . . their past drinking experiences, an intimate knowledge of the places and people the compulsive drinker gets to know, a bag of tricks, ruses, rationalisations, and defences which they have been forced to build up in the course of their compulsive drinking, an odyssey of adventures and mis-adventures too often ending in tragedy, and the sense of a common fate'.[38]

In short 'they are all alcoholics'. One in five of the respondents mentioned this as a reason why A.A. was *most* helpful:

'They have suffered themselves, so they are sympathetic and know the tricks'.

'Those who are there have been heavy drinkers and have given it up and would have a practical experience of the problem'.

Five people just made statements of general approval without specifying in what way help is given:

'They seem to be doing a good job from what I read in the papers'.

while others (11) said that they really did not know in any detail why A.A. were likely to be most helpful. Just over a quarter (27) gave as their reason the fact that it was A.A.'s job or because of their knowledge about such things:

'They know more about the problem of drinking, more than a doctor would'.

'They know what they're doing. Are used to these sort of people'.

or, more specifically, because of their experience:

'They have more experience. As to their methods I don't know'.

All other respondents mentioned specific aspects of A.A. work or organization. The most frequently cited feature (16) was talk, advice or discussion. Closely linked with talk was 'meetings' and 'groups' (9):

It's group therapy that helps them to give it up I think. I've seen programmes on T.V. and read about it'.

'They get up and say they've been a heavy drinker. By what I've read — imagine the others hiss and boo'.

Stress was also given to the fact that A.A. would either tell people to cut down on their drinking or in some way be able to make them do so (10).

Six people spoke of A.A.'s value in providing an immediate link with someone in times of crisis:

> '. . . with them you can get in touch with them right away, where anyone else you have to make an appointment'.

> 'I've seen it on T.V. they 'phone A.A. when they need help and someone is there to talk to them'.

Four felt that A.A. offered some kind of cure or treatment, while another three mentioned the anonymity of Alcoholics Anonymous:

> '. . . they don't advertise who or what you are'.

> 'The fact that they are anonymous . . . '

> '. . . everything is anonymous . . . '

FAMILY DOCTOR (N = 75)

TABLE 5. Reasons why the family doctor is the 'most' helpful

	N	%
Doctor knows the patient/family	15	20·0
Patient knows the doctor	7	9·3
It's the doctor's job. He knows/is experienced	7	9·3
Doctor can refer to experts	28	37·3
Doctor can advise — talk to the drinker	19	25·3
Doctor can advise drinker to cut down	4	5·3
Doctor can give tablets to make drinker cut down	5	6·7
Doctor may know the cause of drinking	5	6·7
Doctor can point out the consequences of drinking	9	12·0
Don't know	4	5·3
Total	75	137·2[a]

[a] Total per cent = more than 100 per cent since some respondents gave more than one reason.

One of the main differences between the family doctor and the other agencies on the list is that the family doctor is involved with a family for the whole range of its health problems. Thus, particular episodes of distress or illness can be placed in the context of knowledge about previous episodes, inter-personal relationships, and the whole round of daily family life. However, in an urban area with a mobile population, like that in which the study was conducted, such intimate knowledge is less likely to be built up.

Nevertheless, this aspect of the ideal family doctor role was stressed by several of the respondents. In fact, one in five (20) of the respondents stressed the value of the doctor's knowledge of the family.

> 'He's closer, he knows the history of the family'.
>
> 'Well he's closest of all the people here (on the list). He's met them before'.

while other people, looking at it from the drinker's point of view, made the reciprocal point that the family doctor is likely to be the most helpful because he is someone who the drinker knows:

> 'You can confide in your doctor. You can talk to him as you know him'.
>
> 'The person knowing the doctor would feel more inclined to talk to him than a stranger'.

A number of people (7) just said that it was the doctor's job to help people with drinking problems without giving any further elaboration on the specific ways in which the doctor could help, while four others said that they really did not know why they felt that the family doctor would be the most helpful.

Among those people who identified specific ways in which the family doctor could help people with drinking problems, the reason mentioned most frequently, by over one third of respondents (28), was the fact that the family doctor could refer the drinker to someone else:

> 'He can send them to somebody else to get their problems sorted out'.
>
> 'They would know what to do and where to send the people. They would know the sources available — advice would be useless he would have to refer the patient to a specialist in this field'.

But in spite of the last respondent, a lot of people (19), *did* think that advice or 'talk' was one important thing which the family doctor could offer.

Apart from giving general advice three respondents felt that the doctor would be able to give advice on how to cut down on drinking, while one felt that something a little stronger than advice might be offered:

> 'He could advise you and frighten you more than anything. If he gave you medicine and said you can't drink with it, you wouldn't dare'.

The possibility of the doctor prescribing something which would enable the drinker to cut down or stop was mentioned by a further five respondents:

> 'I think he can prescribe something, some kind of tablet to stop them from drinking . . . '

'Can give you tablets to put you off taking alcohol'.

The final two reasons for why family doctors would be most helpful were that they might know about the cause of the excess drinking (5), or would know or point out the consequences of it (9).

ALCOHOLISM ADVICE CENTRE (N = 46)

TABLE 6. Reasons why the Alcoholism Advice Centre is the 'most' helpful (N=46)

	N	%
It sounds the right kind of place	6	13·0
It's their job. They know, they're the experts	12	26·1
They advise, talk (unspecific)	7	15·2
They advise on cutting down or stopping drinking	6	13·0
They can refer to experts	5	10·9
They find out the cause of the problem	5	10·9
They treat the problem	4	8·7
They can advise on the consequences of excess drinking	3	6·5
Other reasons	3	6·5
Don't know	1	2·2
Total	46	112·9[a]

[a] Total per cent = more than 100 per cent since some respondents gave more than one reason.

There is no Alcoholism Advice Centre in the study area, nor is there a Drinking Advice Centre. Nevertheless, after A.A. and the family doctor, these were the organizations which were felt to be the *most* helpful for people whose drinking is causing problems. As has been seen from the material on A.A. and family doctors, advice was frequently mentioned as being of importance to the problem drinker. It is no surprise, therefore, that the Alcoholism Advice Centre, and the Drinking Advice Centre, should have been picked out by so many people as the *most* helpful agency.

Several people (6) merely said that it sounded to be the most suitable place. However, the largest category of respondents (11) were those who said that the Alcoholism Advice Centre had people who knew what to do, or that they were the best people because it was their job to deal with such people and problems:

'They deal with those sort of people — know their problem'.

'They know about these things. They're there for that sort of thing'.

Seven respondents spoke of the centre giving advice, but did not specify what the advice would be about or what form it would take. Others however, saw the centre giving advice to cut down or to stop drinking (6):

'They must be the people who can help tell you how to cut down on your drinking. And that's what they're there for. Or if it's gone beyond they must be told to stop to drink'.

and advice on the consequences of continued drinking (3):

'They would make them understand the effects of their drinking—because people are more likely to stop if they know what it's doing to them'.

Compared with the family doctor the Alcoholism Advice Centre staff are clearly seen to be experts since only five people mentioned the centre referring people on elsewhere. In fact four people thought that the centre would itself be able to offer some kind of treatment to the drinker. A further five respondents felt that the advice centre would be able to find out the cause of the problem.

The Most Helpful Aspects of Other Agencies

In addition to Alcoholics Anonymous, family doctors and the Alcoholism Advice Centre, there were four other agencies which were each considered by approximately five per cent of the general population sample to be *most* helpful for someone whose drinking is causing them problems.

The *Drinking Advice Centre,* which like the Alcoholism Advice Centre does not exist in the study locality, was considered to be most helpful because the staff would know what to do:

'They handle them, it's their business to handle people who drink'.

and because it would be able to give the drinkers some advice:

'By taking them under their wing and try and advise them against the amount they're drinking'.

Whereas only five of the 75 people who thought that the family doctor was likely to be the most helpful mentioned the fact that he would be able to discover the cause of the drinking problem, half of those who felt that the *Psychiatrist* would be most helpful gave this as the reason.

'Well he would know what makes these people do the things they do and why they do it'.

'He'd probably get to the bottom of the trouble . . . it's hard to find out just what it is'.

The psychiatrist was also seen as someone who could give a variety of treatments:

'They could sort them out and see if they're worried or depressed'.

' . . . give them some therapy that would help them. Failing that shock treatment'.

' . . . they can relax a person — get them on the old couch — let their mind go blank and get them talking about their drinking habits'.

and in particular help the drinker by talking or giving advice:

'Try and talk them out of their problem'.

'Well advise — I can't sum up in any other word — their personal advice must be accepted and carried out'.

While the psychiatrist was seen as someone who could tease out the causes of problems, *the social worker* was seen as someone who actively deals with problems or gives support to those in some kind of difficulty:

'They deal with people's problems'.

'They will help with the home problems'.

'Those people do try to help. I'm not saying they're successful but they do try'.

In addition to being the people whose job it is to help with the problems, or who do try to be of assistance, the personal and friendly quality of the social worker–client relationship was seen to be important and was mentioned by five of the 12 respondents:

' . . . they're not an official person who is likely to cause resentment'.

' . . . they're more approachable than a priest or a doctor'.

This feeling of confidence was possibly due to the fact that social workers were willing to listen:

'He would sit and listen to the problem . . . '

'Someone who would listen to them . . . '

as well as talk and give advice.

'They talk you out of it and give you ideas of better ways of spending your time and money'.

'They would also talk about the problem'.

Seven out of the nine people who felt that a *priest or clergyman* would be most helpful made specific reference to some aspect of religion, or being religious, when they gave their reasons for their choice. Three spoke of general qualities:

> 'Because he's been saved by Jesus'.
>
> 'Well, I think they have something about them that is different from anyone else, they have a different way of living and are very understanding'.
>
> 'He's religious and he could help'.

two, of praying:

> 'Only by talking and praying for them . . . '
>
> ' . . . and ask them to pray'.

While two others made particular mention of the value of the Roman Catholic priest:

> ' . . . R.C. depends such a lot on their priest. They are able to advise their parishioner what to do'.
>
> 'She's a Roman Catholic and in her situation — they would be most helpful'.

The Samaritans, Probation Officers and Employers were each considered by less than two per cent of the sample to be *most* helpful for someone whose drinking is causing them problems.

The Least Helpful Agencies

TABLE 7. The *least* 'helpful' agencies

Agency	N	%
1. Employer	137	51·7
2. Priest/clergyman	49	18·5
3. Probation officer	31	11·7
4. Social worker	16	6·0
5. Family doctor	11	4·2
6. Psychiatrist	9	3·3
7. Samaritans	4	1·5
8. Drinking Advice Centre	4	1·5
9. Alcoholism Advice Centre	3	1·1
10. Alcoholics Anonymous	1	0·4
	265	
Don't know	21	
Total	286	

The ordering of agencies in Table 7 is almost an exact reversal of the ordering in Table 3. As with the reasons for why people were most helpful, the reasons for why people were *least* helpful differed greatly from organization to organization. A rather large percentage, 7·3 per cent, of people did not know which of the 10 would be least helpful but, as with the most helpful, three agencies accounted for approximately 80 per cent of answers. These three agencies, beginning with employers, are discussed in detail.

EMPLOYER (N = 137)

TABLE 8. Reasons why employers are the 'least' helpful (N=137)

	N	%
Employer isn't interested in employees problems	30	21·9
Employer would, (be likely to) sack drinker	29	21·2
Employer only interested in the firm and the work	27	19·7
Employer only interested in drinking problems if it affects work	16	11·7
Employer wouldn't know what to do, has no expertise	11	8·0
Employer would be unsympathetic	8	5·8
Employer wouldn't know the drinker well enough	5	3·6
Employer wouldn't like people drinking at work	4	2·9
Employer may drink himself	2	1·5
Employee would not want boss to know	18	13·1
Depends on the organization	7	5·1
Nothing to do with his employer	3	2·2
'Other reasons'	7	5·1
Total	137	121·8[a]

[a] Total per cent = more than 100 per cent since some respondents gave more than one reason.

It was to be expected that the employer would be considered to be least helpful for someone with drinking problems. For the employer was the only one of the 10 people and organizations which was not explicitly concerned in some way with therapy or helping. But the extremely low, often hostile, opinion which a large proportion of the respondents had of employers was perhaps rather less expected. A number of people (11) said that the employer would be least helpful simply because he was least likely to have any expert or relevant knowledge. However, twice as many respondents (30) said that the employer would just not be interested in the fact that an employee had a problem caused by drink or would only be interested if he thought that the drinking was interfering with the employee's work (16):

> 'Not many employers are that interested in other people, as long as they work all right'.

'Most employers don't care about their workers so long as they do the work'.

In fact, the employer was portrayed very clearly (27) as someone who is primarily concerned with his firm and making money, and only interested in his employees in so far as they do the work which he wants them to do:

'I think an employer is more interested in what you produce while you are at work and they can't afford to stop and listen . . . they're basically concerned with your output and not what goes on after work'.

'Well I think the majority of employers are more concerned with getting the job done than with employees' problems'.

These people obviously thought that the employer would make a rigid distinction between the employee as worker and the employee's personal problems. The fact that the problem may affect the employee *as* worker was not mentioned. It seems as though drinking problems are considered to be personal matters which are only enjoyed out of working hours!

Apart from those who saw the employer as someone who is uninterested in employees' problems and only concerned with the employee as worker, some respondents (8) felt that the employer would lack sympathy:

'From my own experience my employer would be the last person I'd go to — only cold and business like — no sympathy'.

while over 20 per cent of respondents (29) said that they thought employers would sack employees for drinking problems. Some made the point quite openly:

'He'd give you your cards — the sack'.

'Out of the door, that's what would happen . . . '

Others dressed the point up a little:

' . . . most people are replaceable, and the employer would not consider this was a problem'.

'They would automatically think the person was no longer suitable for the job'.

In addition, some (5) thought that the employer would be least helpful because he would not know enough about the employee, while the employers' own drinking habits were felt by two to be a barrier to effective help.

Given all this, it is hardly surprising that several respondents (18) should say that people definitely would not want their employer to know that they had some drinking problem:

> 'If I had a drink problem I wouldn't tell my employer'.

> 'I don't think the person would go to his employer and wouldn't want him to know about his problem'.

although some people (7) felt that it might depend on the type or size of organization or on the particular employer:

> 'That depends on the size of the business. If the company was large it would be too impersonal. A small firm might be more inclined to help its employees'.

Trice and Roman conclude their excellent review of 'Alcoholism and the worker' by stressing that:

> '. . . attention to the preventive potential of the work world by researchers, alcoholism specialists, managements, and union should be of the highest priority'.[39]

However, the clear unwillingness of the South London respondents to consider the employer as either relevant for or sympathetic to the worker with alcohol-related problems will be a significant barrier to any widespread attempt to base alcoholism recognition or treatment facilities in industrial or other occupational settings.

PRIEST/CLERGYMAN (N = 49)

TABLE 9. Reasons why priests and clergymen are 'least' helpful (N=49)

	N	%
They are too religious or set apart	14	28·6
They just do not know about drinking and associated problems	11	22·4
They just don't give any effective help	9	18·4
They are too critical or moralistic	6	12·2
They can only advise and that doesn't help	4	8·2
They drink/don't drink themselves	3	6·1
People don't go to church or are not religious	10	20·4
'Other reasons'	5	10·2
Don't know	2	4·1
Total	49	130·6[a]

[a] Total per cent = more than 100 per cent since some respondents gave more than one reason.

The swing, over the past century, from considering alcoholism a moral or spiritual problem to considering it primarily a problem of medicine and public health is reflected in the fact that five times as many people considered the priest or clergyman to be *least* helpful than considered him *most* helpful for people whose drinking is causing them problems.

The fact that priests and clergymen are 'religious' and in some way 'special people' made them the most helpful for a small number of people. However, this made them the *least* helpful for many others (14):

> 'He would mean well. It would be from the heart — I don't know — they're not one of us. It's hard to explain'.
>
> 'A priest is only concerned in believing in God'.
>
> 'They have a one track mind that religion'.

In particular, it was felt (6) that they may be too moralistic and critical.

The reason given most often (11), however, was that priests and clergymen just did not know enough about drink, drinkers and associated problems:

> 'Priests wouldn't have the practical experience to deal with drinking'.
>
> 'They don't drink themselves so they don't know anything about it'.

On the other hand two people felt that the fact that priests *did* drink made them least helpful:

> 'They drink themselves so they can't advise you'.
>
> 'Judging by the two I've known they were heavy drinkers'.

Several people (9) considered that, even though a priest or clergyman may be sympathetic or know about some of the problems associated with alcohol consumption, they would not be able to give any effective or practical help. Four people were critical of priests merely giving advice, while one person was particularly emphatic about their inappropriateness:

> ' I suppose he could drive the devil away, but no, no priest. It's not a religious thing'.

But apart from the feeling that the priest or clergyman would be unsuitable, unhelpful or ineffective one in five (10) of respondents felt that they would be least harmful because most people nowadays, and particularly drinkers, are just not religious and don't go to church:

> 'My dad doesn't go to Church so he wouldn't know the clergyman'.
>
> 'A person who was drinking might not even know one (a priest) or where to find one'.

PROBATION OFFICER (N = 31)

TABLE 10. Reasons why probation officers are 'least' helpful (N=31)

	N	%
They only deal with 'criminals'	16	51·6
They wouldn't know anything about alcoholism	5	16·1
They would be too busy	4	12·9
They only deal with young people	3	9·7
They aren't accepted	3	9·7
They wouldn't be sympathetic, listen, etc.	2	6·5
Don't know	2	6·5
Total	31	112·9[a]

[a] Total per cent = more than 100 per cent since some respondents gave more than one reason.

Priests and clergymen were considered to be unsuitable largely because of the kind of people they are or the kind of life they lead. The probation officer was considered to be unhelpful, by contrast, because his professional commitments were seen to lie elsewhere; in particular with law, crime and the courts. Thus, the question of his suitability as a helper did not arise for many respondents. The probation officer just would not be presented with drinking problems:

> 'You'd only come across a probation officer if you got into trouble while drinking — no contact normally with them'.
>
> 'Unconnected with the problem. Probation officers are dealing with people who have fallen foul of the law'.

Others (3) stressed that probation officers only dealt with young people or that probation officers would not know enough about problems associated with drink (5):

> 'I shouldn't have thought it was in his line. He wouldn't be as well equipped to deal with it'.
>
> 'Don't think it would be his branch of the social scene. All the others are more in touch with this problem'.

or that they would be too busy anyway (4). Two people felt that in some way they are 'not accepted by the community' while others criticized their manner and approach:

> 'They wouldn't take much notice'.

'They wouldn't listen'.

'I don't think they would be very sympathetic'.

The Least Helpful Aspects of Other Agencies

In addition to employers, priests, clergymen and probation officers there were three other agencies which were each considered by approximately five per cent of the general population sample to be *least* helpful for someone whose drinking is causing them problems.

Half of the respondents who felt that *social workers* were *least* helpful considered that they just did not know enough about the problems associated with alcohol to be able to give any help:

> 'Most social workers I've come across are good at a lot of things but drink is outside their normal sphere'.
>
> 'Social workers are a generalized group. No specialized knowledge of alcoholism'.

Others made the reciprocal point and stressed 'other problems' which social workers have to spend their time on:

> 'Only go to them for money it seems. For that sort of thing'.
>
> 'I think that a social worker would deal better with family problems than a person that drinks heavily'.
>
> 'Have no faith in social workers. They have too much on their hands. Takes too long to get anything done. You ring up and someone takes a note and that's the last you hear'.

while one person identified a particular 'lack' in the social worker's armoury compared with certain other professionals on the list:

> 'Because they have a simplistic approach. They do not offer any threats. A doctor can threaten ill health or a probation officer can threaten return to prison. A social worker does not have that type of threat'.

Probation officers and social workers were considered to be unhelpful because they did not deal with people with drinking problems in the course of their everyday work. *Family doctors* on the other hand, were considered unhelpful because they are 'such busy people' or at least because they are likely to be too busy for this kind of problem:

> 'Too busy with his own problem patients who don't drink'.

'Because he's busy doing medical problems. Doesn't have time for this sort of problem'.

'The doctor has enough to get on with without listening to that sort of trouble'.

One respondent said that he did not think the doctor 'could help at all', while two queried the kind of help which a doctor would give:

'Well he usually gives pills and things and they don't need that'.

'They just prescribe medicines'.

and three others suggested that the family doctor would not be very sympathetic to the problem anyway:

'Not too nice. More likely to tell you off'.

'. . . he might not be interested, some doctors are not'.

'I don't think they would be bothered to talk about it. You never hear of them helping anybody'.

The majority of the people who said that *psychiatrists* were *most* helpful felt that they could ferret out the particular cause of drinking problems. It was the *lack* of this ability which one respondent gave as the reason for considering psychiatrists least helpful:

'I'm biased against them really, but I can't see a man being able to understand anyone enough to do any good'.

Another, by contrast, thought that, depending 'on how far gone they are':

'They pick their brains . . . too much'.

But even if someone with a drinking problem did go to a psychiatrist, which one person thought would be doubtful:

'Well in the first place you wouldn't go to a psychiatrist would you?'

the mere fact of having been to a psychiatrist might be counter-productive:

'Might make you feel worse, when you got home you might feel "I must be in a bad way to go and see him" and it would make you more nervous and drink more'.

The Samaritans, the Drinking Advice Centre, the Alcoholism Advice Centre and Alcoholics Anonymous were each considered by less than two per cent of the general population sample to be *least* helpful for someone whose drinking is causing them problems.

Any attempt to set up or redesign comprehensive community services for those with drink-related problems will clearly be more satisfactory if it is informed by a consideration of the ideas which members of the general population have not only about the nature of such problems but also about the range and value of help which is actually available. This chapter has identified the importance which is given to Alcoholics Anonymous and to the provision of information and advice, and highlights particular aspects of current medical and social service organization and practice which are considered to be beneficial and others which are seen as unhelpful for people with drink-related problems.

Chapter 6

Signs, Symptoms and Diagnoses

'Picking a Derby winner and making a diagnosis have much in common. The inspirational punter relies on "having a feeling" or a pin stabbed at a race card. Some doctors use similar methods for diagnosis. They and the punters are over-generous in remembrance of success, there is always a good excuse for the horse or diagnosis that was left at the start'.[1] *Editorial: J. Royal Coll. Physicians, London.*

The question of how diagnoses are arrived at, and of what the social consequences are of being diagnosed as having some particular illness condition or other, has received a good deal of attention.[2] In relation to alcoholism there are, in addition, a great many shopping lists of signs and symptoms designed to help medical professionals and others to recognize people who might be in need of their services. Not only that, but through newspaper articles, popular books, television programmes and health education campaigns the general public is increasingly being made aware of certain questions which they can ask of themselves and their intimates in order to check whether drinking is beginning to cause them some kind of problem.

Max Glatt, for example, includes in his very informative book for the general population[3] the Seligman 35 item questionnaire of 'warning signs'. Alcoholics Anonymous in their pamphlet entitled *Who Me?* list 20 questions which any drinker should ask himself'[4] These range from

'Do you lose time from work due to drinking?'

'Is drinking making your home life unhappy?'

and 'Do you drink alone?'

to 'Has your physician ever treated you for drinking?'

and 'Have you ever been to a hospital or institution on account of drinking?'

The pamphlet suggests that 'if you have answered YES to any *one* of the questions there is a definite warning that *you may be an alcoholic*'. Two yeses mean that 'the chances are that *you are an alcoholic*', while answering yes to three or more questions indicates that '*you are definitely an alcoholic*'. Kessel and Walton[5] present an even longer list of 53 warning signs related to various 'stages in being an alcoholic' while the Criteria Committee of the American National Council on Alcoholism recently drew up a series of 93 physical signs and aspects of personality and behaviour which they suggest could be symptomatic of alcoholism.[6] Clearly, the formal aids to the everyday professional and lay diagnosis of alcoholism are many and various.

The focus of this chapter is not, however, these public statements of what is or is not to count as a reliable sign of alcoholism. The aim is, rather, to display something of the way in which those people who are actually involved in the helping services perceive problems associated with alcohol consumption. The first part of the chapter discusses the range of signs and symptoms which general practitioners, social workers and probation officers in the study locality said would alert them to a possible drinking problem in their patients and clients, and then looks at how professionals actually recognized one particular recent case in which alcohol was causing some kind of problem. The focus then shifts to the question of general practitioner referrals to a psychiatric hospital out-patient department and to how diagnoses are in practice arrived at in a specialist setting.

Signs and Symptoms: the Professionals' view

Once we move away from the exhaustive and exhausting formal lists of diagnostic criteria to the question of what the professional actually does or can do in the diagnostic situation the literature is much more sparse. Catanzaro, however, attempts to provide some simple guide lines for the therapist, and suggests that:

> 'The most important aspect of making the diagnosis of alcoholism is to be *highly suspicious of it* whenever a patient presents with chief complaints which fall into one of the following five categories, or, in the case of the physician-therapist, when the physical examination reveals signs commonly associated with chronic alcoholism:
>
> (1) Social maladjustment disorders: e.g., increased marital discord, failure to advance on the job, failure to get along with associates;
> (2) Psychiatric disorders: e.g., nervousness, depression, loss of sexual drive, promiscuity, ~~homosexuality~~, suicide attempt, insomnia;
> (3) Neurologic disorders, often vague in character: e.g., blackout spells, amnesia, peripheral neuritis, chronic brain syndrome, Korsakoff's and Wernike's syndromes;
> (4) Orthopedic disorders: e.g., multiple fractures of mysterious origin, commonly of the ribs, arms and skull, often the result of one of

the occupational hazards of drinking, i.e., falling from a bar stool or tripping over a small object on the bedroom floor while intoxicated.

(5) Gastrointestinal disorders: e.g., peptic ulcer, gastritis, gastrointestinal bleeding, chronic indigestion, pancreatitis, cirrhosis and hemorrhoids.

Such findings by the physician or physical examination as a ruddy, weather-worn complexion, spider angiomata, "liver palms", hepatomegaly, upper abdominal tenderness, cachexia, mental confusion, odor of alcohol on the breath, and other physical findings commonly associated with chronic alcoholism would certainly lead the physician to suspect alcoholism.[7]

He then goes on to suggest that, once the therapist is suspicious of alcoholism, it may be two or three more visits before sufficient rapport is established to confront the patient with a diagnosis of alcoholism. It is, nevertheless, the initial 'suspicion of alcoholism' which is the crucial point in the diagnostic process.

As part of the South London study the general practitioners, social workers and probation officers were all asked to say 'what sort of things might generally lead you to suspect that a patient/client might have a drinking problem'. Table 1 sets out the main 'warning signs' which were reported by each professional group.

TABLE 1. Warning signs which would alert the professional

Warning signs	G.P.s %	S.W.s %	P.O.s %	All Professionals N	All Professionals %[a]
Smell of drink	45·2	39·3	52·2	37	45·1
Money problems	3·2	53·6	30·4	23	28·0
Other people's report	29·0	25·0	21·7	21	25·6
Family problems	19·4	28·6	26·1	20	24·4
Physical signs	22·6	25·0	21·7	19	23·2
General appearance	16·1	10·7	39·1	17	20·7
Work problems	16·1	14·3	13·0	12	14·6
General disorganization	9·7	7·1	8·7	7	8·5
Empty bottles	3·2	17·9	—	6	7·3
Unreliability	—	3·6	17·4	5	6·1
Sick certificates	16·1	—	—	5	6·1
DK or difficult	3·2	21·4	4·3	8	9·8
N =	31	28	23	82	

[a] Total per cent = more than 100 per cent since several respondents mentioned more than one warning sign

Apart from financial problems, which were mentioned by very few general practitioners, the major signs mentioned by each professional group were very similar. However, general practitioners were, not surprisingly, the only ones to mention frequent sick certificates as a warning sign (6):

> 'Series of sick certificates'.
>
> 'Monday morning certificates for diarrhoea and sickness'.
>
> 'Frequent sick certificates'.

while three of the probation officers mentioned that the nature of 'the offence' which brought them into contact with their client might indicate that drinking was causing some kind of problem. However, this was only mentioned in conjunction with other signs, as by the following officer who put it at the end of his long list:

> 'The state they come to appointments, if they smell of drink. General way of dress, most men dress up before they come to the probation office. If they have a lot of financial problems. Hear about it from other clients or from wife. Trembling hands. Can look at offences. A lot of offences are committed while under the influence'.

It is clear from Table 1 that the sign which would make the professionals most suspicious is, quite simply, if their patient or client smells of drink at the time of their consultation. Several of the other signs, however, such as unreliability, financial problems, family problems and general appearance would not, by themselves, be any more likely to suggest alcoholism than any one of a dozen other 'problems' of everyday living. So, in order to tie the question of recognition of alcohol problems a little more firmly to actual practice, each professional was asked in some detail about a particular recent case which they knew well. One of the questions in this section of the interview was 'how did you come to know that drinking was causing a problem?'

Once the discussion shifted from signs which might, in some hypothetical situation, suggest the possibility of an alcoholism diagnosis to a focused consideration of specific cases then it soon became clear that the local professionals did very little 'recognizing' of alcohol problems at all. They tended, rather, to pick up or accept the prior diagnoses or definitions of the patients themselves, or their intimates, or other professionals or officials involved with the patients at some time in the past.

As Table 2 shows, approximately one third of all professionals picked up the fact that alcohol was causing some kind of problem for their patient or client from the records and reports of other professionals who had been previously involved:

TABLE 2. Recognition of an actual case

Source of knowledge that drink was problem	G.P.s %	S.W.s %	P.O.s %	All Professionals N	All Professionals %[a]
From others					
From case notes and reports	20·0	33·3	63·2	21	36·2
From patient's/client's intimates	43·3	44·4	5·3	18	31·0
From patients/clients themselves	13·3	11·1	26·3	10	17·2
The professionals themselves					
Smell of drink	13·3	—	5·3	5	8·6
Just 'known' for a long time	6·7	11·1	—	3	5·2
Physical signs	6·7	—	—	2	3·4
Other reason	10·0	—	5·3	4	6·9
N =	30	9	19	58	
No case	1	19	4	24	

[a] Per cent = slightly more than 100 per cent since some professionals mentioned more than one source

'Inherited him from ex-partner, problem already known'.

'In court enquiry report'.

'From the probation officer in Coventry who passed on the case'.

'I came to know from previous reports. Drinking problem mentioned on discharge from borstal'.

'Other social worker's reports. Seven admissions to hospital due to drink'.

The other major sources of knowledge were the family and friends of the patient or client:

'Wife called to say that husband — a representative — had exceeded expense account and that her husband saw drinking as a necessity'.

'Mother-in-law rang to tell me that her son was worried about his wife's drinking'.

'Wife 'phoned to say that he was depressed and angry. She asked me to go and see him. He was on strike and had no money so was unable to go and drink'.

while the drinkers themselves were the primary source of information about the problem in some cases:

> 'Patient told me. He thought it was upsetting his relationship with the family'.
>
> 'He said so. "I can't leave it alone". He was convinced it wasn't alcoholism though, just a temporary thing'.
>
> 'She told me. She was an Amytal addict. I refused to prescribe it. She said "I'm turning more and more to drink" '.
>
> 'Client told me straight away. "Put me in a safe place. I'm not strong enough to face problems" '.

In only about 15 per cent of cases did the professionals claim to have recognized themselves that alcohol was causing some kind of problem. Five mentioned that they had smelled drink on their clients breath, while two general practitioners mentioned certain physical signs. But even in one of these the patient's wife was said to have mentioned the problem:

> 'He came to the surgery complaining of gastro-enteritis. Duodenal ulcer operation 10 years ago. Lots of sick-certificates for gastro-enteritis. Wife mentioned drinking problem'.

A small number of other signs were also reported:

> 'Car accident when drunk. Suspicion before that. He is a journalist'.
>
> 'Vicar turned up and she beat him'.
>
> 'See him in a pub. Complained of aches and pains in the leg. Florid appearance. I knew he had been in the Army. I asked him how much he was drinking'.
>
> 'Tie up between booze and prostitution. She drank to cover up her problems'.

Diagnoses

As well as asking about the identification of the particular case under discussion respondents were asked at the end of the interview whether they would describe their patient or client as either 'a normal drinker, heavy drinker, a problem drinker or an alcoholic'. They were then invited to say why they described their patient in that way and, whether they had identified a particular case or not, to explain what they felt to be the difference between an alcoholic and a problem drinker. Table 3 sets out the professionals' definition of their discussion cases and also displays the main categories of distinction between the alcoholic and the problem drinker.

TABLE 3. Definition of the cases and distinction between alcoholics and problem drinkers

a Definition of the case	G.P.s	S.W.s	P.O.s	All Professionals	
	%	%	%	N	%
Normal drinker	3·3	—	—	1	1·7
Heavy drinker	10·0	—	10·5	5	8·6
Problem drinker	10·0	66·7	42·1	17	29·3
Alcoholic	63·3	11·1	42·1	28	48·3
DK	13·3	22·2	5·3	7	12·0
N =	30	9	19	58	
No case	1	19	4	24	

b. Difference between an alcoholic (A) and a problem drinker (PD)	G.P.s	S.W.s	P.O.s	All Professionals	
	%	%	%	N	%[a]
A is dependent, PD is not	44·4	29·2	21·7	24	32·4
A is dependent, PD drinks in *response* to problems/crises	3·7	16·7	26·1	11	14·9
A is dependent, drink *causes* problems for PD	7·4	—	17·4	6	8·1
It's only a matter of degree	11·1	16·7	13·0	10	13·5
No difference	3·7	12·5	4·3	5	6·8
DK	11·1	8·3		5	6·8
Other difference	18·5	16·7	17·4	13	17·6
N =	27	24	23	74	
Question not asked/answered	4	4	—	8	

[a] Per cent = slightly more than 100 per cent since some professionals mentioned more than one source

At the heart of most of the distinctions lay the notion of dependence or addiction. Sometimes this was stated quite baldly:

> 'An alcoholic is someone who can't do without it. They become literally addicted'.
>
> 'Alcoholics are grossly dependent'.
>
> 'An alcoholic is dependent. Life couldn't continue without it'.

'The Alcoholic has become pretty physically dependent upon drink'.

while other people spoke of it in terms of the alcoholic losing or having no control whereas the problem drinker is still to an extent in control:

'Alcoholic has none of his controls left. Problem drinker's controls are still to a limited degree successful. They may ebb and flow but there's something there'.

'Alcoholic can't stop. Problem drinker can stop under pressure'.

Certain of the other professionals, as well as making the dependence–non-dependence distinction also made a distinction between two types of problem drinkers; those who drank in *response* to some problem or life crisis (11):

'Alcoholics are dependent on alcohol, they don't need a reason. The problem drinker drinks to forget'.

'Alcoholic has a real addiction, not necessary conscious. Problem drinker doesn't have to drink. Drinks when problems are acute. Resorts to drink rather than having to do it'.

'I regard an alcoholic as someone who consistently drinks and can't stop, whereas the problem drinker drinks in response to problems. In his own eyes he's a therapeutic drinker'.

and those for whom drinking *causes problems* (6):

'Alcoholic is totally psychologically and physically dependent. Needs a drink every day just to get through the day. Suffers withdrawal symptoms without alcohol. For the problem drinker drink is abnormal. It interferes with the normal course of his life. It's disfunctional to his marriage. He's physically unaffected'.

'An alcoholic is controlled by drink. The problem drinker's drinking affects family, friends, because of spending too much money or being drunk. But he can still abstain at will'.

Ten of the respondents felt that the distinction between alcoholics and problem drinkers was one of degree rather than of kind:

'They are different stages. The distinction is blurred'.

'Not really sure. Problem drinker is on the way anyhow, at a different stage'.

'Problem drinker is just a degree of problem on the way to being an alcoholic'.

'Problem drinker could lead to becoming an alcoholic. It is like a first and secondary stage of an illness'.

'Not sure of the difference. One slides into the other'.

while others (5) felt that there was no difference at all:

'I wouldn't see a great distinction between them, they are the same'.

'Doubt if there is a difference. In practical terms none'.

In contradiction to this last remark, by a young social worker, it could be argued that *in practical terms* there is a great difference between being considered by some member of the helping professions to be an alcoholic and being considered as someone whose drinking is causing them problems, or who is drinking in response to problems. The focus of any immediate therapeutic attention, and the goal of any long term therapeutic strategy is likely to be ultimately bound up with the therapist's view of the patient or client as being or not being an alcoholic and, in particular, as being or not being 'dependent on' or 'addicted to' alcohol.

One way of approaching the question of how therapists see the nature of particular problems is to look at public statements about cases. In order to do this, part of the South London study was conducted in the out-patient department of a psychiatric hospital where access could be had to the case notes and records of people who presented with or were referred to the department with some alcohol-related problem.

As well as containing the details of the presenting problem the case-notes revealed the universe and distribution of referral agencies which advanced patients to the department during the year of the study. For, of course, one way of categorizing the clientele of an organization is to consider from where they come. This may seem an obvious thing to do, but it is not insignificant. For as Freidson reminds us:

'In more cases than may be at first apparent, whether or not one will be diagnosed or treated in a certain way depends in part on what is "actually" wrong and in part on the professional agent one chooses and the referral system in which one is located'.[8]

Of the 2,686 new patients registered in the study period the case records of 207 of them mentioned some drink-related problem. Of those 207, 40 per cent were referred by general practitioners, 20 per cent were self referrals, while four other small categories — other hospitals, probation service, social work agencies and Alcoholics Anonymous — accounted for approximately 10 per cent of referrals each.

The fact that as many as one in five of the cases were self-referred is not surprising since the emergency clinic at hospital H is open 24 hours a day, no appointment is needed, if one's case is considered urgent it will be attended to immediately, diagnosis and treatment facilities are at hand, and quick in-patient admission is possible. Indeed, given all this, it is easy to see Roth's point when he suggests that:

> '. . . perhaps we should stop asking why people come to an emergency department, and instead ask why anyone gets his care anywhere else'.[9]

But in addition, of course, the accounts of the case, and in particular the correspondence between the referral agents and the hospital staff, were of interest in themselves in that they gave some indication of what information was made available, to whom, when. For accounts are made and called for when there is thought to be something to be explained.

Accounts of behaviour, especially in an area like that concerning alcoholism where key working definitions are the source of much discussion and debate are clearly of particular interest. Similarly, the presence or absence of an expected or requested account, may indicate the nature of the relationship between the individuals or organizations concerned. For accounts are only given to those to whom we feel accountable. In short, relationships between those who communicate are in part revealed by those very communications.

The process of becoming an alcoholic is in part the process of the construction of a diagnosis. However, the process by which a person is deemed an alcoholic is poorly understood. The notion that it is due to some inherent quality of the individual remains to be demonstrated'.[10] Similarly, it remains to be demonstrated that any particular type of drinking behaviour will inevitably be labelled and reacted to as 'that of an alcoholic'.[11] As this chapter has already shown, it is also the case that general practitioners and other helping professionals seldom diagnose alcoholism; they simply validate the judgements of the family, the drinker or whoever is presenting the 'problem'.[12] This occurs especially where there are clear indications that the subject conforms to the stereotype of Skid Row alcoholic,[13] or where the subject's drinking is reported to be jeopardising in some way their social, and particularly economic, standards'[14] Then the professional helps the family and the drinker to settle upon a label which in all likelihood will be 'alcoholic' or perhaps 'problem drinker', for want of a less firm designation.[15] The question now arises of how often the staff of specialist alcoholism clinics diagnose alcoholism, as opposed to confirming a prior diagnosis.

Butterfield and Wadsworth in their study of Guy's Hospital out-patient referrals,[16] noted that in 20 per cent of the referral letters which they analysed no diagnosis was mentioned. The letter merely requested the specialist to 'please see and advise'. 'It was assumed', they said, 'that since no diagnosis was mentioned the general practitioners did not wish to commit himself to an explanation of the patient's complaint'. Clearly, the willingness with which general practitioners commit themselves to a diagnosis, or to an explanation of the patient's complaint, was one of the areas of interest in the present study.

The case notes of half (42) of the people referred to the clinic by general practitioners were analysed. In 12 of them the doctor unequivocally defined the patient as 'an alcoholic' or as having 'alcoholism'. For example:

> 'I would be grateful if you would help this lady who is an alcoholic'.
>
> 'This man is an alcoholic'.
>
> 'Thank you for seeing Mrs. X, she is an alcoholic . . . '

In four of these 12 cases no substantiation or justification of the unequivocal diagnosis was given. The designation was made and the remainder of the letter was concerned with the implications of the complaint, details of current or past treatment, and requests for help and advice. In four other cases, justification appeared to have been given in terms of reference to lapses at other medical or helping agencies:

> 'This man is an alcoholic who was doing very well at St. X. He relapsed on Friday . . . '
>
> 'Thank you for seeing Mrs. X. She is an alcoholic who has recently been under hypnotherapy . . . '
>
> ' . . . X has been an alcoholic for many years. He was for some time under Doctor A at B clinic . . . '

The implication appears to be that a person who has at some time in the past been under treatment for 'alcoholism' is, by definition, 'an alcoholic'. The question of the criteria for the initial, or continuing, definition of the condition being, therefore, superfluous. In the remaining four cases the unequivocal diagnosis was supported in a variety of ways; the amount of money spent on drink being considered by the doctor to be excessive, a reported complaint by the patient's wife, or a statement about the large amount of drink being consumed per day.

Apart from these 12 letters, other general practitioners introduced the drinking problems of their patients in a variety of ways. One, while not mentioning alcoholic or alcoholism, implied an abnormal drinking pattern when he referred to his patient as 'drinking to excess', while another referred to his patient in slightly stronger terms as 'a habitual drinker to excess'. Only one family doctor acknowledged some difficulty over defining alcoholism when he wrote:

> 'Thank you for seeing this patient for me. He is indeed a problem. I suppose if you define an alcoholic as a man who cannot stop drinking, then Mr. X is certainly an alcoholic . . . '

The unwillingness to call Mr. X an alcoholic in spite of the fact that:

'He drinks $\frac{3}{4}$–1 bottle of whisky a day . . . he also suffers from gout . . . '

and that alcohol is:

' . . . gradually changing his personality and he is becoming aggressive and belligerent to his daughters . . . '

was probably due to the fact that:

'fortunately his alcoholism has not intruded into his ability in his responsible job . . . '

As Pattison has pointed out,[17] many doctors seem reluctant to define as alcoholic a person who is working and retaining his social and, particularly economic, standards, while Blane and coworkers have suggested[18] that alcoholics not conforming to the popular Skid Row stereotype may be missed diagnostically. Only one doctor referred a patient with a drink-related problem, while at the same time stating categorically that 'he is not an alcoholic'. The reason why this man was not considered to be an alcoholic was that 'He does not drink on Mondays or Tuesdays'.

A second major category of letters referred to drink in a way which suggested that the general practitioner thought a problem might be developing, or that a current problem might worsen. Phrases such as 'heavy drinking', 'started to drink heavily' and 'has started drinking', are typical of this signposting of a *potential* alcoholism diagnosis. In a third category of letters some mention of drink was made *in passing* in conjunction with other specific diagnoses or problems:

' . . . depression, fits of temper and drinking',

' . . . tends to be violent and has started to drink'.

In one case, the letter explained in some detail how 'this patient has become very dependent upon drugs', and right at the end of the letter added 'P.S. when not on pills she consumes large quantities of brandy'.

Finally, in 10 letters there was no mention of alcoholism or any other drink-related problem. However, mention *was* made in either the case notes or in the specialist's reply to the general practitioner. Reasons for these referrals were many and varied, ranging from; ' . . . increasingly anxious as regards his loss of libido . . . ' via ' . . . severe depression' to ' . . . very mixed-up, and has made a half-hearted attempt at suicide . . . '.

As well as presenting diagnoses, or signposting potential diagnoses, general practitioners made statements about the cause and consequence of the drink-related problems which they referred. Some made explicit causal statements:

' . . . a recent history of heavy drinking due to family trouble'.

while others presented the patient's views on the problem:

> 'this man reports he has been drinking heavily for four months since domestic upheaval'.
>
> 'He says that he drinks to relieve chronic anxiety'.

Other accounts were two-step. That is, they identified a particular event, made a causal link between the event and a subsequent problem, then implicitly attributed the drinking as a response to that problem:

> 'He was in the R.A.F. and was a P.O.W. in Belsen, which he attributes as the cause of the voices . . . he says that he gets the voices at times when he is not drinking'.

Statements about the consequences of drinking fell into two main categories, first broadly social:

> 'She has now left him as she was finding life intolerable with him'.
>
> 'He is now employed as a casual worker in the Post Office after having previously been manager of a business'.

and second broadly physical/psychological:

> ' . . . gastritis with a liver three fingers enlarged',
>
> ' . . . has been getting confused as well as suffering from auditory hallucinations'.

However, the presentation of material on cause and consequence was not a uniform feature of all letters. Rather it was specifically presented in relation to those patients whose problem was defined as 'heavy drinking', 'excess drinking', 'drinking to excess' and so on. In other words, the middle category between those who were defined unequivocally as alcoholic and those about whom merely a passing reference to drink was made.

It seems as though these statements as to cause and consequence were presented by the general practitioner as background, or filling-out, material in order to make the presented picture of the patient as full as possible. In order, that is, for the specialist practitioner in the hospital to confirm or reject what can be conceptualized as the general practitioner's 'offer' of an alcoholism diagnosis. The offered diagnosis can, thus, be either taken up by the specialist practitioner, ignored or specifically rejected.

Since, by and large, it is conventional for hospital staff to enter into correspondence with the general practitioners from who patients are referred, it was possible to inspect pairs of letters, where they existed, in order to discover the extent of coincidence between diagnoses or other drink references.

From an inspection of the 30 available pairs of letters, it was clear that there was a broad measure of agreement between the placing of patients in broad alcohol-related categories. For instance, all those whom the general practitioners had referred to unequivocally as alcoholic, or having alcoholism, were similarly referred to by the specialist in his reply. However, in four cases a 'heavy drinking' reference had been taken up by the specialist and transformed into alcoholism. While, in one case it was not taken up and no further mention of drink was made.

In four of the cases where there was *no* mention of alcoholism or drink at all in the general practitioner's letter, the specialist made reference to it in his reply. In one case the diagnosis given in the reply was 'chronic alcoholism'. As the specialist said:

> 'Mr. X has been consuming 15–19 pints of beer daily for some years, as you know . . . occasional blackouts . . . hallucinations . . . , a feeling of being persecuted (The G.P's reason for referral), is probably a direct outcome of his chronic alcoholism . . . '

Whether the phrase 'as you know', after the report of Mr. X's consumption of '15–19 pints of beer daily', is a thinly disguised rebuke to the referring doctor which should read 'as you know *or ought to have known and told me*' is a matter we can merely speculate upon.

In spite of the small number of open disagreements over diagnosis the overall coincidence between the general practitioners' and the specialists' interpretation of their patients' drink-related behaviour may be rather more apparent than real. This is suggested by the fact that in six cases drink was not mentioned in either the referral letter or the reply from the specialist. The designation of these cases as coming within the overall category of 'patients with drink-related problems' came after a close reading of the case notes. From these it soon became clear that replies to family doctors from the hospital were, in some cases, designed merely to confirm the doctor's initial diagnosis, rather than to reveal the diagnosis which had informed the out-patient or in-patient care at the hospital. To take the most clear example, Mr. X aged 56 was referred to the emergency clinic at hospital H with a letter from his doctor addressed to 'Consultant Psychiatrist, Urgent'. It read:

> 'Dear Doctor,
> This patient has been strange for the last three weeks, worse last weekend. He says somebody is following him and went to the door last night and other odd ideas. Very quiet, not aggressive. Would you please see and advise'.

Mr. X was, in fact, admitted immediately as an in-patient. A letter, subsequently sent from the hospital to his general practitioner, spoke at length of depression, paranoid ideas, the investigation which had been carried out and the treatment which had been given. The patient was 'returned to your care'. There was no mention at all of alcoholism, drink or any drink-related problem. However, the in-patient case notes referred in the initial formulation to ' . . . a 56 year-old alcoholic man of low intelligence' while the 'internal instructions to the sister or nurse in charge' described the patient as 'an alcoholic' and asked for:

> 'evidence of disorientation, memory loss, also of hallucinations and delusions and incipient D.T.'s . . . '

The instruction ended by saying that the patient 'will no doubt try to get a drink'.

Becoming an alcoholic is, in part, the process of the development of a diagnosis of 'alcoholism' or designation as 'an alcoholic'. The current analysis has shown that where a patient is designated unequivocally by the referring doctor as 'an alcoholic' then this diagnosis tends to be accepted, upheld and confirmed by the specialist clinic. In other cases, however, there is much more room for manoeuvre. Some letters, in which a fuller picture of the patient was presented, were clearly 'offering' the possibility of an alcoholism diagnosis. Others made only passing reference to drink, while still others did not mention alcoholism or drink at all. The specialist practitioners' replies revealed either a *public* acceptance of an 'offered' diagnosis or a *public* pick-up of a passing reference to drink.

Those letters in which the specialist did not reveal the diagnosis which informed the hospital care which was given to the patient, but merely returned the general practitioner's description of the patient's problem, were in a sense *private* diagnoses of alcoholism. The question of the implications of such private diagnoses, for subsequent intraprofessional communication and for the relationship between the patient and his family doctor, is one which can only be raised here. However, where the specialist upgraded either an offered diagnosis or passing drink-reference into a firm diagnosis of alcoholism, it is assumed that the general practitioner would adopt that diagnosis and present it himself on any subsequent referral. In the very small number of cases where information was available on the re-referral of such patients this was seen to be so. Similarly, since the diagnosis is then clear, and to an extent 'decided upon', the whole host of statements about cause and consequence tend to disappear. In short, the process of the construction of the diagnosis of alcoholism, and thus the process of becoming an alcoholic, has gone a stage further.

Chapter 7
The Referral Process

'It is not difficult to perceive that to lay bare the rationale of practice in referral on the one hand and retention on the other could be a rewarding and revealing exercise'. *McLachlan*[1]

General practitioner referrals to the out-patient department of a psychiatric hospital in the study locality were discussed, in the previous chapter, with particular reference to the question of how diagnoses of alcoholism are offered and picked up in everyday medical practice. However, referral behaviour is a research topic of particular interest not only for what it reveals about the referral agent's definition of the problem which is being presented. For the act of referral, by definition, links together representatives of different sets or categories of people such as units, departments, organizations, agencies or occupations. Thus, the act of referral is also of interest in that it is likely to reveal something of the nature of the relationship between those different sets or categories of people.

The increase in the numbers of emergency and out-patient clinic attendances in England,[2] America[3] and elsewhere[4] is not new. Nor is the realization that, in spite of this increase, health surveys still report that large proportions of their general population samples have some aberration or disorder considered by medical professionals to be well worthy of attention. These two facts of current medical life cause much concern among those practitioners and administrators responsible for, or who wish to shape the future of, the medical services. They also, of course, raise issues which are of interest to the sociologist. Two general questions which immediately suggest themselves are, first: 'what are the grounds for deciding that some case is worthy of referral on to some other professional?' and, second: 'how do the staff of particular agencies decide upon the legitimacy or acceptability of any referral which is made to them?'

The first part of this chapter discusses the views of the professionals in the study locality on certain features of referral, such as the range of agencies to which they had referred in the past and their reservations about passing on information. The second part of the chapter draws again on material from the case notes of the psychiatric hospital in the study locality to throw light on some of the decisions made by those to whom referrals are made. For just as 'noticing alcoholism' and 'referring someone to an alcoholism clinic' will not be understandable unless placed in the context of ideas about what counts as alcoholism, the range and nature of available help and treatment, and what is an appropriate referral of particular people to particular organizations, so the staff of organizations to which people with drink-related problems are referred will have their own ideas about what counts as an appropriate referral, and will have routines for handling those referrals which are considered to fall outside this category and for discouraging further referrals of that type.

Making Referrals and Passing Information

In Chapter 4 it was noted that a large proportion of the 82 study professionals felt that they themselves had little to offer someone whose drinking was causing them problems. General practitioners certainly felt that referral was their most important resource while one in five of them felt that it was the *only* thing they had to offer. Twenty-eight per cent of social workers felt that they had 'little if anything to offer', while 61 per cent mentioned referral, of whom one in three saw it as their major resource for helping their clients who had drinking problems. Half of the probation officers said that their best way of helping their clients with drinking problems was to refer them on.

TABLE 1. Professionals' referral of the discussion case

	G.P.s	S.W.s	P.O.s	All professionals	
	%	%	%	N	%
Referred to:					
Psychiatrist	43·3	22·2	26·3	20	34·5
Other	6·7	11·1	10·5	5	8·6
Did not refer because:					
Patient/client already referred	3·4	33·3	10·5	6	10·3
Patient/client refused referral	20·0	11·1	10·5	9	15·5
No need to refer	26·7	—	21·1	12	20·7
No point in referring	—	22·2	21·1	6	10·3
N =	30	9	19	58	
No case	1	19	4	24	

In order to tie this general feeling of helplessness to particular situations, each professional was asked, in relation to the specific case which we focused on in the interview, whether they had referred the patient on to some other professional or organization for help or advice. As Table 1 shows, approximately 50 per cent of the cases had been referred on elsewhere, and 80 per cent of these had been referred on to a psychiatrist. Of the others, two had been referred to a general hospital, one to a general practitioner, one to a reception centre and one to Alcoholics Anonymous.

Of those who had not been referred, one in five were already in contact with other helping agencies, usually a psychiatrist, while one in four of the patients and clients had refused to be referred anyway. There were a number of cases (12) in which the patient was not considered *to need* referring on:

'No deterioration or self-neglect'

'His drinking is not so heavy now'

'I had the impression he was cutting down anyway'

and a few (6) where the professional thought that there would be *no point* in referring, either because of the client:

'Waste of time, I question his ability to talk about his problems'

or because of some other professional's weakness:

'None of the medical bods seem to be able to define his problem. In his records he's a criminal psychopath'.

In addition to considering the particular case which acted as a focus for detailed questions the professionals were asked whether they had ever referred anyone with a drinking problem to four particular agencies: the

TABLE 2. Professionals' referral to particular agents

	G.P.s	S.W.s	P.O.s	All professionals	
	%	%	%	N	%
Psychiatric hospital	80·6	17·9	56·5	43	52·4
Client's general practitioner	N.A.	25·0	26·1		(13)25·5
Half-way house	—	10·7	60·9	17	20·7
Alcoholics Anonymous	41·9	10·7	34·8	25	30·5
None of them	19·4	53·6	17·4		
N =	31	28	23	82(51)	

local psychiatric hospital, their client's general practitioner, a local half-way house for people with drinking problems and Alcoholics Anonymous.

As Table 2 shows, general practitioners and probation officers were most likely to have referred someone with a drinking problem to the local psychiatric hospital, and also to Alcoholics Anonymous, while three out of five of the probation officers had also referred people to one of the local half-way houses which provide accommodation for homeless alcoholics. It is also clear from Table 2 that over half of all the social workers who were interviewed had never referred anyone with a drinking problem to any of the four agencies. This may, in part, be due to the fact that many of the social workers were only very recently qualified and would, therefore, have had very little experience of referring anyone to anywhere. On the other hand, it may be due to a greater reluctance to refer clients in any situation. With this in mind, all the professionals were asked whether they had any reservations about making referrals to other agencies and organizations and also whether they had any reservations about passing on information about their patients or clients.

Table 3 shows that approximately half of all the professionals had no reservations about referring. Among those who did, the most common reason was if the patient or client was unwilling to be referred or was considered to be unmotivated for treatment (20):

'I only refer if the patient appears to be motivated'

'No point unless the client is willing'

'It would depend if the client was willing'

TABLE 3. Reservations about making referrals

	G.P.s	S.W.s	P.O.s	All professionals	
	%	%	%	N	%
No reservations about referral	53·6	50·0	39·1	38	48·1
Reservations about referral:					
If client is not willing/motivated	7·1	35·7	34·8	20	25·3
To voluntary organizations	7·1	7·1	8·7	6	7·6
To psychiatrists	7·1	3·6	4·3	4	5·1
To social workers	10·7	—	4·3	4	5·1
To all *except* psychiatrists	10·7	—	—	3	3·8
Other reservations	3·6	3·6	8·7	4	5·1
N =	28	28	23	79	
No answer	3			3	

'You have to accept what the man wants. That puts the restriction on action'.

Others were reluctant about referring to particular agents or organizations, such as voluntary bodies (6):

'I feel they are lay people dealing with semi-science'

'With non-professional agencies, I'd want to be sure they had something to offer'

psychiatrists (4):

'Always reservations about referring clients to a psychiatrist. Because a lot are pill practitioners. Hospital H has the additional sin of swift rotation of registrars so you can't get a relationship going'

'Concerned about referring people to a psychiatric hospital. Being in a closed environment doesn't help them outside'

and social workers (4):

'Strong reservations about social workers'

'Social workers have no medical knowledge, and anyway people should be taught to stand on their own feet and not have some social worker taking responsibility'.

In addition, three of the general practitioners said that they would *only* refer to psychiatrists.

Table 4 shows that even more of the professionals had reservations about passing on information than had reservations about making referrals: approximately two thirds of each professional group.

The biggest cause for reservation was the reluctance to pass information without the patient's or client's consent (30):

'With patient's permission only'

'It's a thorny thing. If things are written down they get out. If client stresses it's confidential I keep it to myself'

'Thorny question. If my client refused I wouldn't give it'

'I would pass on information only if the client agreed. I would try to get the client to agree, but if it came to the crunch I wouldn't pass it on'

TABLE 4. Reservations about passing on information

	G.P.s	S.W.s	P.O.s	All professionals	
	%	%	%	N	%
No reservations about passing information	37·9	32·1	34·8	28	35·0
Reservations about passing information:					
Without patient's/client's consent	24·2	46·4	43·5	30	37·5
To social workers	24·2	—	—	7	8·8
To 'non-professional' agencies	10·2	10·7	—	6	7·5
To A.A.	—	—	8·7	2	2·5
To psychiatrist	3·4	—	—	1	1·3
Because of confidentiality	—	—	13·1	3	3·8
Depends on agency	—	10·7	—	3	3·8
N =	29	28	23	80	
No answer	2			2	

'Ask the client, he may have revealed more to me under the influence than he meant to'.

General practitioners, in particular, were worried about passing information about their patients to social workers (7):

'I telephone rather than write. Social workers and agency personnel are not aware of the confidentiality of information. I am frightened of losing the patient's trust'.

'I wouldn't give information to a social worker'

'I'm not entirely happy about social workers. They are not bound by professional secrets. They're gossipy'

while others were unhappy about giving information to 'non-professionals' (6):

'Very difficult. Voluntary agencies particularly I fear passing on information'

'Would want to know why they wanted it. Difficult with voluntary bodies'.

Two probation officers said that they would not give information to Alcoholics Anonymous and one general practitioner was:

'only willing to divulge details to a psychiatrist of my own choice'.

But in spite of the reservations which professionals have about referring to particular agencies and about passing on information about their patients and clients, and in spite of the many and various difficulties of defining alcoholism in any particular case, and in spite of their unwillingness to be referred to specialist agencies, there are still many people with alcohol-related problems who do get referred on by general practitioners, social workers, probation officers and others. As we have seen in earlier sections, the psychiatrist is the person to whom most agents have referred at some time in the past. The next section, therefore, concentrates on the question of how referrals, once made, are handled at the local psychiatric hospital.

Handling Referrals to a Specialist Setting

Patients are referred to out-patient departments and specialist facilities not only in response to the disorders which they are considered to have, or because of the availability of the service but also in the light of any of a whole range of functions of the facility as the referral agent sees it at that time. The World Health Organization, for example, delineated the main functions of a hospital out-patient department in the following way:

'i Early diagnosis for the detection of undiagnosed diseases
ii Ambulatory (and domiciliary) treatment
iii The admission to hospital of those patients who need it
iv The care and medical rehabilitation, when necessary, after discharge from hospital
v The promotion of health of the individuals under their care by means of health education
vi The training of medical and nursing students
vii The keeping of records and the collection of data for epidemiological and social research'.[5]

One major omission from this list of out-patient department functions is the opportunity for the generalist to seek confirmation from a specialist practitioner about diagnosis and advice about treatment and prognosis. Several studies[6] have shown this to be a major purpose of out-patient referrals. Similarly, referral in order to reassure the patient was also identified[7] as a minor but significant category.

In order to look at how referrals were, in practice, handled in a specialist setting the case notes and records of all newly registered patients at a psychiatric hospital in the study locality were analysed. From an inspection of the referral letters during the study year, six main types of material were identified; dealing with:

(1) The certainty of the referral agent's diagnosis — this material was drawn upon in the final section of the previous chapter in the discussion of diagnosis and general practitioners' referrals,

(2) The referral agent's views as to the causes of the particular drink-related problem under discussion or drinking problems in general,

(3) Their views about other problems which had been caused by their patient's or client's drinking habits,

(4) Assumptions about the possibility of help for, or treatment or even cure of, particular drink-related problems,

(5) The question of motivation,

(6) The reason or justification for the referral of the case to Hospital H at that time.

From the material in the hospital case-notes two simple preliminary facts about the handling of referrals emerged. First, only five per cent or so of the cases were explicitly rejected. That is, nearly all the cases were accepted, where *accepted* means that hospital H accepted responsibility for them. Either an in-patient or out-patient treatment programme was initiated or the patient was discharged as not being in need of medical treatment — but that decision was made at hospital H. The second feature to emerge was that in approximately 50 per cent of the cases which were accepted, the referral agent was discouraged from making further referrals. This was done either by making no reply to the referral letter or by replying and explicitly discouraging further referrals of that type.

In addition, it was clear that whether or not cases were accepted, and whether or not further referrals were discouraged, could *not* be explained in terms of either the agreed *seriousness* of the case or the particular *source* of the referral. Thus, two quite straightforward questions about these referrals are raised.

(1) Why were certain cases rejected and how were these rejections handled?

(2) Why were certain referral agents, both medical and non-medical, discouraged from making further referrals — where *discouraged* means either explicitly discouraged by being rebuked, or implicitly discouraged by not being replied to or corresponded with?

It was suggested earlier in the chapter that, given estimates of need based upon health survey research, specialist medical facilities are scarce. In the alcoholism services, given current official estimations of the number of alcoholics or people with alcohol-related problems, and the likelihood that such people will be considered to have a 'medical' problem, the scarcity of specialist medical facilities is particularly acute. In 1974 there were less than 400 'alcoholism treatment-unit' beds in England for a problem said to affect anywhere between 200,000 and 500,000 individuals. So however the definitional questions in relation to diagnosis are handled, there is 'scarcity of facilities' par excellence. Thus, practitioners in specialist facilities are called upon to make everyday decisions about, for example, which among many suitable cases for in-patient treatment shall receive it. Similarly, since many people recognize and seek advice about their own or other people's alcohol-related problems, decisions have to be made about appropriate channels of referral *to* specialist medical facilities. In short, specialist medical practitioners act as gate-keepers, in that they must control not only access but the amount and type of contact. This is the nature of the case in *any* specialist medical facility but appears to be particularly acute in relation to alcoholism.

It could be argued that a major reason why cases in any medical setting are accepted is that the medical professional is *obliged* to accept them, on the grounds that, quite simply, it is the task of a practitioner to give help when it is needed; it is not a question of choice but one of duty. As the International Code of Medical Ethics puts it:

> 'A doctor must give care as a humanitarian duty unless he is assured that others are willing and able to give such care'.

Clearly, the question of being assured of others' willingness and ability is complex, but the implication is that a medical professional will provide care if it is needed unless it can be guaranteed elsewhere. In the case of people referred for specialist medical attention from non-medical sources this is clearly a consideration of no little importance. Cresswell[8] shows how the emergency clinic at hospital H 'straddled between hospital and community', as he puts it, gradually came to accept that it must be ready to assume clinical responsibility for its patients.

A second *core* feature of the obligation to accept a case applies specifically to a practitioner in specialist medical settings and is the reciprocal part of one of the basic principles of the Hippocratic Oath, namely that any medical practitioner should 'defer to specialist assistance whenever this is in the best interests of the patient'. Clearly, this only has meaning if specialist practitioners accept the complementary obligation to *provide* that assistance.

In addition to the *obligations* of the medical practitioner in hospital H, there is an administrative rule in respect of catchment area referrals. In short, hospital H has an obligation to care for those persons who live within a particular area around the hospital. But this should not be taken to mean that referrals cannot be accepted from *outside*. In fact, only about 15 per cent of people referred to hospital H in the study year with some drink-related problem came from *within* the catchment area.

Given that specialist practitioners have to exercise control over scarce resources, given the nature of medical professional obligations and given an administrative rule, it was possible to discern three typical modes of response, by hospital H, to referrals from a whole range of medical and non-medical sources. These are set out in Table 5.

TABLE 5. Handling referrals to a psychiatric hospital

	Modes of response to referrals	The specialist's obligation	Main sources of referrals	% of all cases (approx.)
A:	Accept the referral + Maintain contact with the agent	Controllable obligation	G.P.s Probation officers (I)	60%
B:	Accept the referral + Discourage further referrals from that source	Uncontrollable obligation	Probation officers (II) A.A. Social workers Other hospitals (I)	35%
C:	Reject the referral + Discourage further referrals from that source	No obligation	Other hospitals (II)	5%

A: Accept the Referral and Maintain Contact with the Agent

The first mode of response was that in which hospital H accepted the case and maintained some kind of contact with the referral agent. Further referrals were not encouraged — in a situation of scarce resources who would do that — but further referrals were not discouraged. Most of the cases in this category came from *general practitioners.* In fact they represented an easily recognizable common mode of referral; namely of 'a generalist deferring to special assistance'. Such assistance may be to confirm 'offered' diagnoses, to provide specialist treatment, or to give advice on how the generalist might himself manage the case.

However, the *style* of the referrals and the subsequent correspondence reveal that the specialist practitioner was given a great deal of room for manoeuvre. While certain of the general practitioners' referral letters contained a great deal of information and opinion about the cause and consequences of the presented alcohol-related problems, and often contained detailed statements about the patient's 'motivation for treatment' and explanations of why the referral was made 'at that time', there was almost never any indication of the *type* of treatment which was being sought. Nearly 50 per cent of the general practitioners letters contained no statement or even phrase from which any explicit or implicit assumptions about the ability or the readiness of the specialist practitioner to alleviate the presented condition could be ascertained. While it might be said, of course, that working in a psychiatric out-patient clinic, by definition, signifies a readiness to deal with or at least to look at patients with alcohol-related problems the potential referral agent is still faced with the problem of what counts for the specialist as 'a problem'. It was seen in the previous chapter that where a non-disease diagnosis such as 'heavy drinking' was proffered the general practitioner was much more likely to present other material concerning assumed causes and consequences than he was in the cases where a specific disease diagnosis — such as alcoholism — was mentioned. General practitioners appeared to feel that a report of heavy or excessive drinking without substantiation was unacceptable as a 'problem' in a referral to an out-patient department, whereas an assertion that 'this man is an alcoholic' without substantiation *was* acceptable.

Of the remaining letters some contained indications that the doctor thought the specialist could offer help or treatment, while others contained reports of the patients' assumption as to the help, treatment and cures which could be provided. Almost all letters contained standard phrases of the 'please see and advise' kind;

'Thank you for seeing this case'

'Thanks for seeing him for me'

'I should be most grateful for your help and advice'.

Others, however, contained statements about help which were rather stronger in their request for help than the conventional phrase:

'I am seeking your advice to help him'

'I wonder if you can do anything to help'

'I would be personally grateful if you can help him'

'I would be grateful if you could help this lady who is an alcoholic'

'I would be grateful for any assistance you can give him'

'I would be very grateful if you would kindly help'

Only one letter contained any indication of the broad kind of treatment which the general practitioner felt was necessary.

'She obviously requires a great deal of help at this stage and I am sure she should be under observation as an in-patient'.

In addition to the general practitioners' assumptions about help, other letters reported the *patients'* requests for help. Two revealed that the patient assumed some kind of in-patient treatment would be available or, at least a possible option:

'She would like to go into hospital in England'

> 'He is however prepared to accept help although he does not wish it to interfere with his job which he is afraid to risk if he is admitted for treatment'

while several letters report patients' assumptions that a cure for drink-related problems is available. Quotation marks in one letter reveal that, while reporting her views, the doctor himself did not share the patient's optimism:

> 'This man who is an habitual drinker to excess has expressed the desire to be cured of the habit'

> 'This man . . . has been an alcoholic for many years . . . and would like expert advice as to how he can be cured of his habit'

> 'She would like to go away somewhere for a "cure". Her husband is an alcoholic but he has been "cured" '.

The success of any treatment programme concerned with alcohol-related problems is intimately linked with the readiness of those involved to recognize that they have some 'problem' and to recognize also the part which they must play in any scheme of treatment or rehabilitation. This complex question of 'motivation' and the readiness to comply with certain therapeutic rules and procedures lies at the heart of most treatment programmes and is certainly a dominant theme running through the literature on alcohol-related problems, and is discussed further in the next chapter.

Briefly stated, however, a widely held notion is that drinking alcoholics are not free agents but rather slaves to their compulsion and are not at liberty to decide whether they want treatment or not.[9] Often held simultaneously is the view that the alcoholic must be 'ready' before he can be helped and that, therefore, any attempted treatment without his motivation is doomed to failure.[10] But how, in fact, do these slaves ever shake off their chains? How does any course of treatment ever start? Apart from those people who have quite clearly written one thing and then in their work been informed by quite different assumptions, certain writers have overcome the problem by distinguishing between 'initial' motivation for treatment, and motivation for the continuation of treatment once it has been embarked upon. As Glatt states:[11]

> ' . . . no treatment of alcoholics can succeed unless they are "motivated" and want to get better. But that is quite different from claiming that such "motivation" must be present at the time treatment is initiated'.

One practical outcome of this position is, of course, compulsory treatment. For Glatt claims that while they are drinking such people are unable to make rational decisions and so one may therefore ask:

'. . . whether society has the right to stand by and watch him go to his grave while debating whether or not one should intervene'.

Glatt, in this way, directs our attention straight to the essential legal–moral nature of the discussion. He, in fact, phrases it in political philosophical terms. But, in whatever terms it is phrased it is not a purely medical decision and must be made in conjunction with legal–political procedure and debate.

However, the question of the implications of assuming that alcoholics cannot make rational decisions, and that the correct 'motivation' is a necessary prerequisite to the commencement of any treatment programme, are points of vital concern in any study of out-patient referrals for alcohol-related problems. For beliefs about the role of 'correct motivation' clearly affect readiness to refer in any particular case. Similarly, a statement about motivation may be seen by the referral agent as an essential piece of information to place before the specialist practitioner to whom the referral is made.

In 20 out of the 42 referral letters written by general practitioners some explicit or implicit statement about motivation was made. First, there were those which dealt with motivation to stop drinking. Second, were those which referred to the patients' motivation to embark upon treatment, and third were those which spoke of motivation in non-specific terms. Within each of the three categories the letter could be written in terms which revealed or implied that the general practitioner felt the patient's motivation to be either good, bad or somewhere in between.

Thus, concerning drinking, one patient was referred to as:

'. . . very anxious to stop'

while of another the doctor wrote merely that:

'I feel on about three occasions he managed about two months free of drinking'.

On the other hand one patient had:

'. . . never gone longer than three months without a drink'

while another was:

'. . . still drinking — and averring that he had stopped'.

As to the patients' motivation for treatment one was described as:

'. . . very anxious to obtain further treatment for her condition before the situation worsens'.

Two others were referred to in terms which suggested that the doctor was not quite convinced of their commitment:

'He is prepared to accept help'

'On previous occasions he was not keen on seeking psychiatric advice but suddenly today he came asking if he could see a psychiatrist!'

While several other patients were, by implication, given less chance of successfully embarking on a programme of treatment:

'Since coming to the area he has not sought help but things have become so bad that now he has no alternative'

'She discharged herself from X hospital after five days and was readmitted after a week to X hospital again but has since discharged herself after only two days'

The third category of statement was that which referred in general terms to motivation and the patient's readiness to alter behaviour in some way. One doctor, in moderately optimistic terms, wrote that:

'I feel he now knows that he has come to the end of the road and must do something about it'.

Two others offered some indication of a change in outlook on the part of the patient:

'. . . he is very contrite to a certain extent'

'He *says* he is getting in touch with A.A. . . . his appearance has improved a great deal'

While one general practitioner was rather less than enthusiastic when he wrote that:

'. . . I do not think he is prepared to do very much for himself'.

It is a matter not only of theoretical but practical concern to discover the sources and consequences of different types of illness behaviour. In the case of a chronic condition, such as the development of some alcohol-related disorder, the problems for both the potential patient and for the medical professional are many and varied. General practitioners, for instance, may find it particularly difficult to separate any presented symptom or disorder from the pattern of illness behaviour or social processes which brought the patient into contact with him at a particular time. Clearly this is a potential problem in relation to those drink-related problems which are defined solely in social or emotional terms. As Zola has pointed out[12] the general practitioner may interpret the emotionality of the patient as an indication of the severity of the illness rather than as an indication of the demands of a pattern of illness behaviour which encourages the complaint to be presented emotionally.

In the same way, people seeking care and those from whom they seek it may have quite different and, at times, conflicting interests. Some patients may be more concerned with primary symptoms, pain and social incapacitation, than with any underlying organic disease. A member of the medical profession, on the other hand, may be more keen to concentrate upon clinical illness than on the concomitant physical discomforts of its symptoms or on its social consequences. These differing orientations may lie behind the differential readiness with which conditions or problems are presented to primary medical care facilities and also behind the differential referral of those conditions to specialist facilities such as those available at hospital H.

It might be assumed that all patients were referred to hospital H because general practitioners felt that those particular cases with which they were faced could best be dealt with in that setting. However, only one letter made any reference which could be interpreted as a reason for referring a patient specifically to hospital H. The letter was addressed to a named member of the staff. Whether or not the following statement represents anything more than conventional intraprofessional flattery is impossible to say:

> 'Conscious of the fact that I will never achieve anything very much on my own I have persuaded him to agree to see your good self . . . '

A related theme in the general practitioners' letters concerned the timing of the referral. Twenty of the letters made explicit statements about this. In any non-acute condition the question of what happens to trigger off self or professional referral is a matter of interest both to those who want to offer explanations for illness behaviour and to those who have to provide, administer or work in treatment facilities of various kinds. Several letters spoke of long-term problems:

> '. . . and has been an alcoholic for many years'.

> 'He is an alcoholic of some 10 years'.

The question which immediately springs to mind and must also be assumed to spring into the mind of the specialist practitioner at hospital H is 'why refer now?'. What is so special about, for instance, the 21st September 1974 which distinguishes that date from the 20th September 1974 or the 20th September 1964? Similarly, if the case was not referred in 1964 why was it not left until 1984?

Several letters offered reasons or justifications for the timing of the referral. The first were in terms of changes in patients' expectations or attitudes. The second were in terms of changes in the doctor's assessment of the case, and the third, in terms of the response to the action or pressure of significant lay others. Finally, one letter stressed that referral was made for the strictly short-term surveillance of a local student during a long vacation.

The first set of statements expressing an implied explanation for the timing of the referral reported a request from the patient for specialist treatment, or a change in their circumstance or attitude toward treatment:

> 'I would be grateful if you would help this lady who is an alcoholic. She would like to go away somewhere for a "cure" '.
>
> 'She would like to go to some hospital in England'.
>
> 'She is unable to obtain an appointment with the doctor she was under since he moved away'.
>
> 'On previous occasions he was not keen on seeking psychiatric advice but suddenly today he came asking if he could see a psychiatrist!'

The second set of implied reasons for referral were those in which the general practitioner noted some recent deterioration in the patient's social, physical or psychological state.

> 'I would value your opinion as he appears to be going downhill'.
>
> 'I believe she is potentially suicidal by now'.
>
> 'She requires a great deal of help at this stage and I am sure she should be under observation as an in-patient'.
>
> ' . . . and has been an alcoholic for many years. This has recently developed into a major problem and he has now drunk himself into debt'.

The third category were those letters which report some recent domestic change which, after being reported by a significant lay other, had highlighted a long-standing problem:

> 'He admits that he is drinking heavily — his wife says he is in the pub all day except for a short interval in the betting shop. She has now left him as she was finding life intolerable with him'.
>
> 'They had been married for 13 years and he had always been a heavy drinker but she felt recently that she could not accept this any longer'.

In spite of the range of information and opinion which was presented in the general practitioners' referral letters there was almost never a specific request for either action or facilities. The cases were in greater or lesser detail described, and then merely presented with a general request to 'please see and advise'. In such a situation, therefore, the specialist practitioner's room for manoeuvre is extensive. In addition, he knows that the case can be returned to the care of the general practitioner who will take up again complete medical responsibility for it. Thus, core obligations are easy to satisfy and only such strain on resources will be exerted as the specialist practitioner sees fit. In such cases the specialist will maintain contact with the referral agent, he will thank him for the referral and in all probability send a letter giving details of the diagnosis and treatment, opinion and advice as to future management of the case.

Another set of referrals which came into Category A: 'accept the referral and maintain contact with the agent' were those cases sent by *probation officers* in relation to legal proceedings at magistrates courts. The first point to make about probation-service referrals to the psychiatric hospital is that they are of two main types. The first are people, for whom the officer has some case responsibility:

> 'The above named is on prison-after-care to me at this office . . . '

The second are those people referred by probation officers for a psychiatrist's report in relation to remand requirements at a magistrates court.

> ' . . . she appeared at X magistrate's court and pleaded guilty to stealing about £40 from one of her friends, . . . she was remanded for a probation officer's report and a psychiatrist's report until . . . '

The correspondence between the probation officer and the specialist in the relatively small number of remand cases was open, full and courteous. Both had a part to play vis-à-vis the legal process. From the specialist's point of view the procedure — providing a court report — would be circumscribed and short-term and, thus, make no great demands upon resources, while for his part the probation officer, unlike the general practitioner, was as likely to offer help as to request it:

> 'Please telephone me if you want any further information'.
>
> 'I am prepared to "have a go" again if you feel it is worth it'.

Again, as with the general practitioner referrals, the specialist practitioner is accepting *controllable* cases which do not put any strain on resources. However, not all probation-office referrals were of this type. Others came into category B where the nature of the relationship between the officer and the hospital psychiatrist, as revealed by the correspondence, was quite different.

B: Accept the Referral and Discourage Further Referrals from that Source

The nature of the relationship between *probation officers* and specialists was quite different when patients were referred direct to hospital H for 'purely medical', as opposed to 'medical-in-a-legal framework', reasons. In every case the patient was seen and courses of treatment were initiated. The cases were, in a sense, 'unrefusable', in that it was clear that at least certain aspects required medical attention which could *not* be provided by the referring agency. Hospital H was, thus, obliged to accept the case.

In contrast to the general practitioners, most of the probation officers' referral letters contained sparse information, apart from diagnosis, relating to the six 'areas of interest'. As far as certainty of diagnosis is concerned alcoholism was mentioned as a primary problem in only two cases. Each time the diagnosis was supported by a medical-organizational reference:

> 'It appears that X has been increasingly dependent on alcohol as a temporary solution to his difficulties and there has been a progressive deterioration in his condition. He used to be in touch with Dr. A. at the B alcohol clinic . . . It may be that he needs psychiatric help as well as treatment for alcoholism'.
>
> 'I understand that he was being treated for alcoholism in 1969 at X mental hospital . . . and subsequently went to A.A. . . . '

Other cases referred to 'anxiety', 'nervousness' and 'drinking', in rather more general terms:

> ' . . . she accepts she drinks a lot and she is probably on the edge of alcoholism'.

By and large, however, the cases from probation officers were presented as unhappy, disturbed or disturbing people:

> ' . . . a social and behavioural problem rather than someone suffering from any form of mental illness'.

Statements as to cause or consequence of the client's drinking were rather few and far between, while indications of the patient's motivation were general rather than specific and, unlike the general practitioners' letters, geared to reporting the patient's desire for help rather than offering an opinion about its likely sincerity. Such statements as there were were short:

> 'He is asking for help'
>
> 'She accepts that she drinks a lot'
>
> 'He has attended A.A.'.

All, that is, apart from one rather flowery opening to a letter which ran:

> 'It is with Mr. X's knowledge and consent — indeed at his request that I tried to get him such help — that I am writing to you today . . . '

Requests for help were made in general terms:

> 'I should be most grateful if you could do something to help this man'.
>
> 'Perhaps you could help him in this matter'.
>
> 'Hoping you will be able to help'.

Although one letter did make a tentative request for specific and short-term treatment:

> 'I wonder if some temporary prescription could be given to him . . . as he is going to have to function on his own for a while at least and I don't feel that he is capable of absorbing the A.A. programme unaided for the moment'.

In spite of the sparseness of the specific medical or drinking-problem material which was presented, all of these probation-office referrals were accepted as legitimate by hospital H. Since the cases could not, by definition, be sent back to a referral agent who could accept medical responsibility for them, the specialist practitioner was not so easily able to control the referral situation. The medical buck had stopped there. Clearly, the hospital's ability to control scarce resources would be seriously undermined if this category of cases expanded. Further referrals of this kind were, therefore, discouraged. No replies were sent to the majority of probation officers who referred in this way. In one case a reply *was* sent but only in order to rebuke the referring officer who had sent a patient, with a very short accompanying letter, to the emergency clinic.
The referral letter said:

> 'Mr. X has suffered from nervousness for some years now, and finds that the only way he can face a new day and new people is by taking two or three pints of beer. Perhaps you can help him in this matter.
>
> Yours sincerely,
> ABC
> Assistant Probation Officer'

The Duty Registrar replied:

> 'Thank you for referring this patient whom I saw in the emergency clinic on Xth of June. I understand from the patient that his G.P. did not know that he had been referred here. However, I have sent a full report to him and suggested a course of treatment. I think in future it

might be better if you get a patient's G.P. to refer him/her to hospital H who can then give us any medical history that we require when seeing the patient.

Yours sincerely . . . '

The point about the 'medical history' is an important one, but the fact remains that the case was immediately taken out of the probation officer's sphere of influence. What his professional relationship with the patient was is uncertain since he did not reveal it in the short referral letter. However, the reply to the probation officer from hospital H did not mention the diagnosis, or the course of treatment which had been initiated or other action which had been taken. In fact, arrangements had been made for the patient to go to a reception centre, Alcoholics Anonymous had been contacted and an almost immediate appointment to see a consultant who specialized in alcohol-related problems had been made. In the letter to his general practitioner, the patient was described as having 'all the symptomatology of alcoholism' and

' . . . some symptoms of depression and anxiety state which may well have exacerbated his drinking problem which is serious'.

The isolation of the probation officer from his client was further strengthened when, in the hospital's letter to the patient's general practitioner, the officer was not mentioned by name.

'Dear Doctor X, your patient was referred to us by a probation officer at XYZ magistrates court and appeared with a letter written two weeks ago . . . '

Interviews with probation officers in the study area confirmed how resentful many of them are about information being withheld from them by psychiatrists. Comments ranged from the mild:

' . . . psychiatrists could be a little more forthcoming about what they're doing with clients'.

via

'I feel very strongly about not getting information back from other agencies — particularly psychiatrists'.

to the officer who complained bitterly of the:

' . . . out of date ethics — like psychiatrists only accepting referrals via G.P.s — it's a waste of time and nonsense, the medical myth and etiquette. Psychiatrists sometimes send back a bald statement about a client, with no explanation, as if they're handing down a judgement'.

It is hardly surprising that one should say that probation officers 'feel that they are looked down on', or that another should conclude that:

> 'We should all get our heads together for the good of the individual. But . . . psychiatrists make us work very hard for our referrals, and give very little back. I don't think it's worth the bother'.

One 'purely-medical-care' referral from a probation officer which did elicit a reply from hospital H demonstrated one technique for overcoming the inter-professional problem. This case appeared to be, in purely medical terms, less acute than the one from which the officer had been directly cut off by the hospital. But this probation officer presented it rather differently. This was the referral letter which began with the flowery introduction:

> 'It is with Mr. X's knowledge and consent — indeed at his request that I try to get him such help — that I am writing to you today . . . '

It then proceeded to a full case history — including a probation report from Australia where the patient had lived for several years — detailed the current state of the patient, and claimed that there had been a recent change in his motivation toward treatment in particular and life in general. The letter ended by pointing out that the case was special, that the probation officer knew such referral was unusual and tentatively requested the possibility of an appointment:

> 'I wonder if you would be prepared to accept this as a direct referral and consider arranging for him to be seen as an out-patient.
>
> Your sincerely . . . '

Other referrals which fell into the 'unrefusable' category were made from A.A. and from social workers and were handled in much the same way as those from probation officers. *Social workers* rarely wrote referral letters in connection with the small number of cases they introduced to hospital H. If they did write letters they appeared to be merely formal appendages to the main business of the referral which had gone on either through personal contact with a member of the clinic staff or over the telephone with the secretary of the specialist alcoholism clinic:

> 'I have spoken with Mr. A. the social worker at hospital H about this man. I understand that Mr. A. has arranged an out-patient appointment for . . . '

'I would be grateful if you would see Mr. X as arranged over the telephone with Mrs. Y (secretary to the alcoholism clinic) this afternoon. Thank you for your co-operation'.

The only exceptions were those 'direct' referrals made from one local organization which dealt specifically with alcohol problems, several of whose members were closely associated on a working basis with the staff at hospital H. One began by making reference to the fact that the patient was known to the director of the organization. It briefly described the patient's present situation:

' . . . N.F.A. and seems in a very distressed condition . . . He walked out of his job on Friday and was drinking until yesterday . . . ', his standing vis-à-vis the law: 'There is a warrant out for Mr. X's arrest for non-payment of a £50 fine . . . ', and his previous contact with helping agencies ' . . . was in X house but not happy there . . . was in the Y clinic for two periods of one month and a further week during 1971 . . . '. The social worker ends by indicating that he ' . . . would be grateful for your advice' and 'will keep in contact with Mr. X for as long as he wishes'.

Mr. X was then seen by the emergency clinic doctor who passed him on to hospital H social worker, who telephoned a local reception centre to arrange accommodation and inform them of the patient's subsequent specialist out-patient appointment, which was *not,* in fact, kept.

There were rarely any statements from social workers about cause or consequence of drinking, or about motivation or reasons for referral. The only comments which did accompany the simple request for help concerned organizational or situational difficulties associated with the case. In fact, the impression was gained that the point of the referral was, on the one hand, a last resort, or reasonable chance, for someone who had little going for them and, on the other, a tactic used by one social agency vis-à-vis another. The outcomes of these social work agency referrals were rather like those of probation-service referrals. All cases were seen at the emergency clinic and series of consultations were offered. However, few appointments were kept. The cases emerged briefly from the hostel, social work, reception-centre network and then plunged back into it again.

No letters at all were written in association with any of the *Alcoholics Anonymous* referrals to hospital H. These cases were classed as A.A. referrals since each of the patients was either accompanied by a member of A.A. at the time of the emergency clinic attendance or described their attendance as being at the instigation of a member of A.A., and, in particular, the local organizer. Furthermore some cases were explicitly considered by the staff of hospital H to be A.A. referrals.

'. . . this patient who I saw in the E.C. this afternoon. He was referred to us by A.A. . . . '

'Referred by X of A.A. . . . '

'. . . who was referred via X of A.A. . . . '

The role of Alcoholics Anonymous in relation to the support given to and the rehabilitation of self-defined alcoholics is well known and needs little elaboration. However, the nature of the relationship between A.A. and medical organizations and institutions is worthy of close study. The first thing to note about the A.A. referrals is that a much higher proportion of them, as compared with referrals from any other source, were admitted for immediate in-patient care. This could be either as a result of the local A.A. group operating with a much higher threshold of 'referral suitability' than other referral agents, or as a result of the hospital staff considering A.A. referrals as being well motivated towards treatment since they are likely to already operate with a disease conception of alcoholism and a concomitant belief in the necessity for abstinence if all is not to be lost.

Since no letters were available for inspection, no comment can be made about the referral agent's views as to diagnosis, cause, consequence or motivation. However, the case notes, patients' comments and the comments of those who attended with the patients give clues as to the reason for the referral being made at that time.

Six of the eight cases reported the patient as being 'suicidal', and this rather than alcoholism is given as the reason for the referral:

'. . . this morning . . . the Samaritans had been contacted about him following a suicidal attempt . . . '

'. . . definitely suicidal'

'. . . alcoholic, suicidally depressed'.

A further referral which led to in-patient admission was described in the case notes as:

'Certainly an alcoholic with incipient D.T.'s, paranoid, aggressive . . . requiring admission . . . essentially'.

The patient reported that 'I want to kill someone . . . sick of being pushed around . . . by society . . . ' and since he was considered likely '. . . to kill himself' was '. . . admitted for the safety of himself and others'.

The only A.A. referral which did not result in in-patient admission was a:

'. . . woman of 45 suffering from alcoholism of long standing presenting on account of desperate social circumstances to which alcoholism has brought her . . . '

Rather than in-patient admission she was given an out-patient appointment, which she kept, and was referred to a local reception centre. The distinguishing feature of this case may have been that:

> 'although spirits are low she is not suicidal'.

No replies were sent to A.A. from the hospital concerning any of these patients. Whether anyone from A.A. rang the hospital to enquire about the outcome of the referrals is impossible to say. However, it might be expected that there would have been some contact since the cases were by definition, as immediate in-patient admissions, serious. Similarly, the possibility of the local A.A. making contact with the A.A. group in the hospitals to which these patients were referred may have been considered.

Most of the referrals from *other hospitals* were rejected, and these will be discussed in the next section. However, some referrals from other hospitals were 'unrefusable' and were thus accepted. It could be argued that one hospital with scarce facilities can only pass a patient to another hospital with scarce facilities also if it is able to make the case either very attractive or unrefusable. It will be seen later how attempts to make cases attractive failed. However, some referrals were 'successful', and these were the ones in which the referring hospital demonstrated a clear lack of ability to deal with the case itself. One resulted from a 'very difficult' situation in which 'Neither Mrs. X, nor her husband speak English'. Her daughter 'gave me a reasonable history', however, the patient:

> 'is now a little paranoid in her attitude so that she wishes to be seen alone, which means that her only daughter is precluded from interpreting for her'.

consequently

> 'everyone is very anxious that she should be seen by a German-speaking psychiatrist in the hope that this may prove helpful'.

In short, the case was unrefusable in that hospital H was obliged to accept it on the grounds that it could not be assured that others, while they may have been *willing,* were *able* to give the care that was needed.

Most of the other referrals from 'another hospital' which succeeded did so because there were made 'across-specialties'. For example, a consultant chest physician working in a chest clinic wrote in detail about his successful treatment of a patient's tuberculosis. The T.B. treatment began in 1959 and in recent years:

> ' . . . he has kept fairly well as far as his chest is concerned and his tuberculosis has shown no signs of reactivating; his last X-ray here was on the 23rd April, 1971'.

The letter went on to describe the fact that the patient

> '. . . has always been a heavy drinker and has smelt of alcohol on many occasions when he attended the clinic. He admitted in 1965 to drinking 14 pints of beer a day, . . . (the referral to hospital H was made in 1971) . . . he has been unemployable for many years and has let himself deteriorate very badly. He now admits to spending every penny that he can on drink . . . I would appreciate anything you can do for him'.

Again, this could be described as an unrefusable case in that it could not be assumed that it could be handled where it was. Further contact was discouraged in that no reply was sent to the referral agent. All other referrals from 'other hospitals' were rejected and come into the next category.

C. Reject the Referral and Discourage Further Referrals from That Source

The third category is made up of those small number of referrals which were explicitly rejected. All of them came from 'other hospitals'. It could be argued that if specialists are gate-keepers to scarce medical facilities then they are most likely to reject cases which they are not obliged — as defined previously — to accept. The rejected referrals from 'other hospitals' were without exception more serious in terms of reported problems and prognosis than those which were accepted. In one case, for example, the referring hospital described in detail the social, physical, psychological deterioration of the patient and concluded that:

> 'He is a pleasant enough chap who freely admits and discusses his problem and I think sincerely wants a cure. From his recent record I think this will only be possible with prolonged specialist treatment which we are not really able to give . . . '

The letter adds, as a final piece of evidence as to the seriousness of the case that:

> 'If he does not stop drinking now, his prognosis from the point of view of his liver is obviously very poor, and one might expect him to live another five years'.

The reply from hospital H, after the single out-patient visit, repeated the details about the seriousness of the condition and concluded that:

> '. . . as you suggest, it seems imperative now that he should undergo a period of in-patient investigation and management, preferably in a specialized setting'.

but added that:

> 'Unfortunately our waiting list here is fairly long, and since he does not live within the hospital catchment area, I cannot see a bed becoming available within the next two months'

and suggested to the referring hospital that:

> ' . . if you would, therefore, explore the local services, then this might be the best policy'.

As a concession the letter ended by saying that hospital H had:

> ' . . . put his name on the waiting list, and it can certainly stay there if there are no alternatives available'.

Thus, the referral failed. It might be said that the case was over-sold, in that by pressing it as extremely urgent it meant that in fact immediate admission was being asked for. The impression was certainly given that immediate admission was considered to be the only possible course of action. However, once the 'waiting list' response was made by hospital H, backed up by the catchment area rule, the referring hospital's ploy had failed. Even the waiting list 'offer' could hardly be accepted, since that would have been tantamount to admitting that the case was not as urgent as had been suggested. As in all bargains and exchanges the higher the stakes the greater the setback if a move fails.

In a situation in which it is legitimate to pass the case back — because there is specialist cover at the referring hospital — it is difficult to see how a successful referral could be made, especially in cases when the catchment area rule can be invoked as well. This is not to say, of course, that if we know where the patient lives we should be able to predict whether or not a referral will be accepted. Since only 15 per cent of patients with drink-related problems seen at hospital H came from within the catchment area this is obviously not so. But in any case, rules do not work in that way. They do not automatically control action. They are not disembodied standards, but human arrangements to be invoked in particular situations. As Strauss succinctly puts it:[13]

> ' . . . actors define rules as relevant to situations, which means that they must define situations as related or unrelated to specific governing rules. Consequently . . . people expect rules to control their own and others' behaviour. They also counter others' claims to be rule-appliers with claims of their own'.

Referral Behaviour

For much of this chapter attention has been focused on the case notes of people referred to the out-patient department of a psychiatric hospital. The act of referral plays an important part of the process of being diagnosed as, or coming to take oneself to be, an alcoholic. In addition, referral behaviour is of particular research interest since the referral agent does have to, in a sense, come clean about his idea of what counts as alcoholism, alcohol-related problem, an appropriate referral and the appropriate time for making it.

But any attempt to explain why referral agents do what they do must also be informed by a consideration of the activities and practices of those to whom they have referred in the past, or might be likely to refer in the future. The potential referral agents will be to a greater or lesser extent aware of the ideas which the staff who control scarce resources have about 'what counts as' an appropriate referral. Similarly, they will have either experienced or not experienced those procedures for handling referrals which are considered to be inappropriate. For if we are to understand social action in any situation we must attempt to tease out the rules which are taken by particular categories of people as justifications for action, and attempt to explain why certain people's claims to be rule-appliers are more successful than other people's.

David Goldberg,[14] writing about psychiatry in general practice claims that:

'G.P.'s only refer one in 20 of their disturbed patients to a psychiatrist', and suggests that:

> 'If they were only slightly less selective in their referrals, the out-patient service would be brought to its knees'.

It could be argued that just as important in any explanation of why out-patient services are not 'brought to their knees' is the specialist medical practitioner's ability to discourage 'uncontrollable' or 'unrefusable' referrals.

Chapter 8

Treatment 'Success'

'Scientists have not found a specific treatment of alcoholism. One treatment seems to be as good as any other. Indeed, there is no conclusive evidence that any treatment is better than no treatment. Treatments are administered on the faith that they do more good than harm'.
Mulford.[1]

Whenever alcohologists are gathered together at meetings, seminars, conferences, summer schools and the like, they can usually be relied upon to spend a great deal of time discussing two core questions: 'What is alcoholism?' and 'How should alcoholism be treated?'. Answers to the first question range from 'alcoholism is an illness' to 'alcoholism is a moral failing' via 'alcoholism is a crime, a sin, a social reaction, a bad habit, a learning fault, a mistake, a genetic, physical, social or psychological weakness' and many more. While in response to the second question may be heard the claims for 'psycho-therapy', 'counselling', 'milieu therapy', 'hypnosis', 'social support', 'psycho-analysis', 'occupational therapy', 'community action', 'transactional analysis', ''aversive conditioning' and any combination or permutation among them.

An intimately-related core issue which tends to receive rather less attention at such gatherings is the question of what should be the outcome or goal of any treatment programme. In other words, 'to what end' are people who are deemed to have some alcohol-related problem given psycho-therapy, counselling, hypnosis, social support or whatever? What would have to happen for such a 'treatment' to be 'successful'? The aim of this chapter is to discuss some of the issues involved in a consideration of the 'success' of alcoholism treatment. The South London survey was in no sense part of a study of treatments or a treatment trial. Nevertheless it afforded an opportunity to gain some idea of what professionals working in the study locality and members of the general public considered treatment success to be. For while the views of experts and the propaganda of governments and other interested bodies may suggest a particular range of criteria in terms of which to judge the success of particular treatments it is the principles and priorities of those who are actually involved in helping situations which determine the course and outcome of actual problems and conditions.

Treatment 'Outcomes' and 'Treatment 'Goals'

The early development of alcoholism treatment programmes was characterized by a tendency to think in terms of one population of alcoholics, who needed treatment by one best method, with a view to one therapeutic outcome. However, the increasing specialist interest taken in alcohol-related problems over the past 30 years has resulted in a loosening-up of this kind of approach. Jellinek's seminal work clearly encouraged those concerned with alcoholism treatment to think of alcoholism*s* rather than alcoholism, while the rapid increase in medical professional interest, plus the greater sophistication of much clinical research, undermined the search for the one best treatment.

But while alcoholism changed to alcoholisms and treatment to treatments, attention in the professional literature has remained fixed until very recently on only one treatment goal — abstinence. It is certainly true that De Morsier and Feldman,[2] Lemere,[3] Shea,[4] Norvig and Neilson,[5] Pfeffer and Berger,[6] Selzer and Holloway,[7] Fox and Smith,[8] Moore and Ramseur[9] followed by Davies,[10] Lambert,[11] Kendall[12] and many more, report that some alcoholics have been able to 'return to normal drinking'. But these studies merely report 'return to normal drinking' as an *outcome* of treatment, or non-treatment in the cases of Lemere and Kendell, in a certain proportion of cases. 'Return to normal drinking' has rarely been set out explicitly as a *goal* of treatment in any therapeutic setting. In fact, it seems that decisions about the purpose or aims of treatment often go by default. One way of making clear the status of any statement about treatment is to maintain the simple analytic distinction between the *outcome* of treatment: something which 'comes out' at the end of treatment, and the *goal* of treatment: something which the treatment is designed to accomplish. In many papers on alcoholism treatment it is difficult to make out to which of these two very different things the author is referring.

Many of the 'return to normal drinking' studies contained methodological weaknesses, such as those identified by Gillespie,[13] which may have deterred some clinicians from taking 'return to normal drinking' seriously as a treatment goal. But, for whatever reason, the notion that, in Kessel and Walton's terms, 'the "cure" calls for total abstinence from alcohol'[14] appears to be firmly entrenched. As Glatt puts it:

> ' . . . the cardinal rule at the present state of knowledge still remains that the alcoholic has to refrain from taking alcoholic drinks altogether for the rest of his life'.[15]

It could be argued, of course, that books like Kessel and Walton's and Glatt's are not designed to reveal 'the real' goals of treatment as much as to spread certain ideas — such as that 'alcoholics can never drink again' or 'one drink then drunk' — which are intended to make it more likely that the general population, potential or actual alcoholics, or the intimates of potential or actual alcoholics, will act sensibly, present their problems at an early stage, or act in some way which is deemed to be appropriate by those specialists concerned with the treatment of alcohol-related problems. In short, such books may be written with strategic-therapeutic rather than scientific-explanatory aims. Thus, in order to answer the empirical question 'Is abstinence the main goal of alcoholism treatment?' we would need to look at things other than the books written for the general population.

What is really needed, of course, is a study of 'professionals in action' in order to see the way they handle their everyday work, set their goals, make efforts to achieve them, and the way in which that work is received and perceived by those others who are involved. But another way of approaching the question 'Is abstinence the main goal of alcoholism treatment?' is to look at the reports of treatment research. As a preliminary move in this direction let us take the popular collection of papers which were presented at the International Symposium on Alcohol and Alcoholism[16] as a memorial to Jellinek the 'father of the scientific approach to the problems of alcohol'.

Four of the chapters deal with the treatment of alcoholism and make statements about 'treatment goals'. In Chapter 22 'Psycho-therapeutic methods in alcoholism' Guido Solari C. has this to say:

> 'Today, strictly speaking, we cannot cure the alcoholic, we cannot offer to remove his loss of control and make him a normal drinker. We can only help to prevent his abnormality from being actualised. Abstinence, as an improvement criterion, can be discussed but undoubtedly it appears as a condition for the readjustment of the alcoholic patient'.[17]

Significantly, 'abstinence, as an improvement criterion' is *not* 'discussed'. In Chapter 23 'Drugs in the treatment of alcoholism' Gunnar, A. R. Lundquist makes the distinction between:

> 'The medical treatment during the acute stages (which) would constitute the *treatment of a syndrome,* (and) . . . the medical and psychological treatment after the acute stage . . . the *treatment of a person* who must be helped to change his habits and learn to abstain from alcohol.[18]

In Chapter 24 'Alcoholism: the analysis of treatment' Griffith Edwards points out that:

> 'A common element in all the different approaches (today employed in most parts of the world for the treatment of alcoholism) is that the

alcoholic is required to register himself as a patient . . . he is then offered a relationship with the therapist and he will be told categorically that he is not to touch a drop of alcohol again . . . '.[19]

Edwards then goes on to describe a study in which he and his colleagues compared the value of out-patient and in-patient treatment. After discussing the sample, randomization, comparability of groups, size of sample and the treatment, he outlines the rating of the results. Each patient was rated each month. In any month he could earn a maximum of two points. The basis of the rating was as follows:

'2 points: Completely sober for the month under consideration or occasionally drinking without interference with social function.
1 point: Drinking more than occasionally or drinking occasionally causing mild social incapacity (e.g. patients missing a few days work).
No points: Heavy drinking causing considerable social incapacity (e.g. prolonged unemployment, hospitalization, imprisonment).[20]

In Chapter 25 'Evaluation of the results of alcoholism treatment' Horwitz and associates survey three well-known treatment studies by Davies, Shepherd, and Myers[21], by Glatt[22] and by Dintrans and Arce[23] all of which used abstinence as the success or recovery criterion.

'Only one patient was lost during the two-year period of observation. Of the other 49, 10 suppressed all ingestion of alcoholic beverages . . . (Davies et al).

The results can be summarised as follows: one-third practised abstinence during the whole period of observation; one third . . . (Glatt)

The results were: complete recovery, that is total abstinence, in 17·51 per cent; . . . (Dintrans and Arce)'. *Horwitz*.[24]

Clearly, at the level of everyday propaganda and at the level of talking to scientific colleagues there is little doubt that, as Horwitz puts it, 'the goal today in the treatment of alcoholism is complete abstinence from alcoholic beverages'.[25] Nevertheless, while 'total abstinence' is widely taken to be the goal of treatment it is not the case, of course, that this position is never discussed or questioned. Pattison, in particular, has addressed himself to the question of how useful it is to see abstinence as *the* goal of treatment[26] and has recently presented an outline for a 'multi-variate model for treatment' which focuses on the:

' . . . interaction between different populations of alcoholics, who may receive different treatments that may produce different outcomes'.[27]

Very briefly, the thrust of Pattison's paper is that we should consider rehabilitation in terms of total 'Life Health' which in turn he takes to be made up of: (1) Drinking Health (divided into five sub-sets: abstinence, social, modified, controlled and normal drinking); (2) Emotional Health; (3) Vocational Health; (4) Interpersonal Health and (5) Physical Health. He re-emphasizes that not all alcoholics are impaired in each area of Life Health, nor do all alcoholics require rehabilitation in each area of Life Health. Neither does impairment in one area necessarily bear a high correlation with an impairment in other areas of Life Health. Pattison stresses that a change in drinking status is *not* highly predictive of changes in other variables of Life Health, for while it may be reasonable clinical assumption that a person will be able to achieve better adaptation in other areas if his drinking improves there are two confounding sets of observations. One is that drinking may not improve, while there may be improvement in other Life Health areas.[28] The other is that drinking may improve, but at the same time there may be no change or even a deterioration in other Life Health areas.[29] We cannot assume, therefore, that treatment focusing on drinking per se will produce positive effects on other areas of life function. In conclusion Pattison says that there is a clear need to describe:

> '. . . the degree of disability in each area of Life Health, to specify the areas of Life Health to which specific treatments should be addressed, to define the expected degree of improvement that can be expected, and then to develop specific treatment methods for each target area where improvement is to be sought'.[30]

Pattison's paper attempts to tease out and distinguish some of the major elements running through any alcoholism treatment programme. By making explicit the relationship between a whole range of goals and therapeutic strategies he seeks to modify the more traditional view of the role of abstinence such as that put forward in the chapter on alcoholism in the *American Handbook of Psychiatry:*

> 'The goals of treatment may vary with factors in the patient, the therapist, and the therapeutic situation, with reference to all the parameters save one: abstinence must be total and life long'.[31]

Professionals' Views on Abstinence

The views of prestigious professionals in prestigious publications, however, may not be representative of the views of professionals at ground level who make the day-to-day decisions about the goals of treatment in any particular case. The idea that 'abstinence must be total and life long' was held by less than half of the professionals who were interviewed in the study area. Table 1 shows that general practitioners were most likely and social workers least likely to agree with the statement that 'life long abstinences is the only goal in treating alcoholism'.

TABLE 1. Professionals' views on lifelong abstinence

		G.P.s %	S.W.s %	P.O.s %
'Lifelong abstinence is the only goal in treating alcoholics'	Strongly agree	23·3	—	13·0
	Agree	40·0	17·9	34·8
	Uncertain	10·0	28·6	13·0
	Disagree	23·3	32·1	8·7
	Strongly disagree	3·3	21·4	30·4
	N =	30	28	23

This reluctance to see abstinence as the only goal in treatment may be due to the realistic assessment that, in fact, it is only a minority of alcoholics who do stop drinking after treatment. Table 2 also shows that the professionals did not believe it was necessary for an alcoholic to stop drinking before he can be helped.

TABLE 2. Abstinence before treatment and success of treatment geared to abstinence

		G.P.s %	S.W.s %	P.O.s %
'The alcoholic cannot be helped until he has stopped drinking	Strongly agree	6·5	—	4·5
	Agree	16·2	7·1	13·6
	Uncertain	6·5	21·4	9·1
	Disagree	51·6	57·1	63·6
	Strongly disagree	19·4	14·3	9·1
	N =	31	28	22

		G.P.s %	S.W.s %	P.O.s %
'The majority of alcoholics stop drinking after treatment'	Strongly agree	3·4	—	—
	Agree	3·4	—	—
	Uncertain	31·0	31·8	17·4
	Disagree	44·8	59·1	73·9
	Strongly disagree	17·2	9·1	8·7
	N =	29	22	23

As well as agreeing or disagreeing with general statements about treatment goals and outcome, the professionals in the study locality discussed one specific patient or client on their case load who had an alcohol-related problem. At the end of the discussion the general practitioners, social workers and probation officers were asked to say what they felt had been the net result for their client of all the contact which they had had both with them and with other agents. As can be seen from Table 3 almost half of the professionals who were able to identify a specific case felt that the overall effects of their intervention had been minimal, at best.

TABLE 3. Effects of professional involvement

		N	%[b]
Nil, none, no change, no effect		17	29·8
Minimal, short-term change		9	15·8
No change in drinking behaviour		4	7·0
Improvement	non-specific	7	12·3
	in drinking behaviour	7	12·3
	in social relations/situations	11	19·3
Deterioration		4	7·0
	N =	57[a]	

[a] Twenty-five professionals did not have a case about which they could talk fully.
[b] Total per cent = more than 100 per cent since some respondents mentioned more than one effect.

Several respondents (12) merely said that there had been 'no result' of all the professional intervention, while others elaborated the point a little (5):

> 'Nothing really has happened. It's going to be difficult. Client doesn't see it as a problem so it's hard to work out what to do'.
>
> 'Very very little, I don't feel I'm getting anywhere'.
>
> 'Nil for him, we haven't been of any benefit at all, even the probation officer who's known him for some years'.

One in six of the professionals (9) felt that there had been some minimal or short-term improvement, but these professionals were hard pressed to give any solid reason for this:

> 'Pretty minimal really although we have enabled her to keep going out'.
>
> 'Total confusion on my part. The bills are sorted out but danger of repeat situation. I'm not really sure how bad his drinking is'.

'I felt we were beginning to get somewhere, then there was the present incident (fight in a pub). I still don't feel totally unhelpful'.

'Minimal. It may have provoked him to think about his contribution to the breakdown of his marriage'.

Several of the professionals, however, *were* able to report a range of improvements which they felt had resulted from their own work and the work of other agents. Some just reported that the results were excellent or very good (7) while others identified the improvement as being either in the area of drinking behaviour (7):

'No drinking for 18 months'.

'Drinking more controlled'.

'Cut down on drinking, not cut it out altogether'.

or in the client/patient's social situation or everyday social relationships ,11):

'Have kept the family together in a gross way. On balance I think that's good'.

'She's been to see her son. She's coping financially and she seems to be recovering from the break-up of her marriage'.

On the other hand, four of the professionals thought that the situation had declined during the period of their involvement:

'Before Christmas he was in as bad a state as I've ever seen him. All his defences are going. He looks shabby. I saw him staggering — touching the walls of the corridor. His thought processes were disturbed and his concentration going. I thought he was beginning to look like an alcoholic'.

while two felt that their involvement may have been quite counterproductive:

'I have given the client hope of help which may well be a false hope'.

'My presence only exacerbates his behaviour. I'm another one who's seen as against him and for his wife'.

General Population's Views on Abstinence

As well as gaining some idea of the *professionals'* views on treatment success and outcome the South London study provided some material on how abstinence and abstainers are perceived by the *general population.* In Chapter 2 it was seen that only four per cent of the general population sample said that they had never had a drink in their lives while a further seven per cent said that they had not drunk in the previous year. But in spite of this small percentage of non-drinkers, one in five of the general population said that they 'approved' of 'people who do not drink at all'. In addition to giving a general opinion on abstainers, respondents were asked whether they thought that 'people who do not drink at all are missing out on anything?' and if so what it was that they were missing out on. Forty-six (16 per cent) thought that abstainers were missing out on something, and the great majority of them gave reasons which suggested that abstainers were missing out on something good:

> 'It can do you good. It can pep you up'.
>
> 'Weekends in the pub. There is music and you meet people, especially if you are lonely'.
>
> 'Fun. If you're sitting with friends talking and you have a drink you feel good'.
>
> 'I think there's a matching mixture of food and drink. There's a combination of certain dishes with complimentary wines that make a meal complete'.

Since abstainers are a relatively small minority of the population their position can be either supported or undermined by the actions and attitudes of others. For example, they can be openly praised or criticized. A larger population of drinkers, 15 per cent, said that they had 'praised someone for not drinking at all' than said they had 'criticized', four per cent. However, when the abstainers in the sample were asked about the reaction of others to them a much higher proportion, 37 per cent, said that they had 'been criticized for not drinking at all, by someone who does drink' than said that they had been praised, 14 per cent. As well as being criticized for their abstention 38 per cent had in the past year been put under pressure by other people attempting to persuade them to have a drink.

TABLE 4. Results of 'persuasion'

	To stop altogether %	To cut down %
Gave up permanently	4·0	2·3
Gave up for a while	16·0	—
Cut down	20·0	60·9
Carried on as before	60·0	36·8
N =	25	87

However, persuasion is used not only to try to get abstainers to drink but also to try to get other drinkers to stop or cut down. In fact, one in 10 of drinkers said that they had tried to persuade someone to give up drinking altogether' while almost one in three had tried to persuade someone 'to cut down on their drinking'. As Table 4 shows, people appeared to be more successful in persuading people to cut down than they were in persuading them to stop altogether.

Abstinence and 'Other' Goals of Treatment

It is *not* being suggested in this chapter that abstinence has been unthinkingly accepted as the prime goal of treatment. Anyone who has been concerned with the day-to-day treatment of alcoholics knows that this is not the case. But while other goals may have been worked toward, in therapies of various kinds, abstinence has been the goal of treatment which has tended to be made most explicit to the alcoholic and his intimates, to the general public and to various medical-scientific publics. In addition, there is no denying that abstinence is a particularly useful multi-purpose idea for the therapist to have at his disposal. It is fairly easy to define, and in the field of alcoholism which is not short of major definitional problems this is a bonus which is unlikely to be lightly discarded. Further, it is useful at so many different points in the treatment process.

First it is useful as an index of motivation *prior* to treatment. The advantage of this for the therapist is that only those people who have clearly made a key first step — given up drinking — are accepted for treatment. The disadvantage is that those who most need treatment may be least likely to get it.

Second, it is useful as a control and maintenance mechanism *during* specialist treatment.[32] The advantage of this is that it ensures that everyone can have a chance to live in a drink-free environment. The disadvantages are that, again, those who need treatment are most likely to be thrown out of specialist units or hostels, and that it trains people to live in an 'abnormal' environment which they will not be able to maintain outside.[33]

Third, it is useful as an improvement, success of treatment or research *outcome criterion* and as a goal of therapy. The advantage is that, compared with some goals of treatment it is easy to define. The disadvantages are that it is difficult to operationalize for research or follow-up purposes outside 'abnormal' and closed settings,[34] it may only bear a tenuous relationship to the problem(s) which caused the person to be defined as an alcoholic in the first place or which caused him to seek or agree to being treated, and it encourages people to feel that they have failed unless total permanent sobriety has been achieved.[35]

Clearly, the decision to advocate abstinence in any of these ways in relation to any case will be associated with the aetiological theory in terms of which the therapist defines the nature of the particular alcohol-related problem with which he is faced, and depends also on how he weighs up the advantages and disadvantages of invoking the need for abstinence at any particular point in the treatment process.

Apart from abstinence there are two main types of 'other' alcoholism treatment goals. First, there is treatment which could be geared to some form of return to or attainment of 'normal' or 'controlled' drinking.[36] Pattison[37] has discussed the distinction between the two while Offer and Sabshin[38] analyse the concept of 'normality'. Second, there is treatment which focuses on the return to or attainment of adequate or normal social, emotional or intra-psychic functioning. There is some evidence to suggest that alcoholics with controlled drinking show improvement in other areas of Life Health[39] while similar evidence has been accumulated in various behavioural modification programmes.[40] However, there is little point in attempting to catalogue in any detail the myriad 'other' particular goals which treatment of some kind might be designed to achieve or lead toward. Clearly, once this area of the alcoholism treatment process is explicitly loosened-up we shall find as many 'goals' as there are definitions of alcoholism and therapeutic strategies. Nevertheless there are certain consequences of such an explicit loosening-up which we might wish to consider, and certain questions which are constantly posed for those who are involved with any kind of alcoholism treatment.

Loosening-up on 'Goals': Some Consequential Questions

> 'Implicit in the use of a goal achievement model is the ability to define presenting problems in operational terms, to develop terminal goals toward which therapeutic change can be directed, and to establish an on-going system for measuring the direction and magnitude of change'. *Tischler and Riedel.*[41]

It could be argued that the concentration upon abstinence as the primary treatment goal has served to cover up some of the core disagreements or differences of perspective which underlie *any* therapeutic encounter. As has been suggested already the invocation of 'the need for abstinence' can be a common unifying thread running through diverse aspects of any particular treatment process. It can be the common thread linking together different types of treatment and different types of facility, and it can link together, in their common definition of its necessity and importance, drinkers, their intimates and various helping professions which may be involved in any particular case.

The statement by Tischler and Riedel at the head of this section draws our attention to three questions which have to be answered by anyone involved in treatment, and particularly by those who see their treatment in any particular case as 'leading to' something as well as 'being a response to' something. However, it is essential that we do not slip into the trap of seeing these questions in some sort of pre-ordained chronological sequence: definition of the problem, determination of goals, therapeutic intervention, evaluation. We do not, in practice, answer the first question then move on to the second, the third and so on. These questions are independent and a general position on any one of them may determine the presence or the absence of, or the timing of a consideration of, any other. For example, there are many people who see little point in defining or 'seeing' alcohol-related problems of various kinds because of moral–ethical reasons: 'a person certainly has the right to drink himself to death if he wants to', because of medical–administrative reasons: 'I have more valuable/productive things I can do with my time than work on alcohol-related problems', or because of medical–therapeutic reasons: 'there is no point in diagnosing alcoholism because no one can do anything for alcoholics anyway'. Nevertheless, elements of Tischler and Riedel's statement can serve as foci for further discussion.

The Problem, Says Who?

'. . . the ability to define presenting problems in operational terms'.

Intimately related to any question of the goal of treatment is the question of what is being treated anyway. The last section of Chapter 4 focused on certain social consequences of the increasing tendency to operate with a rather ill-defined notion of alcoholism as a disease, while Chaper 6 discussed the question of what is taken by various categories of people to count as alcoholism in particular situations. However, once 'abstinence' is rejected as the only explicit treatment 'goal' then what is taken to be the nature of the particular presenting problem has to be brought out into the open from underneath the overall umbrella of 'alcoholism'. And once this is done we run straight into the question of whose definition of the problem is the 'real' one, or the one which is going to inform the construction of a treatment programme geared to the attainment of certain goals.

On the question of 'whose problem is it?', at the very simplest level we can make the distinction between 'the problem' as it may be presented by a drinker and his intimates and 'the problem' as defined by a helping professional. In response to whose 'problem', in such a situation, is treatment to be initiated? Is it necessary to go through a period of mutual bargaining or persuasion to get to the position where all parties to the therapeutic endeavour agree on what the real problem is? Or does the therapist define what is to be the 'real' problem as of right, because of either his position as 'expert in relation to such problems' or because of his position as the person to whom a request for help has been made? Clearly, the way in which these questions are answered will determine the course of the treatment which is initiated and the type of judgements about its success which will be made at a later date.

It may very well be, of course, that the drinker *disagrees* with the close intimates about the nature of 'the problem'. A may present the problem in terms of B's excess drinking. B may present it in terms of A's lack of understanding or affection. In such a — crudely and simplistically presented — situation four major questions confront us.

(1) Whose problem is the 'real' one to which the therapist should give attention?

(2) If we decide that both are 'real' problems then is that fact itself the 'real' problem, or just another problem?

(3) Who are objects of treatment in this situation?

(4) If there are different 'goals' to be worked toward in resolution of different problems, how compatible are they, and if they are incompatible how is the incompatibility resolved, and further, in what ways does that resolution affect the likelihood of particular goals being achieved?

Up to now we have only considered goals in connection with those problems which are defined in individual physical, psychological or immediate interpersonal terms. Obviously, the range of 'goals' of treatment is greatly extended if 'the problem' is posed in terms of wider interpersonal, social structural or societal terms. A whole new set of definitional, strategic and therapeutic problems arise when 'the problem' of, for example, the Skid Row alcoholic or the habitual drunkenness offender is raised. Here the 'goals' of treatment in relation to any particular Skid Row alcoholic or habitual drunkenness offender may conflict with the 'goals' of sectional, or occupational interests who see 'the problem' and goals toward which intervention should be aimed in entirely different terms. It can be argued that the current move toward the establishment of detoxification centres is designed primarily to solve problems for the police, the medical profession and the courts rather than to solve the problems of those who are likely to be the clients of detoxification centres. There is, of course, nothing wrong in trying to solve police, medical professional, legal or administrative problems. The detoxification issue merely highlights the difficulty of fixing universally acceptable goals for any intervention given that 'the problem' in any particular case or situation is open to incompatible definitions.

The quotation at the head of this brief section draws attention to the need to define presenting problems in operational terms. But the problem of operationalization is secondary to, or is dependent upon the successful resolution of, the question of whose definition of 'the problem' is to count for particular therapeutic purposes in particular situations. Only after this question has been answered can we approach the question of how we can produce comparable, repeatable, explicit descriptions of problems, symptoms and diagnoses.[42]

The Goal, Says Who?

'. . . to develop terminal goals toward which therapeutic change can be directed . . .'

Those involved in any particular therapeutic encounter can either agree or disagree on the nature of 'the problem' and either agree or disagree on 'the goal of treatment'. While there is no information on the proportion of cases in which all those intimately involved agree with each other on both these definitional questions in the field of alcoholism, it is likely to be very small. If this is so then the question of whose goals are going to be the goals of treatment or intervention in relation to any case or situation is of particular importance.

Let us assume that a therapist defines a particular drinker's problem in terms of 'excessive drinking having a deleterious effect on the heart, liver or peripheral nerves' and concludes that permanent abstinence is essential if the condition is not to worsen and the drinker's life not to be shortened by several years. Let us assume also that the drinker and his intimates define the problem in terms of 'the drinking putting an unacceptable strain on family finances' and see cutting down on drinking as the desired goal. A treatment programme geared to, and which results in, the drinker's abstinence may lead to an improvement in family finances as a desired side effect. But what if the drinker becomes increasingly irritable and is sacked after a row at work. There would be those who would claim, not only with the benefit of hindsight, that the goal of treatment should have been a reduction in drinking rather than total abstinence. In other words, that the treatment should have been geared to achieving the goals desired by the drinker and his intimates rather than the goal indicated by the physical facts of the individual case as the therapist saw them. Clearly, such a proposition goes right to the heart not only of theories of alcoholism but of everyday medical practice, responsibility and ethics. For while the therapist can handle, more or less covertly, the problem of multiple definitions of the problem, it is much more difficult to gear a treatment programme to explicitly multiple goals. The therapist has to come clean and justify his position particularly when such impossible-to-reconcile goals as 'abstinence' and 'not abstinence' are the desired future states of affairs for different people intimately involved in the case. In addition, of course, any programme which attempted to take account of varying definitions of 'the optimum goals of treatment' would require knowledge of, access to and involvement in a much wider range of situations related to the everyday life of the alcoholic than any current treatment programme. Such an involvement would put a considerable, and probably unacceptable, additional burden on available resources.

One way of disguising the problem of multiple, and possible incompatible, goals is to retreat behind some global phrase such as adequate social functioning. Unfortunately, this merely pushes the problem of 'goals' one stage further back since we first have to answer the questions 'adequate for what?' and 'says who?'.[43] For example, we might pose the question as:

(1) Is the person functioning 'as well as' at some time in the past?
(2) Is the person functioning 'as well as' others of the same age, sex, class, etc.?
(3) Is the person functioning 'as well as' some ideal healthy perfectly functioning individual?
(4) Is the person functioning 'as well as' he thinks he ought to be?
(5) Is the person functioning 'as well as' his intimates think he ought to be? etc. etc.

The precise nature of these questions, who poses them, when and why, is particularly important in fields such as alcoholism when people whose behaviour is felt to be in need of change may not themselves have any desire to change it. If J. Bloggs, while being aware that his drinking habits are doing him physical damage and causing his wife worry and distress, does not wish to change them, whose claim that there is a need for his behaviour to be changed is the therapist to act upon? Is it his own, Mrs. Bloggs', Mr. Bloggs' employer, neighbour, best friend or who? Once person A's behaviour is deemed fit for medical intervention because person B, C or D is being distressed by it then first, we are only a short step away from compulsory treatment, which we may or may not want to advocate for alcoholics in certain cases and second, it is difficult to see any limit to the call for medical intervention.

If Mrs. Bloggs calls for medical help when she is worried and distressed by, and wants to change, her husband's drinking habits there is no reason to suppose that she will not call for medical help when she is worried and distressed, and wants to change, her husband's habit of watching television rather than washing up, his habits of going to football matches on Saturday afternoon rather than going shopping, or his habit of sleeping with his secretary on Wednesdays rather than with her. And given the history of alcoholism over the past 50 years it is quite likely that the medical profession would see itself duty bound to answer her call.

In the case of television versus washing up, football versus shopping and secretary versus herself on Wednesdays, Mrs. Bloggs has the same options as anyone has for dealing with aspects of their spouse's life which they find unpleasant. They can persuade, or coerce with whatever interpersonal power the relationship affords, or put up with it or they can go. The question is not whether Mr. Bloggs, by sleeping with his secretary, is sick or well but rather how his wife should react to him. There seems to be no more reason why the medical profession or the police, should answer Mrs. Bloggs' call to alter Mr. Bloggs' drinking habits, than it should answer his secretary's call to alter his sleeping-with-her habits from Wednesday to Tuesday and Thursday, or Mr. Bloggs' call to alter Mrs. Bloggs' habit of complaining about his drinking.

Although at one level, the notion of adequate social functioning raises as many definitional problems as it solves it is useful in that it draws us away from the rather sterile debate about abstinence versus normal drinking as 'the goal of treatment' for alcoholism, which at heart is about the degree of dependence which exists between abstinence and clinical improvement. Logically the alternatives are simple[44] but, unfortunately, clinical-experimentally they are difficult to assess.[45] However, the price of taking adequate social functioning seriously as a therapeutic goal is high in terms of time, money and expertise. Even if the notion is restricted to 'adequate social functioning in the family' the problems are immense. Cahn's brief discussion of family therapy makes many of the basic points:

> 'The rationale for this approach is twofold: that individual therapy having proven to have distinct limitations in its effectiveness, new therapeutic systems are needed if the desired behavioral change is to take place; and that, since the family is the primary bio-social unit in our culture, behavior and change are many times possible only when there is change in the family relationships, symbolic transactions, and roles. In this form of therapy the entire family is considered a case and is given treatment as a unit. The treatment objective is to change interaction patterns, since it is believed that the behavioral dysfunction of individuals results from dysfunctions in the total social system (the family as a whole). The therapist does not necessarily focus on any individual in the system, not even on the person(s) whose dysfunction presumably caused the family to seek help.
>
> As in group therapy, family therapy and the therapist's role in it varies from clinic to clinic. For example, the therapist may merely observe the interactional patterns for diagnostic purposes, with a view to convincing the members to rely eventually on individual treatment. Or the family may be viewed as a total social system with its own interactive and organizational form: and psychoanalytic or some other psychodynamic method may be used in a traditional way to interpret the underlying causes for the dysfunctional interactions, in order to effect individual change and thereby restore family "homeostasis". Or yet the family group may be seen as a patient-unit, with the entire treatment addressed to a group as a whole. Here, the family may be viewed as a network of interacting roles, with the therapist attempting to affect a balance in the network of relationships by interpreting to the member(s) what is dysfunctional in the network . . . '.[46]

The Success, Says Who?

> ' . . . and to establish an on-going system for measuring the direction and magnitude of change'.

In any treatment situation the question of what will count as the treatment 'moving along the right lines?' or 'leading toward being or having been a success?' is particularly important. However, at one level, there is nothing very special about such questions since everyone, whether involved in alcoholism treatment or not, is continually involved in 'the process of evaluation'.

Because we are all social and thinking animals we are all committed to understanding our everyday social lives. We all have ideas and theories about the way in which our lives work and are ordered, about what matters to people and what makes them do what they do, about what the effects of our actions are for us, for our intimates and for the wider society. All everyday social life is in essence this understanding, interpreting, attempting to control, bargaining over, theorizing about, anticipating, evaluating, learning from and being mistaken over the causes and consequences of our own actions and the actions of others. The call for 'evaluation' of particular aspects of social life, such as defence programmes, educational systems or treatment processes, is really a call for the everyday evaluation which we all engage in to be made *explicit* and *public*. The literature expounding basic principles of evaluation[47] is not primarily concerned with evaluation per se but with core methodological and technological problems involved in making the evaluative process demonstrable: the need for careful definitions of goals and methods, the need for studies to be replicable and so on.[48]

However, there are some general points which might be considered by anyone interested in, or thinking of becoming involved with, the evaluation of alcoholism treatment programmes. First, it could be argued that evaluation — making public one's goals and making public the criteria in terms of which success is to be judged — is incompatible with certain core values of medical practice. Medical students are confronted by a wealth of detail and an armoury of perspectives based upon different disciplines considered relevant to their applied practice of medicine. In response to this wide ranging and often competing sets of ideas and data Becker and his associates in their book *Boys in White: Student Culture in a Medical School,*[49] argue that the students orient their experience as trainee practitioners in terms of two core values. These values, strongly emphasized by the staff, are *medical responsibility:* 'for the patient's well being . . . the physician is most a physician when he exercises this responsibility' and *clinical experience* 'actual experience in dealing with patients and disease' which acknowledges that medical diagnosis and treatment rest upon the application of multidiscipline based knowledge which can only be learnt by doing it. Just as the good cook 'knows' the correct balance of ingredients and their manipulation without reference to a recipe — and indeed in a way which could not in its entirety be captured in a subsequent description — so the practice of medicine is over and above the application of accumulated knowledge as expressed in 'the text'. An over-emphasis on this particular feature of medical practice results, as Becker observed in relation to the medical schools which he studied, in a situation in which 'argument from experience was quite commonly used and considered unanswerable . . . '. In such a situation 'the only counter-argument that can prevail is by someone who can claim greater experience in the area discussed'. The medical student will learn to rely on feelings and results rather than theories. Sharaf and Levinson noted in their study of psychiatrists in training that:

> 'The dangers of "intellectualising" and "book learning" are stressed. The highest value is placed on emotional experience, and widening the range of the "gut response" as a means of understanding what is going on in one's self and in the patient'.[50]

Against such a background the demands, by the general public or fund givers or government departments, for aspects of the therapeutic process to be made demonstrable for evaluation are unlikely to be acceded to without difficulty.

Second, just as differential definitions of 'the problem' and 'the goal' have to be reconciled so, in any evaluation of treatment, differential definitions of 'success', 'cure' or 'improvement' have to be taken into account. The question which has to be faced, constantly reposed, and constantly reanswered throughout the treatment process is 'success says who?'. Clearly, at the simplest level the alcoholic, the alcoholic's intimates and the therapist may all differ in their ideas about who has benefited in what ways from a particular treatment programme. Is it 'success', to repeat an earlier example, if the therapist's goal of total abstinence by the drinker has been achieved but that the life of those around him is made unbearable by his irritability which eventually leads to him being sacked from his job? With conditions such as alcoholism when interpersonal relationships, their course and their difficulties, are often built into the definition of the condition the question of differential definitions of 'success' cannot be ignored?

Third, one of the biggest barriers to adequate evaluation is that the 'success' of some particular therapy may appear so obvious that it's evaluation is felt to be unnecessary. The history of the use of metrondazole (Flagyl) exemplifies this problem. Briefly, in 1959 it was clinically observed that some patients after being given Flagyl reported discomfort after drinking and also reported that they were less likely to drink.[51] Subsequently a series of uncontrolled studies were done in which series of alcoholics were given the drug and followed-up to see if there was any change in their attitude toward drink or drinking behaviour.[52] There were many fulsome patient testimonials to the efficacy and importance of the drug in alcoholism treatment. However, in subsequent controlled studies when the selection of patients was carefully done, when patients were randomly assigned to active drug or placebo and in which both the patients and the raters were unaware of which preparation had been administered it was found that Flagyl was no better than the placebo. The same glowing references such as 'it absolutely helps. Nobody can convince me otherwise' were found with equal frequency for both preparations.

The most important point about the Flagyl story is that after the *un*controlled studies many clinicians using Flagyl felt that their results were so dramatic that controlled studies were not needed. Schaeffer and associates presented some similarly 'Sobering data on the use of self-confrontation with alcoholics'.[53] There were good theoretical grounds upon which to base the use of video-tape confrontations for alcoholics. In addition, many clinicians were enthusiastic users of the technique and felt that its efficacy was so obvious as to make controlled evaluation a waste of time and money. However, controlled study revealed that patients treated with video-tape confrontation not only failed to show greater improvement than controls but actually fared worse.

The question of treatment success, its definition and its evaluation will not be 'answered' by a series of rather general remarks by a sociologist. Clearly, this chapter has not been a systematic review of the literature or a scholarly critique of specific, practical, technical or methodological problems. On the contrary it has been, by design, a question-raising exercise.

The questions which have been focused on are ones faced by and, either implicitly or explicitly answered by, everyone involved in *any* treatment situation — not just by those concerned with alcohol-related problems. It has been suggested that in the field of alcoholism it seems as though some of the questions are answered too covertly, while others are answered explicitly but without much consideration of the alternative answers which might be given by others intimately involved, or of the implications for therapy of those alternative answers being given.

Appendix

The General Population Survey

The general population survey is based on a random sample of people aged 18 and over in the study locality, which comprises approximately half of one of the South London boroughs. The population of the borough, like that of all inner London boroughs, has fallen throughout the twentieth century, with an 11·4 per cent decline between 1969 and 1971. The Greater London Council's Department of Planning and Transportation Intelligence Unit has recently produced projections based on fertility and migration assumptions using 1971 as a base. These envisage continuing population losses for the borough from the 1971 figure of 262,000 to between 189,000 (high migration and low fertility) and 199,000 (low migration and high fertility) in 1981. The study area in the south of the borough contains 13 of the borough's 23 electoral wards and 148,000 of its 262,000 population.

Sampling

Unless there is sufficient time and money to carry out a complete enumeration of a study area the difficulties of obtaining a representative sample of a general population are many and various. However, techniques for using the electoral register to provide a sampling frame for the general population are well established. The best known and most widely used is that designed for the National Readership Survey, and most probability samples used in general consumer, planning and social survey research employ this technique with minor variations.

The major problem with the above technique is the difficulty of sampling those individuals who are either not on the electoral register or who have changed their address since registration. However, the South London general population survey employed the Blyth and Marchant self-weighting random sampling technique[1] to overcome this problem.

One of the major advantages of any technique based on the electoral roll is that the interviewer goes to every address armed with the name of a specific person to be interviewed. The Blyth and Marchant technique retains this advantage while having a more satisfactory approach to selecting unregistered individuals. It also simplifies the process of selection, and ensures equal probabilities of selection between all individuals.

Setting up the Sample

The total population on the electoral register of the study area was 108,578. Given financial and, in particular, time constraints it was decided to select a basic sample of 400 individuals. This entailed the extraction of every 271st name from the polling district lists of the 13 wards which form the study area. It is after this initial selection stage that the Blyth and Marchant technique diverges from standard procedures.

Using a pro-forma, illustrated in Table 1, the sampling officer prepared a list of all the electors at each of the 400 addresses which had been selected in stage I. The sampling officer then added four stars (*) spaced at regular intervals. The interval between a star and the one below it being equal to the number of electors at the address. The first star appeared against the name of the elector who had led originally to the selection of the address.

TABLE 1. Sampling examples

Example A			Example B		
Elector No.	Elector	Interview*	Elector No.	Elector	Interview*
3061	MORGAN Doris		3061	MORGAN, Doris	
3062	MORGAN, John	*	3062	MORGAN, John	*
3063	MORGAN, Michael		3063	MORGAN, Michael	
'Other adults	SMITH, Janc			SMITH, Jane	
		*		THOMAS, Ann	*
				THOMAS, Brian	
				THOMAS, Sally	
		*			*
		*			*

As with other techniques the interviewer starts by interviewing the starred elector at the address, assuming he or she is still there. With the Blyth and Marchant method the interviewer next lists in descending age order all residents over 18 years old at the address whom the sampling officer has not previously listed. These are the 'other adults'. Interviews are then carried out with any of these individuals whose name happens to fall on the pre-starred lines. In Example 'B' there are four 'other adults' living at the address. John Morgan and Ann Thomas, the two starred people, would both be interviewed.

'It is a very simple matter, say Blyth and Marchant, to show that this procedure leads to all respondents having the same chance of selection. Imagine an address at which n electors were registered. When the interviewer has finished her enumeration, lines 1 to n contain the names of the n electors written in by the sampling officer, lines $n + 1$ onwards contain the names of non-electors added by the interviewer. If the elector on line 1 happens to have been the one selected by the sampling officer then the 'other adults' on lines $n + 1$, $2n + 1$, etc., will automatically be selected, hence their probabilities of selection are necessarily the same as that of the elector on line 1. Similarly the 'other adults' on lines $n + 2$, $2n + 2$, etc., have the same chance of selection as the elector on line 2 and so on. But all electors were given the same a priori chances of selection, whatever their address and wherever they happened to live. Therefore, all respondents have the same chances of selection, and the resulting sample is self-weighting.

Response Rate and Refusals

The crude completion rate, as Table 2 shows, was 70·8 per cent.

TABLE 2. Crude response rate

	N	%
(a) Total addresses issued	400	
Less: Vacant or demolished property	7	
= Effective total of addresses	393	
(b) Effective total of addresses	393	
Plus: Extra 'non-voters' to interview	11	
= Total possible interviews	404	
(c) Total completed interviews	286	70·8
All non-contacts	88	21·8
Refusals	30	7·4
N =	404	

However, this crude completion rate of 70·8 per cent is less than the effective completion rate since approximately half of those in the non-contact category were uninterviewable. As Table 3 shows, some people were dead, others were too young, others were senile or infirm, while others were away from home for the whole of the survey period.

TABLE 3. Non-contacts

Away from home, ill or on holiday for the whole of the survey period	4
Infirm or senile	10
Too young or spoke no English	11
The named person was dead or had moved away and no other resident was eligible for interview	18
Four or more calls at the address	45
N =	88

Of the 88 non-contacts detailed in Table 3, it is only the 45 people for whom four or more calls were made who go into the effective sample, which totals 361. The effective completion rate for the general population survey, therefore, as Table 4 shows, is 79·2 per cent and the refusal rate is 8·3 per cent.

TABLE 4. Effective completion rate

	N	%
Completed interview	286	79·2
Non-contact (4 calls or more)	45	12·5
Refusals	30	8·3
Effective sample	361	

It was part of the fieldwork routine to write down on the cover sheet of the schedule the reason why any respondent refused to be interviewed. Of the 30 who refused, 10 said that they did not like surveys, or the people who conducted them. Others refused because they were too busy, or without giving any reason for their refusal. Some refused on behalf of the intended respondent. One interviewer started an interview but had to give up half way through. She wrote the following account of the episode:

> 'Mrs. B answered the door and seemed very co-operative when I explained the survey. Her husband stood in the passage listening and walked away when I entered. Half way through Section B. II (in which the respondent talks about someone she knows well with a drinking problem) he shouted out her name and she left the room for several minutes. When she returned she asked if the interview would take much longer, as her husband was "hopping mad" because she had let me in. About 10 minutes later she was called again, she closed the door

but I could hear raised voices, mostly his. She came back in, very flustered and said she thought I should pack up and go. She said her husband was "having a go" at her and she was nervous in case he started to "cut up rough". I asked if I could complete the interview another time when he wasn't home but she said "No, he's at home all the time". I wasn't sure if she was worried about my safety or her own but I left'.

Problems of Interviewing

The main general population survey interviewing was carried out in the Spring of 1974 by 12 interviewers from the Greater London Council Social Survey Group under the direction of Mrs. Jennifer Owen. While the G.L.C. reported that there had been few problems in the actual administration of the survey, there are several indicators which suggest that drinking behaviour may have been an area about which it was difficult for the interviewers to ask questions of the general public. There is tentative evidence to suggest that, for both interviewers and respondents, there were feelings of ambivalence towards the content of the questionnaire.

Both the G.L.C. interviewers and those involved in piloting, frequently noted a very defensive reaction on the part of respondents at the outset of the interview, sometimes going as far as attempts to exclude themselves from the area of study. Respondents might, for instance, emphatically play down their drinking behaviour — 'I never drink. I won't be much help to you'. Usually, where an interview was obtained, it became apparent that the respondent had in fact taken alcohol quite recently. However, from the respondent's comments, it appears that their assumption was that if interviewers were asking questions about drinking behaviour, they were looking for alcoholics and they were anxious to dissociate themselves from such implications.

At the same time, many respondents said after the interview that they thought a study of such a 'dreadful problem' as alcoholism worthwhile and, in the words of one of the G.L.C. interviewers, 'treated it seriously, giving considerable thought to their answers'.

It does not appear to have been only the respondents who experienced some discomfort over the area of questioning. One of the G.L.C. interviewers withdrew from the survey after the briefing, and several others, despite their overall assertions that working on the study had been interesting appear to have had their doubts.

Eight questionnaires were completed after the fieldwork and returned by the G.L.C. interviewers, one of which was illegible. Of the rest, three specifically mentioned embarrassment at the nature of some of the questions and feelings of apprehension at the outset of the survey. One felt that 'people might be suspicious' about why they were chosen to answer questions about alcoholism. The other two felt that the questions were too personal and one anticipated difficulties with respondents — 'I thought they would be more hostile towards it than they were'.

Of the four who did not mention such apprehension, one stated that she had found some of the questions difficult to ask. The attitudes to the survey of the remaining four interviewers who did not return their questionnaires are, of course, not known.

It is clear then that a significant proportion of the interviewers did, at some stages of the survey, experience difficulties with areas of the questionnaire. It is possible that, in instances where the interviewers were lacking confidence in their right to ask certain questions, this may have affected the extent to which respondents felt willing or able to discuss their own drinking problems or those of people known to them. For their part, interviewers may have been less positive in their probing than would have been the case if they had not experienced doubts.

Representativeness

In an attempt to assess the representatives of the sample, the material was compared with the 1971 census data for the 13 wards of which the study area was comprised. Tables 5 and 6 show that the overall age and sex breakdowns were adequately representative.

TABLE 5. Sex distribution

	1971 Census		Sample	
	N	%	N	%
Males	52,424	46·6	134	46·0
Females	60,064	53·4	152	54·0
N =	112,488		286	

TABLE 6. Age distribution

	1971 Census		Sample	
	N	%	N	%
18 – 34	34,895	31·0	91	31·9
35 – 54	37,734	33·5	84	29·5
55+	39,829	35·4	110	38·6
N =	112,488		285	
DK			1	

TABLE 7. Age – sex distribution

Age	Males 1971 Census N	Males 1971 Census %	Males Sample N	Males Sample %	Females 1971 Census N	Females 1971 Census %	Females Sample N	Females Sample %
18–24	8,348	15·9	22	16·4	8,554	14·2	13	8·6
25–34	8,875	16·9	28	20·9	9,118	15·2	28	18·5
35–44	8,561	16·3	19	14·2	8,850	14·7	20	13·2
45–54	9,829	18·7	20	14·7	10,524	17·5	25	16·5
55–64	9,714	18·5	17	12·7	10,323	17·2	28	18·5
65+	7,097	13·5	28	20·9	12,695	21·1	37	24·5
N =	52,424		134		60,064		151	
DK							1	

TABLE 8. Completion rate and social status - x - 1971 census wards

Ward	Completion rate N	out of N	= %	% of respondent in social status categories 1–3a %
1	30	35	85·7	27·6
2	24	28	85·7	66·7
3	27	34	79·4	55·6
4	23	31	74·2	36·4
5	22	31	73·3	57·1
6	18	25	72·0	22·2
7	26	37	70·3	58·3
8	17	25	68·0	52·9
9	23	34	67·6	20·0
10	12	18	66·7	50·0
11	14	21	66·7	50·0
12	34	39	61·5	36·0
13	25	46	54·3	32·0
N =	285	404	70·5	
DK Ward	1			
6 Wards with *above* average (70·5%) completion rate				43·9
7 Wards with *below* average (70·5%) completion rate				41·5

Table 7 which displays the age and sex data in more detail, shows that compared with the 1971 census data the sample was *under-represented* by females in the 18–24 age group and males in the 55–64 age group and *over-represented* by people over 65 of both sexes. There is no way of telling, of course, whether the sample or the 1971 census distributions are most representative of the actual study population in 1974.

The completion rate differed for each of the 113 census wards in the study locality. An attempt was made to see whether this introduced any significant social class bias into the sample. The completion rates for each ward were ranked and then inspected to see the percentage of respondents in each ward who were in the higher (1–3a) and lower (3b–5) Registrar General's socio-economic class categories. Figure 8 shows that the percentage of respondents in social class categories 1–3a was about the same in the low completion rate wards as in the high completion rate wards.

References

Chapter 1

1. Catanzaro, R. J., 'Psychiatric aspects of alcoholism', *in* Pittman, D. J. (Ed.), *Alcoholism,* Harper and Row, New York, 1967.
2. Keller, M., 'Problems with alcohol', paper presented to the International Symposium on Alcoholism and Alcohol Problems, Lutheran General Hospital, Chicago, 1973.
3. For a clear brief account of this topic see Kendis, J. B., 'The human body and alcohol', *in* Pittman, D. J. (Ed.), *Op. Cit. 1.*
4. MacAndrew, C. and Edgerton, R. B., *Drunken Comportment: a social explanation,* Nelson, London, 1970.
5. Mandelbaum, D. G., 'Alcohol and culture', *Current Anthropology,* 6, 3, 281, 282 (1965).
6. For a good review of this literature see Mandelbaum, D. G., *Ibid.*
7. Renov, L., *The Civilisation of Ancient India,* Susil Gupta, Calcutta, 1954.
8. Numbers, 28: 7–8.
9. John, 2: 3–10.
10. Luke, 10: 34, I Timothy, 5: 23.
11. Mathew, 26: 27–29, Mark 14: 23–25, Luke 22: 17–18.
12. I. Timothy, 3: 8 see also Titus, 2: 3, Ephesians, 5: 18.
13. Mandelbaum, D. G., *op. cit.* 5, p. 281.
14. Netting, R., *A West African Beer Complex, Unpublished* 1962, cited in Mandelbaum, D. G. reference 5.
15. Parsons, E. C., *Pueblo Indian Religion,* 2 Vols., University of Chicago Press, Chicago, 1939.
16. Heath, D. B., 'Drinking Patterns of the Bolivian Camba', *Quart. J. Stud. Alc.,* **19,** 491, 1958. For other good studies see the bibliography to this article and the article by Mandelbaum cited in reference 5.
17. Honigmann, J. J., 'Dynamics of drinking in an Austrian village', *Ethnology,* **2,** 157–169. 1963.
18. Mulford, H. A., 'Alcoholism a concern (and creation) of every community', *Selected Papers* 18 Annual meeting M.A.A.P., Chicago, 1967.
19. U.S. Department of Health Education and Welfare, *Alcohol and Health,* U.S. Government Printing Office, Washington D.C., 1971.
20. Home Office, *Offences of Drunkenness,* 1973, H.M.S.O., London, 1974.
21. Edwards, G., Hensman, C. and Peto, J. 'Drinking problems among Recidivist Prisoners', *Psychological Medicine,* 1, 5, 388, 1971.
22. Morris, T. P. and Blum-Cooper, L., *Criminal Homicide in England and Wales,* Unpublished report, Legal Research Unit, Bedford College, University of London, 1969.
23. McClintock, F. H., *Crimes of Violence: an enquiry by the Institute of Criminology into cases of violence against the person in London,* MacMillan, London, 1963.

24. Odgers, F. J. and McClintock, F. H., *in* Radzcinowicz, L. (Ed.) *Sexual Offences a report,* MacMillan, London, 1957.
25. Willet, T. C., *The Criminal on the Road,* Tavistock, London, 1964.
26. Home Office, *Offences Relating to Motor Vehicles,* H.M.S.O., London, 1974.
27. For brief discussions of the range of social problems taken to be associated with alcohol consumption see, for example, Kessel, N. and Walton, H., *Alcoholism,* Penguin Books, Harmondsworth, 1965; Pittman, D. J. (Ed.), *Alcoholism,* Harper and Row, New York, 1967 and Glatt, M. M., *The Alcoholic and the Help he Needs,* Part 1, Priory Press, Royston, Herts, 1970.
28. For the most learned, insightful and consistently misunderstood discussion of the problems associated with defining alcoholism, see Jellinek, E. M., *The Disease Concept of Alcoholism,* Hillhouse Press, New Haven, 1960.
29. See. Jellinek, E. M., *The Disease Concept of Alcoholism,* Hillhouse Press, New Haven, 1960.
30. Ireland, Father John. The catholic church and the saloon, *North American Review* LIX, 502, 1894.
31. Glatt, M. M., *op. cit.* 27.
32. Keller, M., 'The definition of alcoholism', *Quart. J. Stud. Alc.,* **21,** 125–134, 1960.
33. Kessel, N. and Walton, H., *Alcoholism,* Penguin Books, Harmondsworth, 1965, pp. 15–16.
34. Kessel, N. and Walton, H., *Alcoholism,* Penguin Books, Harmondsworth, 1965, pp. 16–17.
35. E.g. Glatt, M. M., *op. cit.* 27.
36. E.g. Jellinek, E. M., 'Phases in the drinking history of alcoholics', *Quart. J. Stud. Alc.,* 7, 1, 1946.
37. Kessel, N. and Walton, H., *op. cit.* 27, p. 17.
38. Roebuck, J. B. and Kessler, R. G., *The Etiology of Alcoholism: constitutional, psychological and sociological approaches,* Charles C. Thomas, Springfield Illinois, 1972.
39. Horton, D., 'The functions of alcohol in primitive societies: a cross-cultural study', *Quart. J. Stud. Alc.,* **4,** 199 (1943).
40. Field, P. B., 'A new cross-cultural study of drunkenness', in Pittman, D. J. and Snyder, C. R. (Eds.), *Society, Culture and Drinking Patterns,* Wiley, New York, 1962.
41. Pittman, D. J., 'International overview: social and cultural factors in drinking patterns, pathological and non-pathological, in Pittman, D. J. (Ed.), *Alcoholism,* Harper Row, New York, 1967.
42. Spindler, D. G., 'Alcoholism symposium, editorial preview', *American Anthropologist,* **66,** 341, 1964.
43. Bales, R. F., 'Cultural differences in ideas of alcoholism', in McCarthy, R. G. (Ed.), *Drinking and Intoxication,* Free Press, New York, 1959.
44. Chlotos, J. W. and Deiter, J., 'Psychological considerations in the aetiology of alcoholism', *in* Pittman, D. J. (Ed.), *Alcoholism: an interdisciplinary approach,* Charles C. Thomas, Springfield Illinois, 1959.
45. Bales, R. F., 'Attitudes toward drinking in the Irish culture', *in* Pittman, D. J. and Snyder, C. R. (Ed.), *Society, Culture and Drinking Patterns, op. cit.* 7.
46. Cahalan, D., Cisin, I. H. and Crossley, H. M., *American Drinking Practices: a national study of drinking behaviour and attitudes,* New Brunswick, N.J., Rutgers Center of Alcohol Studies, 1969.

47. E.g. Skolnick, J. H., 'Religious affiliation and drinking behaviour', *Quart. J. Stud., Alc.*, **19,** 452 (1958), Snyder, C. R., *Alcohol and the Jews,* Free Press, Glencoe, Illinois, 1958, Knupfer, G. and Roon, R., 'Drinking patterns and attitudes of Irish, Jewish and white Protestant American men', *Quart. J. Stud. Alc.*, **29,** 679 (1967).
48. E.g. Glad, D. D., 'Attitudes and experiences of American-Jewish and American–Irish male youths as related to adult rates of inebriety', *Quart. J. Stud. Alc.*, **8,** 406 (1947); Bacon, M. and Jones, M. B., *Teen-age Drinking,* Crowell, New York, 1968. Maddox, G. L. and McCall, B. C., *Drinking among Teenagers: a sociological interpretation of alcohol use by high-school students,* Rutgers Center of Alcohol Studies, New Brunswick, New Jersey, 1964, Stacey, B. and Davies, J., 'Drinking behaviour in childhood and adolescence: an evaluative review', *Brit. J. Addict.*, **65,** 203 (1970).
49. E.g. Ullman, A. D., 'Sex differences in the first drinking experience', *Quart. J. Stud. Alc.*, **18,** 299 (1957). McCord, W., McCord, J. and Gudeman, J., *Origins of Alcoholism,* Stanford University Press, Stanford, 1960.
50. E.g. Ullman, A. D., 'Ethnic differences in the first drinking experience', *Social Problems,* **8,** 45 (1960); Whittaker, J. O., 'Alcohol and the Rock Sioux Tribe. 1. Pattern of drinking', *Quart. J. Stud. Alc.*, **23,** 468 (1962), Robins, L. A., Murphy, G. E. and Breckenridge, M. B., 'Drinking behaviour of young urban negro men', *Quart. J. Stud. Alc.*, **29,** 657 (1968).
51. E.g. Dollard, J., 'Drinking mores of the social classes', *in Alcohol, Science and Society, Quart. J. Stud. Alc.*, New Haven, 1945. Riley, J. and Marder, C. F., 'The social pattern of alcoholic drinking', *Quart. J. Stud. Alc.*, **8,** 265 (1947), Straus, R. and Bacon, S., *Drinking in College,* Yale University Press, New Haven, 1952.
52. Lolli, G., Seriani, E., Bannissoni, F., Golder, G., McCarthy, R. G., Mariani, A. and Toner, M., 'The use of wine and other alcoholic beverages by a group of Italians and Americans of Italian extraction', *Quart. J. Stud. Alc.*, **13,** 27 (1952), Edwards, G., Chandler, J. and Hensman, C., 'Drinking in a London Suburb. 1. correlates of normal drinking', *Quart. J. Stud. Alc.*, Supplement 6, 69 (1972), Moore, M., 'Chinese wine; some notes on its social use', *Quart. J. Stud. Alc.*, **9,** 270 (1948).
53. Riley, J. W. and Marder, C., *op. cit.* 51.
54. Mulford, H. A., 'Drinking and deviant drinking. U.S.A. 1963', *Quart. J. Stud. Alc.*, **25,** 674 (1964).
55. Cahalan, D. and Cisin, I. H., 'American drinking practices. Summary of findings from a national probability sample 1. Extent of drinking by population subgroups', *Quart. J. Stud. Alc.*, **29,** 142 (1968).
56. E.g. Bailey, M. P., Haberman, P. W. and Alksne, H., 'The epidemiology of alcoholism in an urban residential area', *Quart. J. Stud. Alc.*, **26,** 19 (1965), Roberts, B. H. and Myers, J. K., 'Religion, national origin, immigration and mental illness', in Weinberg, S. K. (Ed.), *Sociology of Mental Disorders,* Aldine, Chicago, 1967.
57. Keller, M., 'The great Jewish drink mystery", *Brit. J. Addict,* **64,** 287 (1970).
58. Bales, R. F., *op. cit.* 43.
59. Glad, D. D., *op. cit.* 48.
60. *Ibid.*
61. Snyder, C. R., *op. cit.* 47.

62. Edwards, G., Chandler, J. and Hensman, C., 'Drinking in a London Suburb: correlates of trouble with drinking among men', *Quart. J. Stud. Alc.*, Suppl. 6, 94 (1972).
63. Cahalan, D., *Problem Drinkers,* Jossey-Bass, San Francisco, 1970.
64. E.g. Winokur, G. and Clayton, P. J., 'Family History Studies. IV Comparisons of male and female alcoholics', *Quart. J. Stud. Alc.*, **29,** 885 (1968).
65. E.g. Skolnick, J. H., 'A study of the relation of ethnic background to arrests for inebriety', *Quart. J. Stud. Alc.*, **15,** 622 (1954).
66. Ullman, A. D., 'The first drinking experiences of addictives and "normal" drinkers', *Quart. J. Stud. Alc.*, **14,** 181 (1953).
67. E.g. Cramer, M. J. and Blacker, E., 'Social class and drinking experiences of female drunkenness offenders', *J. Health and Hum. Beh.*, **7,** 276 (1966).
68. E.g. Locke, B. Z., Kramer, M. and Pasamanick, B., 'Alcoholic psychoses among first admissions to public mental hospitals in Ohio', *Quart. J. Stud. Alc.*, **21,** 473 (1960).
69. Roberts, B. H. and Myers, J. K., *op. cit.* 56.
70. Roebuck, J. B. and Kessler, R. G., *op. cit.* 38, p. 185.
71. Wittman, M. P., 'Developmental characteristics and personalities of chronic alcoholics', *J. of Abn. Soc. Psychol.*, 34 (1939).
72. E.g. Kinsey, B. A., *The Female Alcoholic,* Thomas, Springfield, 1966; Pittman, D. J. and Gordon, C. W., *Revolving Door,* The Free Press, Glencoe, 1958; and McCord, W., McCord, J. and Gudeman, J. *Origins of Alcoholism,* Stanford University Press, Stanford, 1960.
73. Jackson, J. K. and Conner, R., 'Attitudes of parents of alcoholics, moderate drinkers and non drinkers toward drinking', *Quart. J. Stud. Alc.*, **14,** 596 (1953).
74. Kinsey, B. A., *op. cit.* 72.
75. Moore, R. A. and Ramseur, F. A., 'A Study of the background of 100 hospitalised veterans with alcoholism', *Quart. J. Stud. Alc.*, **21,** 51 (1960).
76. MacKay, J. R., 'Clinical observations in adolescent problem drinkers', *Quart. J. Stud. Alc.*, **22,** 124 (1961).
77. Clinard, M. B., 'The Public drinking house and society', *in* Pittman, D. and Snyder, C. R. (Eds.), *op. cit.* 40.
78. Moore, E. C., 'The social value of the saloon, *Amer. J. Sociol.*, **31,** 1 (1897).
79. Le Masters, E. E., 'Social life in a working class tavern', *Urban Life and Culture,* 2, 1, 27, 1973; and Sommer, R., 'The isolated drinker in the Edmonton beer parlour', *Quart. J. Stud. Alc.*, **26,** 95 (1965).
80. Cavan, S., *Liquor License: an ethnography of bar behaviour,* Aldine, Chicago, 1966, and 'Mass Observation', *The Pub and the People,* Gollancz, London, 1943.
81. Clinard, M. B., *op. cit.* 77.
82. E.g. Wallace, S. E., *Skid Row as a Way of Life,* Bedminster Press, New Jersey, 1965; Bahr, H. M., 'The gradual disappearance of Skid Row', *Social Problems,* **15,** 41 (1967).
83. Dees, J. W. Jnr., *Flophouse: an authentic undercover study of 'Flophouses', 'Cage Hotels', including missions, shelters and institutions serving unattached (homeless) men,* Marshall Jones, Francestown, New Hampshire, 1948.
84. Anderson, N., *The Hobo: the sociology of the homeless man,* University of Chicago Press, Chicago, 1923; and *Men on the Move,* University of Chicago Press, Chicago, 1940.

85. E.g. Peterson, W. J. and Maxwell, M. A., 'The Skid Row "wino" ', *Social Problems,* **5,** 358 (1958); Rubington, E., ' "Failure" as a heavy drinker: the case of the chronic-drunkenness offender on skid row', *in* Pittman, D. J. and Snyder, C. F. (Eds.), *op. cit.* 40.
86. Rosenman, S., 'The skid row alcoholic and the negative ego image', *Quart. J. Stud. Alc.,* **16,** 447 (1955); Bahr, H. M. and Langfur, S. J., 'Social attachment and drinking in skid row life histories', *Social Problems,* **14,** 464 (1967).
87. Wallace, S. E., 'The road to skid row', *Social Problems,* **16,** 92 (1968).
88. Jackson, J. K. and Conner, R., 'The skid row alcoholic', *Quart. J. Stud. Alc.,* **14,** 468 (1953).
89. Rubington, E., 'The bottle gang', *Quart. J. Stud. Alc.,* **29,** 943 (1968).
90. Archard, P., *The Bottle Wont Leave You: a study of homeless alcoholics and their guardians,* Alcohol Recovery Project, London, 1975.
91. Gerard, D. L. and Saenger, G., *Out-patient Treatment of Alcoholics,* University of Toronto Press, Toronto, 1966; Pittman, D. J., 'The open door: sociology in an alcoholism treatment facility', *in* Pittman, D. J. (Ed.), *op. cit.* 1.
92. Otto, S. and Orford, J., *Socialisation for Sobriety: a study of small hostels for alcoholics,* Addiction Research Unit, University of London (Unpub.), 1975; Rubington, E., 'Organisation strains and key roles', Administrative *Science Quarterly,* **9,** 350 (1965).
93. Bales, R. F., 'The therapeutic role of alcoholics anonymous as seen by a sociologist', *Quart. J. Stud. Alc.,* **5,** 267 (1944).
94. Jackson, J. K., Fagan, R. J. and Burr, R. C., 'The Seattle police department rehabilitation project for chronic alcoholics', *Federal Probation,* **22,** 36 (1958); and Lerner, A., 'Interaction among male alcoholic inmates', *Sociology and Social Research,* **38,** 313 (1954).
95. Bales, R. F., *op. cit.* 93.
96. Becker, H. S., *Outsiders: studies in the sociology of deviance,* Free Press, New York, 1963, p. 10.
97. Goffman, E., *Asylums,* Aldine Chicago, 1961.
98. Young, J., *The Drugtakers: the social meaning of drug use,* MacGibbon and Kee, London, 1971.
99. Wilkins, L., 'Some sociological factors in drug addiction control', in Wilner, D. and Kassebaum (Eds.), *Narcotics,* McGraw-Hill, New York, 1965.

Chapter 2

1. *In* Cohen, J. M. (compiler), *The Penguin Book of Comic and Curious Verse,* Penguin Books, Harmondsworth, 1952.
2 Brewers' Society, *Problems Behind the Pint,* Brewers' Society, London, 1970.
3. For a detailed discussion of this issue see Zacune, J. and Hensman, C. (compilers), *Drugs, Alcohol and Tobacco in Britain,* Heinemann Medical Books, London, 1971.
4 Department of Employment and Productivity, *Family Expenditure Survey,* H.M.S.O., London, published annually.
5. See the brief discussion in Moser, J. (compiler), *Problems and Programmes Related to Alcohol and Drug Dependence in 33 Countries,* W.H.O. offset Publication No. 6, Geneva, 1974.

6. Department of Health Education and Welfare, *Alcohol and Health,* Report to the U.S. Congress, D.H.E.W. No. (HSM) 72–9099, 1971.
7. *Ibid,* p. 12.
8. Kirsh, A. D., Newcomb, C. H. and Cisin, I. H., *An Experimental Study of Sensitivity of Survey Techniques in Measuring Drinking Practices* (Social Research Project Rep. No. 1), George Washington University, Washington, D.C., 1965.
9. Cisin, I. H., 'Community studies of drinking behaviour', *Ann. N.Y. Acad. Sci.,* **107**, 607–612 (1963), pp. 608–9.
10. Pernanen, K., 'Validity of survey data on alcohol use', *in* Gibbins, R., Israel, Y., Kalant, H., Popham, R. E., Schmidt, W. and Smart, R. G. (Eds.), *Research Advances in Alcohol and Drug Problems,* Vol. 1, John Wiley and Sons, New York, 1974.
11. Mäkelä, K., *Measuring the Consumption of Alcohol in the 1968–1969 Alcohol Consumption Study,* Social Research Institute of Alcohol Studies, Helsinki, 1971.
12. Kuusi, P., *Alcohol Sales Experiment in Rural Finland,* The Finnish Foundation of Alcohol Studies, Helsinki, 1957.
13. de Lint, J., Schmidt, W. and Pernanen, K., *The Ontario Drinking Survey: a preliminary report,* Addiction Research Foundation, Toronto, 1970.
14. Hochstim, J. R., 'Comparison of three information gathering strategies in a population study of socioeconomic variables', *Proc. Soc. Stat. Sect.—Am. Stat. Assoc.,* **1962**, 154.
15. Room, R., 'Survey versus sales data for the U.S.', *The Drinking and Drug Practitioner,* **3,** 15 (1971).
16. Mäkelä, K., *op. cit.* 11.
17. Cosper, R., 'Interview bias in a study of drinking practices', *Quart. J. Stud. Alc.,* **30,** 152 (1969) and Mulford, H. A. and Miller, D. E., 'The prevalence and extent of drinking in Iowa, 1961. A replication and a evaluation of methods, *Quart. J. Stud. Alc.,* **24,** 39 (1963).
18. Pernanen, K., *op. cit.* 10.
19. See, for example, Straus, R. and Bacon, S. D., *Drinking in College,* Yale University Press, New Haven, 1953, and Edwards, G., Chandler, J. and Hensman, C., 'Drinking in a London suburb. I Correlates of normal drinking), *Quart. J. Stud. Alc., Suppl.,* **6,** 69 (1972).
20. Cahalan, D., Cisin, I. and Crossley, M., *American Drinking Practices: a national study of drinking behaviour and attitudes,* Rutgers Center of Alcohol Studies, New Brunswick, New Jersey, 1969.
21. For details of the sampling, the study area and the interviewing, see the appendix to this volume, and Cartwright, A., Salter, Y., Shaw, S. and Spratley, T. A. *Designing an Experimental and Comprehensive Community Response to the Problems of Alcohol Use,* Maudsley Alcoholism Project Report to the Dept. of Health and Social Security, London, 1975.
22. Edwards, G. *et al., op. cit.* 19.
23. Cahalan, D., Cisin, I. and Crossley, M., *op. cit.* 20, p. 23.
24. Dight, S., *Scottish Drinking Habits,* Office of Population, Censuses and Surveys, Draft Report, 1974.
25. E.g. Cahalan, D., Cisin, I. and Crossley, M., *op. cit.* 20; American Institute of Public Opinion, *Gallup political index; political, social and economic*

trends, Princetown, New Jersey, 1966; and Mulford, H. A., 'Drinking and deviant drinking U.S.A., 1963', *Quart. J. Stud. Alc.*, **25,** 634 (1964).

26. Wallace, J. G., 'Drinkers and Abstainers in Norway: a national survey', *Quart. J. Stud. Alc. Suppl.*, No. 6, 129 (1972).
27. British Market Research Bureau, *Target Group Index,* B.M.R.B., London, 1971.
28. Office of Population, Censuses and Surveys, *Classification of Occupations,* H.M.S.O., London, 1970.
29. World Health Organization, Expert Committee on Mental Health, *Report of the First Session of the Alcoholism Sub-Committee, Annex 2: Jellinek Estimation Formula, World Hlt., Org. Tech. Rep. Ser.,* No. 42, Geneva, 1951.
30. Jellinek, E. M., 'The estimate of the number of alcoholics in the U.S.A. for 1949 in the light of the sixth revision of the international lists of causes of death', *Quart. J. Stud. Alc.*, **13,** 215 (1952).
31. Jellinek, E. M., 'Estimating the prevalence of alcoholism: modified values in the Jellinek formulas and an alternative approach', *Quart. J. Stud. Alc.*, **20,** 261 (1959).
32. Popham, R. E., 'The Jellinek alcoholism estimation formulas and its application to Canadian data', *Quart. J. Stud. Alc.*, **17,** 559 (1956).
33. Seeley, J. R., 'Estimating the prevalence of alcoholism: a critical analysis of the Jellinek formula', *Quart. J. Stud. Alc.*, **20,** 245 (1959).
34. Brenner, B., 'Estimating the prevalence of alcoholism: toward a modification of the Jellinek formulas', *Quart. J. Stud. Alc.*, **20,** 255 (1959).
35. Seeley, J. R., 'How many alcoholics? — Under review', *Alcoholism,* Toronto, **6,** 7 (1959).
36. Jellinek, E. M., *op. cit.* 31.
37. Argeriov, M., 'The Jellinek estimation formula revisited', *Quart. J. Stud. Alc.*, **35,** 1053, 1056 (1974).
38. Schmidt, W. and de Lint, J., 'Estimating the prevalence of alcoholism from alcohol consumption and mortality data', *Quart. J. Stud. Alc.*, **31,** 4, 957 1970.
39. Parr, D., 'Alcoholism in general practice', *Brit. J. Addict,* **54,** 25 (1957).
40. World Health Organization, *Tech. Rep. Ser.,* No. 48, Geneva, 1952.
41. World Health Organization, *op. cit.* 29.
42. Prys-Williams, G., *Chronic Alcoholics,* Rowntree Social Science Trust, London, 1965.
43. Moss, M. and Beresford-Davies, E., *A Survey of Alcoholism in an English County,* Geigy, London, 1968.
44. Office of Health Economics, *Alcohol Abuse,* London, 1970.
45. Cahalan, D., *Problem Drinkers: a national survey,* Jossey-Bass, San Francisco, 1970.
46. Edwards, G., Chandler, J., Hensman, C. and Peto, J., 'Drinking in a London suburb I, II and III, *Quart. J. Stud. Alc. Suppl.*, No. 6, 69, 94 and 120 (1972).
47. Edwards, G., Chandler, J., Hensman, C. and Peto, J., 'Drinking in a London suburb II correlates of trouble with drinking among men', *Quart. J. Stud. Alc. Suppl.*, **6,** 94 (1972), and 'Alcoholics known and unknown to agencies: epidemiological studies in a London suburb', *Brit. J. Psychiat.*, 123, 169 (1973).

48. Efron, V. and Keller, M., *Selected statistics on Consumption of Alcohol (1850–1968) and on Alcoholism (1930–1968),* Rutgers Center of Alcohol Studies, New Brunswick, N.J., 1970, and Harris, L. and Associates Inc., *American Attitudes toward Alcohol and Alcoholics,* Study No. 2138, Report prepared for the National Institute on Alcohol Abuse and Alcoholism, 1971.
49. Edwards, G., Chandler, J., Hensman, C. and Peto, J., *op. cit.* 47.
50. Fillmore, K. M., 'Drinking and problem drinking in early adulthood and middle age: an exploratory 20 year follow-up study', *Quart. J. Stud. Alc.,* **35,** 819 (1974).
51. Straus, R. and Bacon, S. D., *Drinking in College,* Yale University Press, New Haven, 1953.
52. Knupfer, G., 'The Epidemiology of Problem Drinking', *Amer. J. Public Health,* **57,** 973 (1967).
53. Jolliffe, N. and Jellinek, E. M., 'Vitamin deficiencies in alcoholism, Part VII. Cirrhosis of the liver', *Quart. J. Stud. Alc.,* **2,** 544 (1941).
54. Lillenfeld, A. M. and Korns, R. F., 'Some epidemiological aspects of cirrhosis of the liver: a study of mortality statistics', *Am. J. Hyg.,* **52,** 65 (1950).
55. E.g. Seeley, J. R., 'Death by liver cirrhosis and the price of beverage alcohol', *Canadian Medical Association Journal,* **83,** 1361 (1960); Schmidt, W. and Bronetto, J., 'Death from liver cirrhosis and specific alcoholic beverage consumption: an ecological study', *Amer. J. Public Health,* **52,** 1473 (1962) and Terris, M., 'Epidemiology of cirrhosis of the liver: national mortality data', *Amer. J. Public. Health,* **57,** 2076 (1967).
56. Terris, M., *Ibid.*
57. E.g. Brummer, P., 'Coronary mortality and living standard', *Acta Medica Scandinavica,* **186,** 61 (1969) and Cook, P., 'Cancer of the oesophagus in Africa', *British Journal of Cancer,* **25,** 853 (1971) and Rushing, W. A., 'Alcoholism and suicide rates by status set and occupation'. *Quart. J. Stud. Alc.,* **29,** 399 (1968).
58. Schmidt, W. and de Lint, J., 'Estimating the prevalence of alcoholism from alcohol consumption and mortality data', *Quart. J. Stud. Alc.,* **31,** 4. 957 (1970).
59. Ledermann, S., *Alcool, alcoolisme, alcoolisation, données scientifiques de charactère physiologique, économique et social,* Presses Universitaires de France, Paris, 1964.
60. Aitcheson, J. and Brown, J. A. C., *The Lognormal Distribution,* Cambridge University Press, Cambridge, 1966.
61. de Lint, J. and Schmidt, W., 'Alcohol use and alcoholism', *Addictions,* Toronto, **18,** 2, 1 (1971).
62. Room, R., 'Notes on the implications of the lognormal curve', *Drinking and Drug Pract. Surveyor,* Berkeley, No. 7, 18 (1973).
63. Skog, O. J., 'Less alcohol — fewer alcoholics?' *Drinking and Drug Pract. Surveyor, Berkeley,* No. 7, 7 (1973); Miller, G. H. and Agnew, N. 'The Letermann model of alcohol consumption: description, implications and assessment', *Quart. J. Stud. Alc.,* **35,** 877 (1974).
64. Report on a Working Group, W.H.O. and the Finnish Foundation for Alcohol Studies, *Alcohol Control Policy and Public Health,* W.H.O. Regional Office for Europe, EURO 5455 IV, Copenhagen, 1974.

Chapter 3

1. Levy, H., *Drink, an Economic and Social Survey,* Routledge and Kegan Paul, London, 1951.
2. Plaut, R. F. A., *Alcohol Problems: a report to the Nation by the Cooperative Commission on the Study of Alcoholism,* Oxford University Press, New York, 1967.
3. Knupfer, G., 'The epidemiology of problem drinking', *Amer. J. Public Health,* **57,** 973–986 (1967).
4. E.g. Cahalan, D., *Problem Drinkers,* Jossey Bass, San Francisco, 1970; and Edwards, G., Chandler, J., Hensman, C. and Peto, J., 'Drinking in a London suburb', *Quart. J. Stud. Alc. Suppl.,* No. 6, 69 (1972).
5. Keller, M. (Ed.), *Alcohol and Health,* First special report to the U.S. Congress, D.H.E.W. publication No. (HEM) 72–9099, 1971.
6. Cited by Haller, M. H., *Eugenics,* Rutgers University Press, New Brunswick, New Jersey, 1963.
7. Tredgold, A. E., *Mental Deficiency (Amentia),* Bailliere, London, 1908.
8. Edwards, G., 'The status of alcoholism as a disease', *in* Phillipson, R. V. (Ed.), *Modern Trends in Drug Dependence and Alcoholism,* Appeton-Century Croft, 1970.
9. McClearn, G. E., 'The genetics aspects of alcoholism', *in* Bourne, P. G. and Fox, R., *Alcoholism: progress in research and treatment,* Academic Press, New York, 1973.
10. *Ibid.,* pp. 342–343.
11. See e.g. Williams, R. J., Berry, L. J. and Beerstecher, E. Jnr., *Arch. Biochem.,* **23,** 275 (1949); McClearn, G. E. and Rodgers, D. A., 'Differences in alcohol preference among inbred strains of mice', *Quart. J. Stud. Alc.,* **20,** 691–695 (1959); and McClearn, G. E. and Rodgers, D. A., 'Genetic factors in alcohol of laboratory mice', *J. Comp. Physiol. Psychol.,* **54,** 116–119 (1961).
12. Fuller, J. C., *J. Compar. Physiolog. Psychol.,* **57,** 85 (1964).
13. Kakihana, R., Doctoral dissentation, University of California, Berkeley, California, 1965.
14. Wilson, E. C., Respess, J. C., Hollifield, C. and Parson, W., *Gastroenterology,* **40,** 807 (1961); Rodgers, D. A., McClearn, G. E., Bennett, E. L. and Henbest, M. J. *Compart. Physiolog. Psychol.,* **56,** 666 (1963); and Sheppard, J. R., Albersheim, P. and McClearn, G. E., *Biochem. Genet.,* **2,** 205 (1968).
15 Amark, C., *Acta Psychiat. Neurolog. Scand. Supple.,* **1951,** 70.
16. McClearn, G. E., *op. cit.* 9, p. 351.
17. Roe, A., 'The adult adjustment of children of alcoholic parents raised in foster homes', *Quart. J. Stud. Alc.,* **5,** 378 (1944) and *Alc. Sci. Soc.,* **1954,** 115.
18. Goodwin, D. W. *et al.,* 'Drinking problems in adopted and non-adopted sons of alcoholics', *Arch. Gen. Psychiatry,* **31,** 164 (1974); and Goodwin, D. W. and Winckur, G., 'A study of alcoholism in half siblings', *Am. J. Psychiat.,* **128,** 122 (1972).
19. Kaij, L., *Acta. Genet. Med. Gemellolog.,* **7,** 437 (1957) and Vessell, E. S., Page, J. G. and Passanati, G. T., *Clin. Pharmacol. Therapeut.,* **12,** 192 (1971).
20. Vandenberg, S. G., *Acta, Psychiat. Scand. Suppl.,* **219,** 46, 232 (1970).
21. E.g. Nordmo, S. H., 'Blood groups in schizophrenia, alcoholism and mental deficiency', *Amer. J. Psychiat.,* **116,** 460 (1969); and Camps, F. E. and

Dodd, B. E., 'Increase in incidence of non-secretors of ABH blood group substances among alcoholic patients', *Brit. J. Med.*, **1,** 30 (1967).

22. E.g. Cruze-Coke, R. and Varela, A., 'Colour blindness and alcohol addiction', *Lancet*, **2,** 1348 (1965); Sassoon, H. F., Wise, J. B. and Watson, J. J., Lancet, **1970,** 367.
23. Smith, J. W. and Brinton, G. A., 'Color-vision defects in alcoholism', *Quart. J. Stud. Alc.*, **32,** 41–44 (1971).
24. McClearn, G. E. *op. cit.* 9, p. 339.
25. E.g. Lisansky, E. S., 'Etiology of alcoholism: the role of psychological disposition', *Quart. J. Stud. Alc.*, **21,** 314 (1960) and see brief review by Catanzano, R. J., 'Psychiatric aspects of alcoholism', *in* Pittman, D. (Ed.), *Alcoholism*, Harper and Row, New York, 1967.
26. Blane, H. T., *The Personality of the Alcoholic: guises of dependency*, Harper and Row, New York, 1968.
27. Orford, J. F., 'Personality factors in alcoholism: a psychological approach', *Update*, London, 1972, p. 1371.
28. E.g. Blum, E. M., *Quart. J. Stud. Alc.*, **27,** 259 (1966); and Tahka, V., *The Alcoholic Personality: a clinical study*, The Finnish Foundation for Alcohol Studies, Helsinki, Finland, 1966.
29. E.g. Menninger, K., *Man Against Himself*, Harcourt Brace, New York, 1938; and Jones, H., *Alcohol Addiction*, Tavistock Publications, London, 1963.
30. E.g. Kessell, N. and Walton, H., *Alcoholism*, Penguin, Harmondsworth, 1965; and Jones, H., *op. cit.* 29.
31. E.g. Tahka, V., *op. cit.* 28.
32. E.g. Mellor, C. S., 'Drinking behaviour and its correlates', *Update*, **3,** 1145 (1971).
33. Syme, L., 'Personality characteristics and the alcoholic', *Quart. J. Stud. Alc.*, **18,** 288 (1971).
34. E.g. Partington, J. T. and Johnson, F. G., 'Personality types among alcoholics', *Quart. J. Stud., Alc.*, **30,** 21 (1969); and Stein, K. B., Rozynko, V. and Pugh, L. H., *Brit. J. Soc. Clin. Psychol.*, **10,** 253 (1971).
35. McCord, W. and McCord, J., *Origins of Alcoholism*, Stanford University Press, Stanford, California, 1960.
36. Robins, L. N., *Deviant Children Grown Up: a sociological and psychiatric study of sociopathic personality*, Williams and Williams, Baltimore, 1966.
37. Orford, J., *op. cit.* 27, pp. 1377–1378.
38. Albrecht, G. L., 'The alcoholism process: a social learning viewpoint', *in* Bourne, P. G. and Fox, R. (Eds.), *op. cit.* 9.
39. Dollard, J. and Miller, N. E., *Personality and Psychotherapy*, McGraw-Hill, New York, 1950.
40. Bandura, A., *Principles of Behaviour Modification*, Holt Rinehart and Winston, New York, 1969.
41. Lemere, F. and Voegtlin, W. L., 'An evaluation of the aversion treatment of alcoholism', *in* Podolsky, E. (Ed.), *Management of Addictions*, Philosophical Library, New York, 1955.
42. Keller, M. (Ed.), *op. cit.* 5, p. 65.
43. Bandura, A., *op. cit.* 40.
44. Schacter, S., *in* Berkowitz, L. (Ed.), *Advances in Experimental Social Psychology*, Vol. 1, Academic Press, New York, 1964.

45. E.g. Orford, J., 'Aspects of the relationship between alcohol and drug abuse', 29th International Congress on Alcoholism and Drug Dependence, Sydney, Australia, 1970.
46. E.g. Heilizer, F., *J. of Psychol.*, **57**, 457 (1964).
47. Orford, J., 'Psychological approaches to alcoholism', *Update*, August, 1971.
48. McCord, W. and McCord, J., *op. cit.* 35.
49. Menninger, K., *The Vital Balance*, Viking Press, New York, 1963.
50. Fenichel, D., *The Psychoanalytic Theory of Neuroses*, W. W. Norton, New York, 1945.
51. E.g. Tahka, V., *op. cit.* 28; and Machover, S., Russo, F. S., Machover, K. and Plumear, F., 'Clinical and objective studies of personality variables in alcoholism. III An objective study of homosexuality in alcoholism', *Quart. J. Stud. Alc.*, **20**, 528 (1959).
52. Fenichel, O., *op. cit.* 50.
53. Machover, S., Russo, F. S., Machover, K. and Plumear, F., *op. cit.* 51.
54. See for example, McClelland, D. G., Davis, W. A., Kalin, R. and Wanner, H. E., *The Drinking Man: alcohol and human motivation*, Free Press, New York, 1972.
55. E.g. Wilkin, H. A., Karp, J. A. and Goodenough, D. R., 'Dependence in alcoholics', *Quart. J. Stud. Alc.*, **20**, 493 (1959).
56. Keller, M. (Ed.), *op. cit.* 5, p. 64.
57. Horton, D., 'Primitive societies', *in* McCarthy, D. (Ed.), *Drinking and Intoxication*, Free Press, New York, 1959.
58. Bales, R. F., 'Cultural differences in rates of alcoholism', *Quart. J. Stud. Alc.*, **6**, 480 (1946).
59. See Roebuck, J. B. and Kessler, R. G., *The Etiology of Alcoholism: constitutional, psychological and sociological approaches*, Charles C. Thomas, Springfield, Illinois, 1972, for a good discussion.
60. See Becker, H. S., *Outsiders: studies in the sociology of deviance*, Free Press, New York, 1963; and Lemert, E. M., *Human Deviance, Social Problems and Social Control*, Prentice-Hall, Englewood Cliffs, New Jersey, 1967.
61. Roebuck, J. B. and Kessler, R. G., *op. cit.* 59, p. 222.

Chapter 4

1. Jellinek, E. M., *The World and its Bottle*, World Hlth., Geneva, 10 (No. 4), 1957.
2. Jellinek, E. M., *The Disease Concept of Alcoholism*, Hillhouse Press, New Jersey, 1960.
3. Edwards, J. G., 'The Status of Alcoholism as a Disease', *in* Phillipson, R. V. (Ed.), *Modern Trends in Drug Dependence and Alcoholism*, Appleton-Century-Crofts, New York, 1970, p. 161.
4. Moser, J., *Problems and Programmes Related to Alcohol and Drug Dependence in 33 Countries*, World Hlth., Geneva, Offset Publication, No. 6, 1974, p. 44.
5. Gitlow, S. E., 'Alcoholism: a disease', *in* Bourne, P. G. and Fox, R. (Eds.), *Alcoholism: progress in research and treatment*, Academic Press Inc., New York, 1973, p. 8.

6. Mitchell, J. N., 'Alcoholism: to heal and not to punish', *in* Keller, M. (Ed.), *Alcohol and Health: a report to Congress*, D.H.E.W. Publication, No. (HSM) 72–9099, 1971, p. 119 (my emphasis).
7. Dewes, P. B., 'Comment on the alcohologist's addiction', *Quart. J. Stud. Alc.*, **33**, 1045 (1972).
8. Glatt, M. M., *The Alcoholic and the Help he Needs*, Priory Press, Royston, Herts., 1970.
9. Jellinek, E. M., 'Phases of alcohol addiction', *Quart. J. Stud. Alc.*, **13**, 673 (1952).
10. Jellinek, E. M., *op. cit.* 1.
11. Moser, J., *op. cit.* 4.
12. 'The legal status of intoxication and alcoholism', *in* Keller, M. (Ed.), *Alcohol and Health*, D.H.E.W. publication, No. (HSM) 72–9099, 1971, p. 85.
13. S. Rep. No. 91–1069, 91st Congress 2nd Session 3, 1970.
14. In re Jones 432 Pa 44, 246 A.2d 356, 363, 1968.
15. Salzman v United States, 405 F.2d 358 D.C. Cir 1968.
16. State v Fearov 283 Minn 90, 166 NW 2d 720, 1969.
17. Vick v State 453 P.2d, 342 Alaska, 1969. Berger v State 118 Ga App 328 163 S.E. 2d 333, 1968.
18. Room, R., 'Comment on the alcohologist's addiction', *Quart. J. Stud. Alc.*, **33**, 1049 (1972).
19. *Ibid.*
20. Pattison, E. M., 'Comment on the alcoholic game', *Quart. J. Stud. Alc.*, **30**, 953 (1969).
21. Davies, D. L., 'Is alcoholism really a disease?' *Contemporary Drug Problems*, 3, 2, 197 (1974).
22. Blane, H. T., Overton, W. F., Jr. and Chafetz, M. E., 'Social factors in the diagnosis of alcoholism. I. Characteristics of the patient', *Quart. J. Stud. Alc.*, **24**, 640–663 (1963).
23. Pattison, E. M., 'A critique of alcoholism treatment concepts; with special reference to abstinence', *Quart. J. Stud. Alc.*, **27**, 49–71 (1966).
24. Jellinek, E. M., *op. cit.* 2, p. 12.
25. Parsons, T., *The Social System*, Free Press, Chicago, 1951.
26. Robinson, D., *The Process of Becoming Ill*, Routledge and Kegan Paul, London, 1971.
27. Siegler, M., Osmond, H. and Newell, S., 'Models of alcoholism', *Quart. J. Stud. Alc.*, **29**, 571–591 (1968).
28. E.g. Glatt, M. M., *op. cit.* 8.
29. E.g. Davies, D. L., 'Normal drinking in recovered alcohol addicts', *Quart. J. Stud. Alc.*, **23**, 94–104 (1962); Kendell, R. E., 'Normal drinking by former alcohol addicts', *Quart. J. Stud. Alc.*, **26**, 247–257 (1965); and Pattison, E. M., Headley, E. B., Gleser, G. C. and Gottschalk, L. A., 'Abstinence and normal drinking; an assessment of changes in drinking patterns in alcoholics after treatment', *Quart. J. Stud. Alc.*, **29**, 610–633 (1968).
30. Glatt, M. M., *op. cit.* 8.
31. Jellinek, E. M., *op. cit.* 9.
32. Douglas, W. J. B., *The Home and the School*, MacGibbin and Kee, London, 1964.
33. Glatt, M. M., *op. cit.* 8.

34. Zola, I. K., 'Medicine as an institution of social control', *Sociol. Rev.*, 4, 1972.
35. Edwards, J. G., *op. cit.* 3.

Chapter 5

1. Root, L. E., 'Social therapies in the treatment of alcoholics', *in* Pittman, D. J. (Ed.), *Alcoholism*, Harper and Row, New York, 1967.
2. Catanzaro, R. J., 'Basic principles of treatment', *in* Catanzaro, R. J. (Ed.), *Alcoholism: the total treatment approach*, Charles C. Thomas, Springfield, Illinois, 1968. This collection of papers provides a critical discussion of a wide range of therapeutic regimes and techniques which are currently employed in relation to alcohol problems.
3. Glatt, M. M., *The Alcoholic and the Help he Needs*, Priory Press, Royston, Herts., 1970.
4. Block, M. A., 'Treating the acute withdrawal phase and associated complications', *in* Catanzaro, R. J. (Ed.), *op. cit.* 2.
5. Glatt, M. M., *op. cit.* 3.
6. See Nathan, P. E., 'Alcoholism', *in* Leitenberg, H. (Ed.), *Handbook of Behaviour Modification*, Appleton-Century Crofts, New York, 1974, for a discussion of various types of aversive conditioning.
7. For a description of major theories and techniques see Wolmon, B. B. (Ed.), *Handbook of Clinical Psychology*, McGraw-Hill, New York, 1965.
8. Clinebell, H. J. Jnr., *Basic Types of Pastoral Counselling*, Abingdon Press, New York, 1966.
9. Root, L. E., 'Social casework with the alcoholic and his family', *in* Catanzaro, R. J. (Ed.), *op. cit.* 2.
10. For a discussion of the basic theories see Jones, M., *The Therapeutic Community: a new treatment in psychology*, Basic Books, New York, 1953; Candill, W., *The Psychiatric Hospital as a Small Society*, Harvard University Press, Cambridge, 1958. Wilmer, H. A., *Practical Social Psychology: a therapeutic community*, Charles C. Thomas, Springfield, 1958.
11. Cumming, J. and Cumming, E., *Ego and Milieu*, Atherton Press, New York, 1962.
12. Pisani, V. D., 'Milieu therapy and the multi-therapeutic approach', *in* Catanzaro, R. J. (Ed.), *op. cit.* 2.
13. Glatt, M. M., *op. cit.* 3.
14. Thomas, M., 'The group therapies', *in* Catanzaro, R. J. (Ed.) *op. cit.* 2.
15. *Ibid.*
16. Rogers, C. R., *On Becoming a Person: a therapist's view of psychotherapy*, Houghton, Boston, 1961.
17. Thomas, M., *op. cit.* 14.
18. Moreno, J. L., 'Psychodrama', in Arieti, S. (Ed.), *American Handbook of Psychiatry Vol. II*, Basic Books, New York, 1959.
19. Glatt, M. M., *op. cit.* 3.
20. Blacker, E. and Kantor, D., 'Halfway houses for problem drinkers', *in* Catanzaro, R. J. (Ed.), *op. cit.* 2.
21. Silkworth, W. D., 'Alcoholism as a manifestation of an allergy', *Medical Record*, pp. 145–249, 1937.

22. *Alcoholics Anonymous,* Chapter 5, 'How it works', A.A. World Services, New York, 1955.
23. *Ibid,* Appendix 1.
24. McCarthy, R. G., 'Group therapy in an out patient clinic for the treatment of alcoholism', *Quart. J. Stud. Alc.*, **7**, 98 (1946).
25. Fox, R. and Lyon, P., *Alcoholism, its Scope, Cause and Treatment,* Random House, New York, 1955.
26. Block, M. A., *Alcoholism its Facets and Phases,* John Day, New York, 1962.
27. Stone, G. P., 'Drinking styles and status arrangements', *in* Pittman, D. J. and Snyder, C. R. (Ed.), *Society, Culture and Drinking Patterns,* John Wiley and Sons, New York, 1962.
28. Editorial, *Annals of the New York Academy of Sciences,* special edition on, The Person with alcoholism, 1974.
29. Leach, B., 'Does alcoholics anonymous really work? *in* Bourne, G. and Fox, R. (Eds.), *Alcoholism: progress in research and treatment,* Academic Press, New York, 1973.
30. Bailey, M. B. and Leach, B., *Alcoholics Anonymous, Pathway to Recovery: a study of 1,058 members of the A.A. fellowship in New York City;* National Council on Alcoholism, New York, 1965; Edwards, G., Hensman, C., Hawker, A. and Williamson, V., 'Alcoholics Anonymous; the anatomy of a self-help group', *Soc. Psychiat.*, **1**, 4, 195 (1967); and Kiviranta, P., *Alcoholism Syndrome in Finland,* Finnish Foundation for Alc. Studies, Helsinki, 1969.
31. Neill, A. and Hymers, J., *Alcoholism, the Ignored Illness,* Alna, Edinburgh, 1972.
32. For a discussion of the material relating to the effectiveness of legislative control measures see Popham, R. E., Schmidt, W. and de Lint, J., 'The effects of legal restraint on drinking', *in* Kissin, B. and Begleiter, H. (Eds.), *Biology of Alcoholism,* Vol. III, Social Biology, Plenum Press, New York, 1974.
33. *Ibid.*
34. Mäkelä, K., Consumption level and cultural patterns as determinants of alcohol problems. Paper presented to the Thirteenth International Congress on Alcoholism and Drug Dependence, Amsterdam, 1972.
35. See Bruun, K., *op. cit.* 31. Lemert, E. M., 'Alcohol values and social control', *in* Pittman, D. J. and Snyder, C. R. (Eds.), *op. cit.* 27 and Room, R., 'The effects of drinking laws on drinking behaviour', Paper presented to the Annual Meeting of the Society for the Study of Social Problems, Denver, Colorado, 1971.
36. Edwards, G., 'Public health implications of liquor control', *Lancet* 424, 1971.
37. Those in managerial and professional classes 1 and 2 according to the Office of Population Censuses and Surveys, *Classification of Occupations,* H.M.S.O., London, 1970.
38. Bales, R. F., 'The therapeutic role of alcoholics anonymous; as seen by a sociologist', *Quart. J. Stud. Alc.*, **5**, 267 (1944).
39. Trice, H. M. and Roman, P. R., 'Alcoholism and the worker', *in* Bourne, P. G. and Fox, R., *op. cit.* 29.

Chapter 6

1. Editorial, *J. Roy. Coll. Phycns. Lond.*, **9**, 3 (1975).
2. For a short discussion on 'The problem of diagnostic reliability', see Mechanic, D., *Medical Sociology; a selective view,* Chap. 3, Free Press, New York, 1968.
3. Glatt, M. M., *The Alcoholic and the Help he Needs,* Priory Press, Royston, Herts, 1970.
4. Alcoholics Anonymous, *Who Me?* Ps. 129, A.A. Publishing Company, London, Undated.
5. Kessel, N. and Walton, H. J., *Alcoholism,* Penguin Books, London, 1965.
6. National Council on Alcoholism, Criteria Committee, Criteria for the diagnosis of alcoholism, *Amer. J. Psychiat.*, **129**, 127 (1972).
7. Catanzaro, R. J., 'Basic principles of treatment', *in* Catanzaro, R. J. (Ed.), *Alcoholism: the total treatment approach,* Charles, C. Thomas, Springfield, Illinois, 1968.
8. Freidson, E., *The Profession of Medicine,* Dodd Mead and Co., New York, 1971.
9. Roth, J., 'Utilization of the hospital emergency department', *J. Health Soc. Beh.*, **12**, 312–320 (1971).
10. Armstrong, J. D., 'The search for the alcoholic personality', *The Ann. Amer. Acad. Pol. and Soc. Sci.*, **315**, 40–47 (1958).
11. Clark, W., 'Operational definitions of drinking problems and associated prevalence rates', *Quart. J. Stud. Alc.*, **27**, 648–668 (1966).
12. Mechanic, D., 'Some factors in identifying and defining mental illness', *Mental Hygiene,* **46**, 66–74 (1962).
13. Blane, H. T., Overton, W. F. and Chafetz, M. E., 'Social factors in the diagnosis of alcoholism', *Quart. J. Stud. Alc.*, **24**, 640–663 (1963).
14. Pattison, E. M., 'A critique of alcoholism treatment concepts: with special reference to abstinence', *Quart. J. Stud. Alc.*, **27**, 49–71 (1966).
15. Mechanic, D., *op. cit.* 12.
16. Butterfield, W. J. and Wadsworth, M. E. J., 'A London teaching hospital', *in* McLachland, G. (Ed.), *Problems and Progress in Medical Care* 2nd Series, Oxford University Press, London, 1966.
17. Pattison, E. M., *op. cit.* 14.
18. Blane, H. T., Overton, W. F. and Chafetz, M. E., *op. cit.* 13.

Chapter 7

1. McLachlan, G., Introduction to *Problems and Progress in Medical Care,* 2nd Series, Oxford University Press, London, 1966.
2. Blackwell, B., 'Why patients come to a casualty department', *Lancet* 1: 369–371 (1962).
3. Freilich, H., 'Variations in census of emergency-room patients', *Hosp. Topics,* **43**, 45–47 (1965); Miller, D. R., *'The hospital emergency service', J. Kansas Med. Soc.*, **63**, 85–88 (1962); Shortcliffe, E. C., 'The emergency-room and the changing pattern of medical care', *New Eng. J. Med.*, **2581**, 20–25 (1953).
4. Achte, K. A. and Seppala, K. R., 'Emergency cases at Hesperia Hospital, Helsinki', *Psychiat. Quart.*, **38**, 537–543 (1964).

5. W.H.O., 'The role of hospitals in ambulatory and medical care', *Med. Hlth. Org. Tech. Rep. Ser.*, No. 176, Geneva, 1959.
6. Acheson, R. M., Barker, D. J. P. and Butterfield, W. J. H., *Brit. Med. J.*, **2**, 1315 (1962); Oxford Regional Hospital Board, Operational Research Unit, Rep. No. 3, *Hospital out-patient survey*, Oxford, 1962, College of General Practitioners, *Thames Valley Faculty Journal*, No. 5, 1961.
7. Butterfield, W. J. H. and Wadsworth, M. E. J., 'A London teaching hospital', *in* McLachlan, G. (Ed.), *Problems and Progress in Medical Care*, 2nd Series, Oxford University Press, London, 1966.
8. Cresswell, R., 'Some aspects of the development of an emergency clinic at a psychiatric hospital, Unpublished, M.Sc. dissertation, University of London, 1973.
9. Glatt, M. M., *The Alcoholic and the Help he Needs*, Priory Press, Royston, Herts, 1970.
10. Williams, L., *Tomorrow Will be Sober*, Cassell, London, 1963.
11. Glatt, M. M., *op. cit.* 5.
12. Zola, I. K., 'Pathways to the Doctor: from person to patient', Paper presented to the 1st International Conference on Social Science and Medicine, Aberdeen, 1968.
13 Strauss, A. L., Schatzman, L., Bucher, R., Ehrich, D. and Sabshin, M., *Psychiatric Ideologies and Institutions*, Free Press, Glencoe, Illinois, 1964.
14. Goldberg, D., 'Psychiatry and general practice', *Medicine*, **9**, 630 (1972).

Chapter 8

1. Mulford, H. A., 'Alcoholism a concern (and creation) of every community', Selected Papers, 1st Annual Meeting NAAAP, 1967.
2. De Morsier, G. and Feldman, H., 'Le traitment de l'alcoolisme par l'apomorphine: etud 500 cas', *Schweiz. Arch. Neurol. Psychiat.*, **70**, 434–440 (1952).
3. Lemere, F., 'What happens to alcoholics', *Amer. J. Psychiat.*, **109**, 674–676 (1953).
4. Shea, J. E., 'Psychoanalytic therapy and alcoholism', *Quart. J. Stud. Alc.*, **15**, 595–605 (1953).
5. Norvig, G. and Neilson, B., 'A follow-up study of 221 alcohol addicts in Denmark', *Quart. J. Stud. Alc.*, **17**, 633–642 (1956).
6. Pfeffer, A. Z. and Berger, S., 'A follow-up study of treated alcoholics', *Quart. J. Stud. Alc.*, **18**, 624–648 (1957).
7. Selzer, M. L. and Holloway, W. H., 'A follow-up of alcoholics committed to a state hospital', *Quart. J. Stud. Alc.*, **18**, 98–120 (1957).
8. Fox, V. and Smith, M. A., 'Evaluation of a chemo-psychotherapeutic program for the rehabilitation of alcoholics: observations over a 2-year period', *Quart. J. Stud. Alc.*, **20**, 767–780 (1959).
9. Moore, R. A. and Ramseur, F., 'Effect of psycho-therapy in an open-ward hospital on patients with alcoholism', *Quart. J. Stud. Alc.*, **21**, 233–252 (1960).
10. Davies, D. L., 'Normal drinking in recovered alcohol addicts', *Quart. J. Stud. Alc.*, **23**, 94–104 (1962).

11. Lambert B. E. V., '"Social" drinking by the alcohol-damaged', *Svenska Läkavtidn,* **61,** 315–318 (1964).
12. Kendell, R. E., 'Normal drinking by former alcohol addicts', *Quart. J. Stud. Alc.,* **26,** 247–257 (1965).
13. Gillespie, D. G., 'The fate of alcoholics: an evaluation of alcoholism follow-up studies', *in* Pittman, D. J. (Ed.), *Alcoholism,* Harper and Row, New York, 1967.
14. Kessel, N. and Walton, H., *Alcoholism,* Penguin Books, Harmondsworth, Mddx, 1965.
15. Glatt, M. M., *The Alcoholic: and the help he needs,* Priory Press, Royston, Herts, 1970.
16. Popham, R. E. (Ed.), *Alcohol and Alcoholism,* Toronto University Press, Toronto, 1970.
17. Guido Solari, C., 'Psycho-therapeutic methods in alcoholism', *in* Popham, R. E. (Ed.), *op. cit.* 16.
18. Lundquist, G. A. R., 'Drugs in the treatment of alcoholism', *in* Popham, R. E. (Ed.), *op. cit.* 16.
19. Edwards, G., 'Alcoholism: the analysis of treatment', *in* Popham, R. E. (Ed.), *op. cit.* 16.
20. *Ibid.*
21. Davies, D. L., Shepherd, M. and Myers, E., 'The two years' prognosis of 50 alcohol addicts after treatment in hospital', *Quart. J. Stud. Alc.,* **18,** 429 (1957).
22. Glatt, M. M., 'Drinking habits of English middle-class alcoholics', *Acta. Psychiat. et Neurol, Scandinav.,* **37,** 88 (1961).
23. Dintrans, E. and Arce, A., 'Consideraciones sobre et tratamiento antialocholico durrante cinco anos de experimencia en el hospital de rancogua', *Rev. Soc. Med. O'Higgins y Colchuagua,* **3,** 18 (1964).
24. Horwitz, J., Naveillan, P., Marambio, C., Cordua, M., Gonzalez, A., 'Evaluation of the results of alcoholism treatment', *in* Popham, R. E. (Ed.), *op. cit.* 16.
25. *Ibid.*
26. Pattison, E. M., 'Alcoholism', *Psychiatric Opinion,* **1, 2,** 39–42 (1965); 'A critique of alcoholism treatment concepts: with special reference to abstinence', *Quart. J. Stud. Alc.,* **27,** 49–71 (1966); and 'Abstinence criteria: a critique of abstinence criteria in the treatment of alcoholism', *Inter. J. Soc. Psychiat.,* **14,** 268–276 (1968).
27. Pattison, E. M., 'Drinking outcomes of alcoholism treatment: abstinence, social, modified, controlled and normal drinking', *in* Kessel, N., Hawker, A. and Chalke, H. (Eds.), *Alcoholism: a medical profile* proceedings of the 1st International Medical Conference on Alcoholism, Edsall, London, 1974.
28. See, for example, Moore, R. A. and Ramseur, F., *op. cit.* 9; Norvig, G. and Neilson, B., *op. cit.* 5; and Gerard, D. and Saenger, G., *Out-patient Treatment of Alcoholism,* Toronto University Press, Toronto, 1966.
29. See, for example, Flaherty, J. A., McGuire, H. T. and Gatski, R. L., 'The psychodynamics of the "dry drunk"', *Amer. J. Psychiat.,* **112,** 460–464 (1955); Gerard, D. L. *et al.,* 'The abstinent alcoholic', *Arch. Gen. Psychiat.,*

16, 83–95 (1962); and Wilby, W. E. and Jones, R. W., 'Assessing patient response following treatment', *Quart. J. Stud. Alc.,* **23,** 325–334 (1963).

30. Pattison, E. M., *op. cit.* 27.
31. Zwerling, I. and Rosenbaum, M., 'Alcoholic addiction and personality (non-psychotic conditions)', *in* Arieti, S. (Ed.), *American Handbook of Psychiatry,* Basic Books Inc., New York, pp. 623–646, 1959.
32. Bolman, W. M., 'Abstinence versus permissiveness in psychotherapy of alcoholism', *Arch. Gen. Psychiat.,* **12,** 456–463 (1965).
33. See the discussion in Canter, F. M., 'The requirement of abstinence as a problem in institutional treatment of alcoholics', *Psychiat. Quart.* **42,** 217–231 (1968) and Chafetz, M. E., 'The alcoholic symptom and its therapeutic relevance', *Quart. J. Stud. Alc.,* **31,** 444–445 (1970).
34. Neiker, S., *Total abstinence: as an attitude and a behaviour,* Paper presented to the 30th International Congress on Alcoholism and Drug Dependence.
35. Cahn, S., *The Treatment of Alcoholics: an evaluative study,* Oxford University Press, New York, 1970.
36. For a general discussion of normal drinking as a goal of alcoholism treatment see Drewery, J., 'Social drinking as a goal in the treatment of alcohol', *J. of Alcoholism,* **9,** 2, 43 (1974). And for a study of normal drinking in alcohol dependent men see Orford, J., 'A comparison of alcoholics whose drinking is totally uncontrolled and those whose drinking is mainly controlled', *Beh. Res. and Therapy,* **2,** 565 (1973).
37. Pattinson, E. M., *op. cit.* 27.
38. Offer, D. and Sabshin, M., *Normality: theoretical and clinical concepts of mental health,* Basic Books, New York, 1966.
39. Pattison, E. M., Coe, R., Rhodes, R. A., 'Evaluation of alcoholism treatment: a comparison of three facilities', *Arch. Gen. Psychiat.,* **20,** 478–488 (1969).
40. Mills, K. C., Sobell, M. H. and Shaefer, H. H., 'Training social drinking as an alternative to abstinence for alcoholics', *Behav. Ther.,* **27,** 18–27 (1971); and Sobell, M. B. and Sobell, L. C., *Individualised Behaviour Therapy for Alcoholics, California Mental Health Monog.,* 13 Sacramento, California, 1972.
41. Tischler, G. L. and Riedel, D. C., 'A criterion-oriented approach for evaluating the quality of patient care', *in* Proceedings of the 2nd Annual Conference NPAAA (1972) DHEW (N14 74–676) 1973.
42. For discussions of some core issues of operational methodology, particularly in relation to diagnoses see Schmidt, H. O. and Fonda, C. P., 'The reliability of psychiatric diagnosis: a new look', *J. Abnorm. Soc. Psychol.,* **52,** 262–267 (1956); Beck, A. T., Ward, C. H., Mendelson, M., Mock, J. B. and Erbaugh, J. K., 'Reliability of psychiatric diagnoses', *Amer. J. Psychiat.,* **119,** 351–357 (1962); Ward, C. H., Beck, A. T., Mendelson, M., Mock, J. B. and Erbaugh, J. K., 'The psychiatric nomenclature; reasons for diagnostic disagreement', *Arch. Gen. Psychiat.,* **7,** 198–205 (1962); Babigan, 'Diagnostic consistency in a follow-up study of 1215 patients', *Amer. J. Psychiat.,* **1965,** 895–901; Lyerly, S. B. and Abbot, P. S., *Handbook of Psychiatric Rating Scales* (1959–1964) NIMH, 1966; Mulford, H. A. and Wilson, R. W., *Identifying Problem Drinkers in a Household Survey,* U.S.

Government Printing Office, 1966; Silverman, C., *The Epidemiology of Depression,* The Johns Hopkins Press, Baltimore, 1968. Kendell, R. E., Cooper, J. E., Gourlay, A. J., Copeland, J. R. M., Sharpel, L. and Guzland, B. J., 'Diagnostic criteria of American and British psychiatrists', *Arch. Gen. Psychiat.*, **25,** 123–130 (1971); Feighner, J. P. *et al.*, 'Diagnostic criteria for use in psychiatric research', *Arch. Gen. Psychiat.*, **26,** 57–63 (1972).

43. For a study in which 'social functioning' is used as both a descriptive and an outcome variable see *The International Pilot Study of Schizophrenia,* Vols. 1 and 2, World Health Organization, Geneva, 1974 and 1976.
44. Feinstein, A. R., 'Boolean algebra and clinical taxonomy: I Analytic synthesis of general spectrum of human disease', *New Eng. J. Med.*, **269,** 929–938 (1963).
45. Bolman, W. M., *op. cit.* 32.
46. Cahn, S., *op. cit.* 35.
47. See Herzog, E., *Some Guidelines for Evaluative Research: assessing psychosocial change in the individual,* DHEW Children's Bureau Publication, 375, 1959; Suchman, E. A., 'Evaluative research: principles and practice *in Public Service and Social Action Programs,* Russell Sage Foundation, New York, 1967; Levine, J. Schiele, B. and Bovthilet, L. (Eds.), *Principles and Problems in Establishing the Efficacy of Psychotropic Agents,* PHSP, No. 2138, U.S. Government Printing Office, Washington D.C., 1971; Weiss, C. H., *Evaluation Research: methods of assessing program effectiveness,* Prentice-Hall, Englewood Cliffs, N.J., 1972; Rossi, P. H. and Williams, W. (Eds.), *Evaluating Social Programs: theory practice and politics,* Seminar Press, New York, 1972. Among many.
48. For a detailed discussion of many of the problems and principles of evaluation in relation to alcoholism treatments see Schucket, M. and Cahalan, D., 'Evaluation of alcohol treatment programs' (forthcoming in collection of commissioned papers. Publication details not yet available 1976).
49. Becker, H. S., Hughes, E. C., Geer, B., and Strauss, A. L., *Boys in White: student culture in a medical school,* University Chicago Press, Chicago, 1961.
50 Sharaf, M. R. and Levinson, D. J., 'The quest for omnipotence in medical training', *Psychiatry,* XXVII, 141, 1964.
51. Goodwin, D. W., 'Metronedazole in the treatment of alcoholism: a negative response', *Amer. J. Psychiat.*, **123,** 1276–1278 (1967).
52. Goodwin, D. W. and Reinhard, J., 'Disulfiram effects of trichomonicidal drugs: a review and double-blind study', *Quart. J. Stud. Alc.*, **33,** 734–740 (1972).
53. Schaeffer, H. H., Sobell, M. B. and Mills, K. C., 'Some sobering data on the use of self-confrontation with alcoholics', *Behaviour Therapy,* **2,** 28–29, 1971.

Appendix

1. Blyth, W. G. and Marchant, L. J., 'A self-weighting Random Sampling Technique', *J. of the Market Research Society* 15.3. 157–162, 1972.

Author Index

Subject Index